PAYING ATTENTION:
Visitors and Museum Exhibitions

by Beverly Serrell

American Association of Museums
1998

P R O F E S S I O N A L   P R A C T I C E   S E R I E S

PAYING ATTENTION: VISITORS AND MUSEUM EXHIBITIONS

Paying Attention: Visitors and Museum Exhibitions
    Beverly Serrell
    Roxana Adams, Series Editor

    ISBN 0-931201-46-2 (paper)

AMERICAN ASSOCIATION OF MUSEUMS

This project was supported, in part, by the

National Science Foundation

Opinions expressed are those of the authors and
not necessarily those of the Foundation

TABLE OF CONTENTS

ACKNOWLEDGMENTS

This project got off to a good start largely due to the efforts of Britt Raphling. She figured out how to log in the data and produce histograms and scattergrams for visual summaries. She supported my ideas even before I could articulate them very clearly.

I owe many thanks to the museum studies advocates who met in Albuquerque in 1993 and agreed to go back to their respective institutions, try out the methods I outlined, and send me data: Susan Ades, Sandra Bicknell, Florence Bramley, Suzanne Bubic, Robyn Einhorn, Ava Ferguson, Ellen Giusti, Kim Hunter, Lisa Mackinney, Patty McNamara, Maureen Otwell, Ann Peabody, Deborah Perry, and Paula Schaedlich. Randi Korn and Margaret Menninger shared data from their studies over the next years, as did many others who are listed in Appendix A.

The scope of this study could not have been as wide without the support of the National Science Foundation. In one year, the sample size was doubled with the help from funds available to hire data collectors across the country. My NSF advisory committee, consisting of Barry Aprison, John Scott Foster, Kathleen McLean, Patricia McNamara, Ed Miller, Lisa Roberts, Charlie Walter, and Linda Wilson, were patient and candid. Their guidance and feedback were essential for keeping me on task.

My distinguished colleagues and vocal critics, Zahava Doering and Harris Shettel, took the time to read earlier drafts and argue with me at great length. Their objections and differences of opinion have helped me clarify and hone my ideas. Praise feels good, but criticism, even when it hurts, forces me to think harder.

I couldn't produce any writing without the help of many editors. Karen Furnweger, Ann Hofstra Grogg, Lori Heringa, and Claudia Lamm Wood were faithful and available beyond the call.

Finally, thanks to the person who has listened from start, criticized, edited, praised, argued, and pried me away from the computer late at night, Gary Mechanic, one of the most diligent museum visitors I know.

Beverly Serrell
Chicago, 1998

FOREWORD

Whereas it was once thought self-evident that museums were worthwhile institutions, they are increasingly faced with an unprecedented demand to explain to their resource providers exactly what sorts of results they are capable of producing. In part this problem is definitional. Museums need to be able to explain in ways they have not hitherto had to do just what it is they are trying to accomplish. In perhaps equal part, however, the problem is also methodological. Once a museum has defined what it is trying to do, how can its actual effectiveness be judged?

It seems to me that Beverly Serrell's work bears directly on this second issue, and support for its publication could not be more timely. The development of some baseline against which to judge the actual behavior of exhibition visitors will be central to any evaluation of effectiveness. Not incidentally, the use of Serrell's methodology will also permit museums to experiment with ongoing exhibitions in an effort to remedy whatever deficiencies may surface. In a field for so long characterized by intuitive assessments (not to mention collegial kindness), Serrell's work offers the hope of finally gathering some concrete and genuinely useful data. As this foreword should make clear, I'm a great enthusiast for what she's doing. It will help us all.

Stephen E. Weil
Deputy Director, Hirshhorn Museum
Washington, D.C., 1996

EXECUTIVE SUMMARY

aying Attention: Visitors and Museum Exhibitions examines the fundamentals of a museum visit: the amount of time spent and the number of stops made by visitors. These critical measures are indicators of learning in museum exhibitions. In the past, museum practitioners have made assumptions about the amount of attention visitors pay to exhibitions based on single exhibits or small samples of data. This research offers a large database of the duration and allocation of visitors' time in 110 museum exhibitions.

The three main purposes of the study are to:
1. Develop a methodology for studying the effectiveness of educational exhibitions defined by how thoroughly visitors use them;
2. Create a database of visitor use of educational exhibitions;
3. Generate a model for interpreting the data and establishing some parameters of relative success.

The theoretical assumptions that support these objectives are based on educational and cognitive psychology. "Time on task" is positively related to the amount of learning, and intrinsic motivation to pay attention is a prerequisite for constructing personal meanings in an informal learning environment.

By incorporating existing, long-standing evaluative methods with new ideas and approaches, this study efficiently and systematically collected data from a diverse sample of museum exhibitions. Data were analyzed using simple, descriptive statistics (e.g., mean, median, percentages, histograms). As a result, a new model for comparing exhibitions using two visitor behavior indexes—how much time per unit area was spent (SRI) and how thoroughly visitors investigated the whole exhibition (%DV)—is introduced.

Although the exhibitions in the data set were not drawn using probabilistic sampling methods, there are nevertheless some broad-brush patterns that emerge from visitors' duration and allocation of time in exhibitions:
- In 80% of the exhibitions, the average total visit time was less than 20 minutes regardless of the size or topic of the exhibition.

- Frequency distributions of time spent in exhibitions show that most visitors spend relatively little time and fewer visitors spend longer times.
- Visitors typically stopped at about one-third of the exhibit elements.
- In general, the amount of time visitors spent in an exhibition was directly and positively related to the number of elements at which they stopped.
- Comparisons across groups of exhibitions suggest that time and stops differed among three subgroups of the data (large exhibitions, old or prerenovation exhibitions, and dioramalike exhibitions), but did not differ significantly among exhibition topics or types of museums.
- Among the 110 exhibitions in this study, exceptionally thoroughly used exhibitions were uncommon. These included exhibitions that charged a fee, were newly opened, contained elements that were extremely captivating, or attracted an audience that was apparently very intentional about being thorough.

This study provides a practical, empirical look at the interaction of visitors and exhibitions and will serve as a reference for future time-and-use studies. It is based on the premise that thoroughly used exhibitions are likely to be more effective educational experiences. While time and stops are only indirect indicators of learning, those observable behaviors are more easily and systematically collected and assessed among a diverse sample of museums than other more direct learning-outcome measures.

I. INTRODUCTION

Today we have some pretty good ideas about our visitors: who they are, why they come, what they like and dislike about museums, and how they hear about exhibitions. We have applied cognitive psychology, leisure studies, and marketing techniques on the exhibit development process. And, we have observed, interviewed, tested and invited comments from visitors before and after they have viewed and interacted with the displays. From these efforts we have discovered many of the basic principles of good exhibition design. This study is part of a new wave of collaborative, multi-site summaries that will further our understandings.

DEFINING AND MEASURING THE EFFECTIVENESS OF EXHIBITIONS

I have always been interested in how to evaluate and define the effectiveness of exhibitions. As a science educator whose classrooms are informal museum settings, I want to know the impact of my efforts. Because most of the exhibits I have worked on are for nonprofit institutions and are supported by grants, I want to be accountable to funders.

My thinking was strongly influenced by two experiences early in my museum career while I was working at Shedd Aquarium. One was a workshop on evaluation at the Smithsonian Institution led by Chandler Screven, and the other was Harris Shettel's 1973 *Museum News* article, "Exhibits: Art Form or Educational Medium?" These two encounters clarified the need for shared definitions of success and made me acutely aware of the gap between a museum's often lofty educational intentions and the failure to realize those objectives with actual visitors.

In the workshop with Screven, I remember being surprised by the discrepancy between an exhibit's intent and the actual exhibit experience. Our assignment was to write interview questions for a summative evaluation of an exhibition. We had a brochure that clearly outlined the topic, messages, and layout of the displays.

I thought we could develop our questions from that information. The brochure was clear, succinct, and complete, so why bother to go across the street and look at the exhibition? But we did, and the exhibition turned out to have very little to do with the abstract concepts presented in the brochure. The stated ideals, which led me to have certain expectations about what I would see and do, were not the same as what I experienced in the exhibition. It was frustrating.

Shettel's 1973 article made a very strong case for the need to have clearly defined, measurable objectives for evaluating educational exhibitions. The situation that he described then is the same today: Exhibitions are often deemed successful based on criteria that are vaguely defined, subjectively measured, and not shared across different kinds of museums in a consistent way.

HOW THIS STUDY GOT STARTED

This study began with a paper published in 1990 that examined visitor behavior in the taxonomic Hall of Birds at the Field Museum of Natural History in Chicago prior to its renovation (Serrell and Becker 1990). The hall contained more than 500 bird mounts in 7,000 square feet of space. It was an old exhibition consisting of repetitive cases of birds that filled the hall with little supporting interpretive materials other than small identification labels. Conventional thinking of the time had led us to the assumption that visitors in the bird hall would budget their time in one of three ways: a transient style (visitors who moved quickly, stopping infrequently); a sampling style (people who stopped briefly here and there); or a methodical style (visitors who studied many exhibits). Other reports and visitor studies have described visitors in similar ways, for example, "streakers," "browsers," "studiers." While these styles reflected individual motivations and interests, it was assumed that distribution of visitors would be roughly equal—one-third of the group in each category. The data, however, failed to confirm this notion (Serrell & Associates 1992). Instead, we found several surprising results:

1. Visitors' time in the exhibition represented a continuum of time spent and stops made, not easily divisible into modes, styles, or types.
2. The majority of people spent less than 10 minutes and made stops at less than 30 percent of the cases.
3. Nowhere near one-third of the visitor population fell into the methodical category.

Had we gotten these results because we used a "bad" example (an old hall), or was this typical of visitor behavior in many exhibitions?

In 1991, in an evaluation of the traveling exhibition "Darkened Waters: Profile of an Oil Spill," we initially observed that more visitors than usual were taking their time to look, stop, read labels, talk, point, and interact. In exit interviews, visitors said they liked the exhibition and found it personally meaningful, and there was ample evidence that visitors understood the exhibition's messages. Systematic observations revealed that half of the visitors spent more than 8 minutes in this 2,000-square-foot exhibit, and they stopped and looked at 51% of the exhibit elements. My clients, the Pratt Museum in Homer, Alaska, and exhibit developer Kathleen McLean, were clearly disappointed by the data. "Is that all?" they asked. Yet, in my experience, when compared with many other exhibits, it seemed that this one was definitely working better than most. Peer reviews agreed with this perception (Garfield 1992). But the time-and-stops statistics did not look as good as the exhibit developers expected or hoped. What had they hoped for? What had they based those hopes on?

Here, again, was an example of the discrepancy between intent and reality. While the developers of "Darkened Waters" did not expect that everyone would be totally enthralled with the exhibits, they apparently were not ready for how low the numbers looked.

THE 51% SOLUTION

After these experiences, I speculated that the specific "Darkened Waters" data (average time spent, exhibition size, elements used, and impact on visitors) could be benchmark criteria for successful exhibitions—ones that effectively engage visitors' attention and create memorable experiences for them. Thus, the "51% Solution" was born. Three criteria for defining the success of an exhibition using visitor behavior as a measure were stated as questions:

1. Do 51% of the visitors move at a rate of less than 300 square feet per minute?
2. Do 51% or more of the visitors stop at 51% or more of the exhibit elements?
3. Can 51% of a random sample of cued visitors, immediately after viewing the exhibition, express (in questionnaire feedback) general or specific attitudes or concepts that are related to the exhibition's content objectives?

These criteria were certainly not absolutes, but they provided serviceable guidelines. Fifty-one percent seemed reasonable because it represented a simple majority, and it left ample room for accommodating the diversity of visitors' demographic and psychographic profiles.

The first two questions are answered by tracking a sample of visitors throughout an exhibition to determine the total time visitors spend and the number of elements they stop at. The size of the exhibition is divided by the average time spent to determine square feet per minute. To answer the third question, evaluators administer a questionnaire to visitors after they have seen the whole exhibition to gauge what they found memorable.

In 1992, "The 51% Solution: Defining a Successful Exhibit by Visitor Behavior" was presented in a poster session at the American Association of Museums' annual meeting in Baltimore and published in that year's Current Trends in Audience Research and Evaluation (Serrell 1992). Further refinements of that idea were presented and discussed at a visitor studies conference held in London and published in Museum Visitor Studies in the 90s (Bicknell and Farmelo 1993).

At the Visitor Studies Association conference held in Albuquerque in 1993, I organized a session during which 24 participants volunteered to collect and share tracking and timing data from their institutions, as expressed in the first two criteria of the 51% Solution. The plan was to consistently collect, process, and summarize all the data in an effort to create a broader database, using the basic methodology of tracking and timing. These efforts formed the first multi-institutional empirical visitor research agenda in which everyone agreed to use the same methodology. For the most part, practitioners who submitted data did not have trouble defining their exhibit elements, constructing a floor plan, or tracking and timing 40 or more visitors in the exhibition. The greatest problem was finding the staff and time to conduct the study. (It is ironic that we lack the time to find out how visitors spend time.)

By 1994, the observational techniques for collecting data for time and stops had, for the most part, been well defined, but methods for gathering self-reported impact data proved illusive. Even though a postvisit questionnaire had been used successfully in a wide variety of settings (Raphling and Serrell 1993), the techniques for analyzing data relating to impact on visitors' learning were not refined to the point that they could be applicable to a wide variety of museums. A decision was made to proceed with the study in two parts: The first would relate to time and stops and deal with the question of thoroughness of use; the second part (still in progress) would relate to the important but more complicated and challenging question of learning.

Over the next year and a half, I continued to gather data from projects I was working on. In addition, colleagues shared data from other institutions. As the project progressed, I realized that a grant was needed to help generate a more robust database. An application to the National Science Foundation (NSF) for a Small Grant for Exploratory Research resulted, in 1995, with a one-year award, from March 1995 to February 1996.

The NSF grant made it possible to complete a large research effort on the first two criteria: How much time do visitors spend in exhibitions, and what percentage of the available elements do they use? The key to acquiring comparable data was to apply the same strategy with the same set of definitions to each exhibition studied. The grant allowed us to coordinate explicitly shared strategies and definitions as well as to gather data across a wide variety of sizes and types of museums. From these we could make some general conclusions.

An added bonus of the NSF grant has been the assistance of an advisory committee that has continually challenged me to articulate my opinions clearly and to distinguish between the evidence and my assumptions.

THE BENEFITS OF MEASURING TIME

By knowing more about the current trends of visitors' time and use of exhibitions, museum practitioners can better predict or anticipate patterns and make better decisions in the future. In addition, criterion-referenced benchmarks (e.g., "51% of the visitors will stop at more than half of the elements") can now be determined realistically.

The logic of the methods presented and discussed in this report and the usefulness of the findings and the model are ultimately meant to help us be better critics of our craft and to avoid mistakes. Similar to other endeavors to enlighten and strengthen education in museums, the model created from the data provides objective empirical guidelines that can "help us to catch ourselves up and check ourselves, if we start to reason or to behave wrongly; and to criticize ourselves more articulately after we have made mistakes" (James 1969, 293). The underlying purpose of this research is to help make educational exhibitions better.

The gap between exhibit developers' intentions and the extent to which those intentions are understood by the audience remains a central issue in museum practice today. The factors of time and use can be studied unobtrusively and systematically with a well-established method of tracking and timing. This is a realistic, fundamental, and practical way to measure and compare the relative success of exhibitions and to establish what makes them work. As a first step, the factors of time and use must be isolated so that they can be easily and empirically measured by museum practitioners who are not highly trained in educational evaluation.

This report provides information that can support or question common beliefs about how visitors use exhibitions. The process of examining the data can, at the least, prompt us to verbalize these previously unspoken beliefs. It is my intention that the patterns revealed in the data can help set parameters for designing exhibits that work for real, not ideal, visitors.

Before we do any more research on how visitors learn in informal museum exhibitions, we should create exhibitions that visitors choose to experience thoroughly. Then we will be able to use those exhibitions as laboratories for investigating what visitors are really learning.

II. PURPOSES OF THIS STUDY

As museum practitioners, part of our job is to encourage diverse populations in the activities of learning and discovery and to adapt our exhibitions to reach the largest possible audience in an engaging and cost-effective way. We want visitors to feel that the time they invest is well spent. One general indication that visitors are satisfied in this way is their thorough use of an exhibition.

The term "thorough use" means that visitors stay a relatively long time and use a high proportion of the available elements. The measure of "relatively long" and "a high proportion" can be determined by descriptive statistics—looking at what the data say is low, normal, average, high, or exceptional.

THE NOTION OF THOROUGH USE

This study investigates and compares a diversity of museum types, visitor variables, and design considerations all at once. It creates two indexes—one that incorporates two important visit variables (time spent and stops made) and one that uses two exhibition variables (square footage and number of elements, i.e., conceptual and physical groupings of objects, art, specimens, phenomena, and interpretive devices). As summative evaluation measures, these indexes reflect the amount of time visitors spend in the given display area and the proportion of visitors who use the exhibition fully ("diligent visitors"). Together, these fundamental variables effectively capture an important measure—how thoroughly visitors used an exhibition. This focus is not intended to dismiss other variables as unimportant or to suggest that understanding how visitors use exhibitions is simple. These measures are proposed as practical, immediately applicable methods for thinking about how visitors use exhibitions and for gauging progress toward the goal of thorough use of exhibitions.

This study is based on the notion that thorough use is an appropriate evaluative measure in a field that lacks a commonly shared, systematic way of measuring the impact of educational exhibitions on visitors.

THREE MAIN PURPOSES

There were three main purposes for this study:

1. To develop a methodology for studying the effectiveness of educational exhibitions defined by thoroughness of use.

   The methods were applied to assessing the duration and allocation of visitors' time in museum exhibitions in a way that makes sense to museum practitioners, is easy to learn (can be used by someone with little or no experience in visitor studies), and uses unobtrusive procedures, relatively small samples, and inexpensive strategies that will work in a variety of settings.

2. To create a database of visitor use of educational exhibitions.

   After collecting and summarizing data using the methodology, researchers noted patterns of visitor behaviors that emerge from the data.

3. To generate a model for interpreting the data and establishing some parameters of relative success.

   The model establishes standards of success defined by visitor behaviors indicating thorough use (time spent in the exhibition and stops at exhibit elements). The model uses numerical indexes—a sweep rate index (SRI) and the percentage of diligent visitors (%DV)—to compare one exhibition to another or to compare the same exhibition in two (or more) different venues.

The first purpose will be addressed in Chapter IV, "Methods," showing that tracking and timing studies are easy to do with a minimal amount of training. A detailed explanation is found in the workbook in Appendix B.

The second purpose will be addressed in Chapter V, "Findings." The third purpose will be addressed extensively in the final chapters—"Discussion of Methods and Findings," "Selected Case Studies," and "Conclusions and Implications for Museum Practitioners."

APPLICABILITY

The methods and purposes of this study are most relevant to thematic exhibitions that have educational
objectives and intend to reach a broad audience. Criteria for thorough use provide realistic quantifications of
the seemingly unquantifiable question about what visitors are learning. The methods and conclusions put
forth here will not apply to all museum exhibitions,
however. Measures of thorough use might not be appropriate, for example, in exhibitions that:

• have no overarching themes to be communicated;
• are designed not for a broad audience, but targeted to
  a small, specific group of visitors with prior knowledge of the subject;
• are intended as a resource room, library, play area, or
  discovery center where visitors are expected to have
  in-depth experiences with a single element or few elements.

Museum professionals need to consider the purposes,
definitions, and intentions of this study to determine if
these measures are appropriate for their exhibitions or
educational efforts.

A WORK IN PROGRESS

This study is a work in progress, and ideas and interpretations are presented in the hope that they will
encourage continued data collection, further analysis,
and lively discussion. They are certainly not the whole
answer, or the only way to look at the issue, but they are
a good place to start.

III. TIME AND LEARNING

Museum professionals seldom concur on what visitors should learn from exhibits or on the "right way" to sample visitors, ask questions, and summarize data. These issues are complex, and exhibitions are highly variable. Time data, on the other hand, are less fraught with methodological problems. With time data in hand, museum practitioners have stronger empirical grounds from which to answer the more difficult questions about what visitors are getting out of exhibitions.

THEORETICAL AND EMPIRICAL CONSIDERATIONS

The present study assumes that there is, in general, a positive correlation between time and learning. The theoretical assumptions that support this research are based on educational and cognitive psychology. Basically, "time on task" is positively related to the amount of learning. "Time on task. . . has been found to be one of the most useful predictors of educational or training effectiveness, and has been used for this purpose in countless studies" (Shettel 1995, 11). In museums, it stands to reason that the more time people spend using an exhibition, the more opportunities they can create for themselves to learn. Likewise, if you do not see visitors paying attention, it is unlikely that exhibition-based learning is taking place.

Motivation to pay attention is a prerequisite for creating personally meaningful situations in both formal and informal learning environments. In museums, unlike schools, learners' motivation to pay attention and become engaged usually comes from inside themselves, not from someone else telling them to do it. Motivation is sustained by interactions with the exhibition environment, including the social interactions with a visitor's companions, that generate intrinsic personal satisfaction. "When complex information is presented in a way that is enjoyable—intrinsically rewarding—the person will be motivated to pursue further learning" (Csikszentmihalyi and Hermanson 1995, 35). What people bring to the experience and what the museum offers need to be a good fit.

Time by itself is not important. It is an indicator. Studies showing positive correlations among time, visitor behaviors, and learning have been conducted recently in museum settings by Borun (1996, et al. 1995), Doering et al. (1994), Giusti (1994, 1993), Korn (1993), Litwak and Cutting (1994a), Raphling (1997), and Serrell (1993a). Direct comparisons among these studies are not possible due to the different goals and methods used, but nevertheless, in general, visitors who engage in learning-related behaviors, such as reading, interacting with exhibits and each other, and visiting more places within one exhibit, spend more time. Researchers have concluded that:

- "It can be seen that there is a clear correlation between learning level and observed behaviors. . . . It would appear that if we observe specific learning behaviors, we can correctly infer that learning is taking place," says Borun et al. (1995).
- The places where most visitors stop are often the places most often recalled in exit interviews (Serrell 1993a). Korn notes that, "In many cases, those works at which visitors stopped most frequently were recalled as most memorable. . . . There are definite trends in visitors' responses, and in most cases they support the behavioral data" (Korn 1993). In "Ocean Planet," the exhibit element that was by far the most popular was also the one visitors found most interesting and emotional (Bickford, et al. 1996).
- In exit interviews, visitors who showed evidence of comprehending the main message of the exhibition tended to spend a longer time (Litwak and Cutting 1994a; Giusti 1994). "Visitors whose responses were rated 'High' and 'Medium' spent slightly more time in the exhibit than did those whose responses were rated 'Low'" (Raphling 1997b).

This relationship between observations of visitor behavior and the feedback received in exit interviews suggests that behaviors can be indicative of interest, engagement, and memory. Just as important, the lack of time spent can be a clue that an exhibition is not working well, although few museums probe deeply enough to discover why. "The majority of visitors to the reptile house do not appear to be showing as much interest in our exhibits as we would like them to" (Marcellini and Jenssen 1988, 337) is a conclusion rarely encountered in print.

Of course, numerous other variables are important to consider when evaluating the success and impact of an exhibition, but many of them are less tangible than time. The study of learning in museums requires feedback through direct contact with visitors, for which no single methodology is widely accepted or easy for untrained staff to use.

OBJECTIONS TO THE USE OF TIME AS A MEASURE OF LEARNING

Time spent may not always indicate learning. In fact, if learning is equated with an epiphany—an "ah ha!" experience—very little time will have elapsed. Certainly epiphany experiences that take place in an instant are possible, but are the majority of museum visitors having them? As George Hein suggests, "Moments of profound insight can be traced back to longer periods of preparation" (Hein 1996). Most visitors, I contend, need appropriate and carefully planned help in an exhibition to have even one modestly epiphanous "a-ha" moment.

Others argue that time spent indicates level of difficulty rather than interest and enjoyment. While this relationship is probably true for a few individuals (especially in school), it does not apply to most museum-goers who are operating in a free-choice environment. They do not have to stick with confusing or difficult assignments. If visitors do not find exhibitions enjoyable, provocative, or personally meaningful, they will turn their attention elsewhere. "Attention," as Mihaly Csikszentmihalyi points out, "is a scarce resource—perhaps the most precious scarce resource there is" (Csikszentmihalyi and Hermanson 1995, 36). In an experimental study of visitors' perceptions, John Scott Foster found that visitors who stayed longer rated exhibits as easier to understand (Foster 1992).

EVIDENCE FROM THE LITERATURE

Studies of visitors' time in museums have been reported for more than 80 years by many museum practitioners. The literature documents a variety of methods for gathering time data, including hidden cameras, floor sensors, and unobtrusive observers. Comparisons of exhibitions in different studies are difficult, however, since data are reported in different ways, such as time per individual exhibit element or time of total visit to the entire museum. In some studies, certain kinds of data are missing, such as the size of the gallery, number of components, or whether the subject was a child or adult. The lack of defined terms creates problems for comparisons. Large and complex studies that are beyond the capabilities of smaller institutions prevent some techniques from being widely applicable or reproducible.

The following examples illustrate some of the difficulties encountered and questions raised when literature reviews seek comparable data on visitors' use of museum exhibitions:

- In an art museum, Melton (1933) reports that "the average proportion of paintings observed seldom deviates from values between 20% and 35%" (a finding that is strongly corroborated by this study) and gives an average time of 72.1 and 70.8 seconds, but he does not say how large the room is. Would the same usage hold true for a different type of museum?

- A tracking-and-timing study in a science museum gallery (Brooks and Vernon 1956) reveals that visitors tend to "flit from one thing to another, stopping to press buttons or turn handles, and treating the Gallery more as an amusement arcade than as a source of scientific information." The audience studied was unaccompanied children. Would the same hold true for adults?

- In a science museum, Eason and Linn (1976) report average viewing times as "five minutes total on the four demonstration machines and ten minutes total on the four activity booths," but their research used students in organized school groups. Are these behaviors comparable to those of casual adults or of family groups?

- The scope and methods of Shettel's extensive study of "Man in His Environment" at the Field Museum

(1976), while comprehensive and detailed, are not within the grasp of most museums' evaluation budgets. Can a large study be scaled down to meet the needs of a small institution?

- Beer (1987) combines data from 10 different sites, all of them small museums. "They were small (a maximum of four galleries), so that observations could be made at most or all of the exhibits during the study." She concludes that visitors entirely skip almost half (43%) of the displays (a finding that suggests a much higher proportion of stops than found by Melton or this study), but she combines data by type of display rather than by institution.
- Falk's widely quoted generalization that virtually any museum label or exhibit will yield a bimodal pattern of visitor attention (either they like it or they don't) (Falk and Dierking 1992) is based on only three examples (Falk 1984). But what is the definition of "bimodal"?

CONFIRMING, CHALLENGING, AND CHANGING ASSUMPTIONS

The following are some of the common, but not universal examples of visitor behavior in exhibitions that have been observed by others (e.g., Miles 1993; Melton 1933, 1935; Marcellini and Jenssen 1988; Bitgood et al. 1991; Beer 1987; Falk and Dierking 1992) and have been confirmed during this study (including data on traffic patterns that are not reported here):

- Visitors generally turn right and follow the right-hand wall through a gallery.
- Fewer people move into the center to explore island exhibits.
- Exhibit elements near an exhibition's entrance often get more attention than those at the end.
- Large exhibitions have different averages for total time spent than small ones.
- The exit has a strong attraction; visitors often leave at the first opportunity.
- The time available for holding visitors' attention is very limited.

Recent research on people's shopping behavior in malls has revealed some strong trends, some of which resemble visitor behavior in museums. For instance, people need to adjust and "decompress" in the first 12 to 25 feet inside the door of a store, and once inside, they usually turn right. In addition, the chances that shoppers will buy something are directly related to how long they spend shopping, and how long they spend shopping is directly related to how deeply they get pulled into the store (Gladwell 1996). Museum practitioners can certainly learn from studies of visitors to entities that are not museums. Many museums have benefited from visitor-service guidelines developed by entertainment industry professionals, for example, at Disneyland.

Other assumptions held by museum practitioners that may be less true than commonly thought are addressed by the findings of this study. Data will be presented regarding the most common overall patterns in the frequency distributions of time data; visitor browsing patterns and the relationship between time spent and number of stops made; and patterns of visitor time and use according to museum type and size of exhibition.

Time data can clarify and perhaps change some assumptions. The large database of time and stops data collected systematically from many types of exhibitions for this study allows us to develop a model of thoroughness of use. We are able to make some estimates about average levels of thoroughness and determine which exhibits tend to be exceptionally low or high in usage according to what visitors tell us with their feet. Using the database, we can translate statements like "They stayed a long time and looked at everything," into actual numbers that allow us to perceive variations in how thoroughly visitors use exhibitions.

In shopping malls, the currency is money: Spending it enables a purchase. In museums, the currency is attention, and paying attention—which requires spending time—is a prerequisite for comprehension.

While tracking and timing studies do not reveal long-term learning, they can predict it. It takes time to use an exhibit, and it takes time to accomplish short-term learning, which is the foundation for long-term learning. But how much use and how much time are typical, possible, or realistic?

The study of time deserves more attention because it has never been examined systematically or thoroughly. This study challenges, refines, and advances the existing ideas, issues, and theories held by museum practitioners about visitors' time and use of exhibitions and the implications that time holds for visitors' informal learning. As a multi-site, multi-discipline study, it accomplishes for the museum profession what none of the smaller, unsystematic, fragmented, and isolated research studies (e.g., single case studies) have been able to do.

IV. METHODS

The first purpose of this study was to create a method of collecting data that could be widely shared. To accomplish this goal, only a few key variables were collected for each exhibition. Each variable is readily available, easy to measure, and can be objectively defined. Two of the variables relate to the exhibition being studied:

1. Exhibition size, measured in square feet

2. Number of elements (exhibit units/activities/ planned stops), defined uniquely for each exhibition

The other two describe the exhibition in terms of the behaviors of the people who visit it:

3. Total amount of time (in minutes) spent in the exhibition by each person in a randomly selected, representative sample of 40 or more adult visitors

4. Total number of stops each visitor made at the available elements

These four variables reflect, in the simplest terms possible, the degree to which visitors were engaged. In general, if visitors stopped often and spent a relatively long time, they were defined as having paid a lot of attention. If visitors looked around briefly, stopped infrequently, and exited at the first opportunity, for whatever reason, they were defined as having paid less attention. That is, they were not engaged in behaviors that showed evidence of being engaged in the exhibition.

DEFINITIONS OF SIZE, NUMBER OF ELEMENTS, TOTAL TIME, AND NUMBER OF STOPS

Even these seemingly straightforward variables are fraught with definitional problems due to the high variability of museum exhibition topics, modalities, and visitors' intentions. Nevertheless, these four factors—exhibition size, number of elements, total time, and number of stops—can be applied across most exhibition types by adhering to specific guidelines.

EXHIBITION SIZE

Exhibition size is measured in square feet from visible wall to visible wall, including the interiors of cases and dioramas. Closets or other behind-the-scene features (e.g., audiovisual equipment space) not visible to visitors were excluded, but if these spaces were relatively small, they were included in the total space. (Exhibitions with many large dioramas will be discussed as a special category in the "Findings" chapter.)

NUMBER OF ELEMENTS

Elements are all the physical spaces where there is something for self-guiding visitors to do, conceptually and physically. For example, elements include places to stop to look more closely at an object or phenomenon, read a label, interact with a device, or watch an audiovisual program. Elements vary greatly in size and detail, e.g., a small, simple mechanical interactive and a large, complex, naturalistic diorama. Another factor in defining elements is the way in which visitors use them. Preliminary observations of visitor behavior can help delineate discrete activities.

Specific elements are usually defined by the exhibition's developers, and the list of elements should account for everything in the exhibition's space. Often several similar things are lumped together by shared intent (e.g., a case of objects plus a label, all on a single topic, or three similar examples even if in different places). Distinctly different modalities are often kept as separate elements (e.g., a case of objects and a 3-minute video about them). In Appendix C, a variety of floor plans with their elements drawn in show a range of possibilities.

The majority of exhibitions in this sample included some form of interactive elements, although science exhibitions usually included more than those in art museums. It was not possible to categorize whole exhibitions as interactive or not.

TOTAL TIME

The total time spent by a visitor is the elapsed time in minutes and seconds from the moment the person crossed the threshold into the exhibition until he or she exited. Fractions of minutes were rounded off (e.g., 5 minutes 23 seconds became 5 minutes; 6 minutes 45 seconds became 7 minutes). When more than 1 minute was spent involved in something other than paying attention to exhibits, or walking and glancing, that was noted on the data sheet for possible exclusion from total time. Rare instances of time spent "changing the baby's diaper," "taking a nap," or "talking on cell phone" were not included in total time, whereas, "Visitor sat down and read brochure for 2-3 minutes" was counted. Thus, total time accurately reflected the time a visitor spent paying attention to the exhibition's elements or briefly traveling among them.

NUMBER OF STOPS

A stop at an element is defined as a visitor's stopping with both feet planted on the floor and head or eyes pointing in the direction of the element for 2 to 3 seconds or more. A person returning to a previously visited element does not count as an additional stop. Thus, if a person stopped at least once at every available element, the number of stops for that visitor and the number of elements in the exhibition would be the same.

Time at stops was not recorded or tabulated by element. Measuring the amount of time at every element a visitor stops at in an exhibition makes data collection and analysis more complicated than was necessary for the basic variables measured and compared in this study. In some exhibitions, time at certain elements (e.g., a video, demonstration, or complex interactive) was relevant to other specific evaluative questions that were being investigated, but in cases where the museum's was undertaking its first visitor study, keeping data collection simple made the process easier.

DEFINITIONS OF VISITORS AND EXHIBITIONS

In addition to the definitions of the four variables researched in this study, it was necessary to define some very basic terms: visitors and exhibitions.

VISITORS

In this study visitors were defined as free-ranging adults (people who appear to be of any age over approximately 16 years old) in any kind of informal social group (e.g., alone, with friends, with family). Each of the 40 or more visitors in each sample was observed as an individual, and his or her behaviors in the exhibition that were recorded by trained observers. Adults in tour groups and children in school groups were not included.

Other studies of visitor behavior in museum exhibitions have recorded detailed interactions among members of family groups, or they have compared the behaviors of the sample using demographic groups, such as males and females, adults in adult-only groups versus family or multi-generational groups, visitors on weekdays versus weekends, in the peak summer visiting season or in the less-crowded fall. This research embraced the diversity of all these subgroups as one group, called "visitors."

EXHIBITIONS

Exhibitions and exhibits are considered two different entities in this study. The latter is one element or component of a larger group or a single, stand-alone experience. The former is a group of elements, planned as a cohesive unit, under a specified theme or topic. Often the distinction between the two is not made clear in museum studies reporting. Many researchers have measured visitors' time and responses to individual exhibits, or sections of exhibitions, whereas this study looks at the entire experience visitors have in one complete exhibition. For the purpose of this study, an exhibition is considered to be educational if it has some intended themes or messages to communicate to visitors. Exhibitions with no interpretive materials were not part of this study.

For additional definitions, see the workbook in Appendix B.

UNDEFINABLE TERMS AND UNMEASURABLE VARIABLES

If a term could not be defined, it could not be measured or compared. For example, the question, "Do visitors stay longer in interactive exhibitions?" could not be answered because we could not define what an interactive exhibition was. Interactive exhibit elements were included in most of the exhibitions in this database, but what, really, does "interactive" mean for a whole exhibition? It is not just "hands-on" touching of artifacts or manipulating mechanical or electronic devices; it can also mean "minds-on" with a static element. The term interactive is much easier to define and apply to individual elements than to whole exhibitions.

Other words commonly used in describing exhibitions such as: "linear exhibitions," "open-ended exhibitions," "constructivist exhibitions," and "density of elements" turned out to be operationally undefinable terms, and thus could not be measured and included in this study's data analysis:

- "Linear" was hard to define because to some people, an exhibition with a title and an introductory sign would be considered linear. To others, any exhibition where visitors have free choice to select and manage their own time budgets (how much time they want to spend and where to spend it) would be considered nonlinear. In fact, visitors can use most exhibitions in a nonlinear way by skipping around or backtracking to elements previously visited. Very few museum exhibitions—and none in this study—literally forced visitors to look at one element at a time in a prescribed sequence.

- "Open-ended," like "interactive," was easier to apply to a single exhibit element than to a whole exhibition. The term is often used to describe an interactive element where there is more than one or multiple outcomes possible, rather than one answer or solution.

- "Constructivist exhibitions" are characterized as being learner-centered, open-ended, multi-modal, and social, and they are developed with considerations for the complex interactions of the visitors' previous experience and personal interest. This definition is complicated by the issue of the difference between the museum's intent and the actualization of that intent. Few good examples of constructivist exhibitions exist, even according to constructivists. Besides, many museum practitioners who do not call themselves constructivists would agree with the desirability of exhibitions with "constructivist" characteristics.

- "Density" can be computed (square feet divided by number of elements), but it is problematic because elements are uniquely determined within each exhibition and vary greatly in size and complexity. For example, imagine a 3,000-square-foot exhibition in an art museum with 24 small, detailed paintings accompanied by interpretive labels on the walls; then imagine a maritime history museum with 24 large cases holding intricate ship models with interpretive graphics in the same 3,000 square feet. The art museum exhibition would feel more open and spacious;

the maritime exhibition would look and feel crowded, but the two would be computed as having the same density.

COLLECTING THE DATA

The basic method of tracking and timing involves noting the visitor's path on a map or floor plan of the exhibition. (See samples in Appendix C.) The data collector, using one data sheet per visitor, unobtrusively observed the behaviors of one visitor at a time, noting the path he or she took in the exhibition and where he or she stopped. Demographic data were based on the collector's observations and included the visitor's approximate age, gender, and whom he or she was with (e.g., alone, with a group, what kind of group). Data were collected during different times of the day (usually in the afternoons on weekdays, to avoid conflicts with school group programming) and on different days of the week to balance out variables, if any, between weekend versus weekday visitors. People who spent less than one minute or who made no stops were not included in the analysis.

The sampling procedure was a convenience sample that strived for a cross-section of casual visitors, selected without any known biases. In most cases, visitors were selected as the first adult person to cross an imaginary line when the data collector was in position to begin the next observation. No record was kept of the number of visitors crossing the line during the observation period. This statistically important detail would have required having twice as many data collectors working, thereby doubling the staff time and costs to conduct a study.

The data for the 110 exhibitions that are included in this study came opportunistically from several sources: summative evaluation studies conducted by Serrell & Associates commissioned by a variety of museums from 1990 to 1997; summative evaluation studies conducted specifically for this project by Serrell & Associates, supported in part by the National Science Foundation during 1996 and 1997; and summative evaluation studies conducted by other evaluators (in-house and independent contractors) that had been reported in the literature or shared informally with the author.

The 110 exhibitions represented typical fare in museums across the board, although certainly every exhibition, like every visitor, is unique and has its own set of complex variables. There were no blockbusters (timed-ticketed, exceedingly popular temporary exhibitions). Submitting data to this study did not constitute an endorsement of the analysis or interpretations of this report; rather, it was considered a contribution in the spirit of cooperation toward improving museum visitor studies. While the sample of 110 exhibitions was a sample of convenience and cannot be called "representative," an effort was made to include a diverse set of examples, with an emphasis on science-related museums and topics.

The specific data collected for this study included the name of the institution; the title of the exhibition; size of the exhibition in square feet; number of elements; and total time and total stops for 40 or more visitors. From the floor plan, it was possible to determine if the exhibition was dioramalike, that is, if some (or many) elements had very large footprints in terms of square feet occupied on the floor plan. It was also noted whether the exhibition was a permanent or a temporary installation, and if it was old or recently renovated. The type of museum (e.g., history, natural history, art) was determined by the institution's formal name, and the exhibition's subject or topic (e.g., science, history, art) was determined by its title. When multiple topics or types were encountered (e.g., science and art, history and science), the most prominent one was used.

The variables of this study can be readily measured by staff or volunteers without academic training. A workbook (see Appendix B) provided detailed definitions, instructions, and examples for how to use the research methods, and it functioned well for most people without additional technical support. Refinements based on data collectors' feedback during the study helped make the workbook as thorough as possible. For example, a participant in the study recommended that guards be informed when data collectors are at work observing visitors so the guards would be suspicious and throw the data collectors out (a case study is reported in Dritsas 1996).

Gathering all the time and stops data necessary to describe one exhibition in this database usually took one person 40 hours or less; processing it took another 10 to 20 hours depending on the level of detail.

DATA ANALYSIS

Analysis of the data beyond the basics used in this study takes longer and depends on the amount of additional data collected and recorded on the floor plan, including time at individual stops, behaviors at each stop, and analysis of the popularity of individual elements. A museum could collect and process a wealth of data using these relatively simple methods; however, this research study made use of the summary statistics only.

It is important to keep in mind that the descriptive analysis of this study is based on the behaviors of a sample of visitors. It does not and cannot predict the behavior of any individual person, nor does it try to represent any single "average visitor." Rather, the summary statistics reflect a distribution of data from a reasonable sample, from which a descriptive model can be generated. The point was to look for patterns, tendencies, and general conclusions that could provide useful information quickly and efficiently. The model shows where we are now, based on this sample, and offers a way to compare this data with data gathered in the future.

Exhibition size, number of elements, visitors' total time, and number of stops were analyzed in several commonly used, relatively simple statistical ways:

1. Raw data from the tracking sheets were transcribed into a computer database, listing the data as rows for each visitor and columns for total time and total stops.

2. Descriptive statistics for the range, mean, median, and percentiles were computed for each variable for each exhibition using the Statview program on a Macintosh computer.

3. Frequency distributions—histograms—were produced to see patterns of data for each variable. Visitors' time data were summarized as a frequency distribution to give a more complete picture of the sample overall rather than simply calculating the mean.

4. Correlations or relationships between sets of variables were shown as scattergrams and analyzed for regression values.

Breaking data samples into subgroups of members/nonmembers, first-time visitors/frequent visitors, or high prior knowledge and interest/low prior knowledge and interest requires the obtrusive intervention of interviewing visitors after tracking to gather this information. This intervention is more time-consuming: additional time is needed for conducting interviews and gathering larger samples to accommodate refusals (e.g., 40 tracked visitors would yield fewer than 40 interviews). This research project aimed to be a broad brush stroke of time and stops data for audiences as a whole. It purposely strove to keep the research techniques easy to learn and unobtrusive to administer.

SCATTERGRAMS OF VISITORS' DATA

Data on the number of stops each visitor made were converted from raw numbers into percentages, that is, each visitor's total stops were divided by the total number of elements available to stop at. This conversion enabled one exhibition to be compared to an exhibition with a different number of elements.

A scattergram is a good tool for seeing data from a whole set of observations in one glance, with each dot on the scattergram representing one visitor. (Examples are shown in Chapter 5 and Appendix G.) The dots typically spread from the lower-left quadrant (lowest time, lowest percent stops) to the upper-right quadrant (highest times, highest percent stops). Visitors represented by dots in the upper right were the ones who used the exhibition more thoroughly. Scattergrams of individual exhibitions can be compared for the relationship of time spent and stops made (correlations and regressions) and for the relative number of points in different quadrants of the scattergram.

ANALYSIS OF VARIABLES BETWEEN EXHIBITIONS

Each of the four variables (exhibition size, number of elements, total time spent by visitors, and number of stops visitors made) can be summarized and analyzed by exhibition and then shown as a scattergram with a correlation of two variables (one on each axis), where each dot on the scattergram represents one exhibition

(instead of one person). This type of scattergram is useful for looking at relationships between exhibition variables, such as size and average time or number of elements and percentage of stops.

DEFINITIONS OF SRI AND %DV

To summarize the data from the four variables and to make comparisons among exhibitions, two indexes were developed for this study: the sweep rate index and the percentage of diligent visitors:

- **Sweep Rate Index (SRI):** For each exhibition, the average total time visitors spent was divided into the exhibition's square footage. SRI is a square-feet-per-minute index and allows exhibitions of different sizes to be compared fairly. It represents the amount of space-per-time used by the sample of visitors as they visually and physically sweep the area of the exhibition. The lower the SRI, the more time visitors spent per unit of area.
- **Percentage of diligent visitors (%DV):** This index is obtained by calculating the percentage of visitors who stopped at more than half the elements. The percentage of diligent visitors is a gauge of how thoroughly an exhibition was used. The higher the %DV index, the more thoroughly the exhibition was used.

Even though SRI and %DV are measures of visitor behavior, these measures serve to describe characteristics of the exhibition; they are not measures for discovering who stopped, why, or for how long at each element. The focus is on thorough use, which we assume is an appropriate objective for most exhibitions.

On scattergrams comparing SRI and %DV among exhibitions, the points represent exhibitions (not people). Those in the lower-right quadrant have slower sweep rates (higher time per unit space) and a higher percentage of stops. On the SRI-%DV scattergram, the lower-right quadrant is where the points (dots) for the most thoroughly used exhibitions appear. As defined in this study, a thoroughly used exhibition is one in which both SRI and %DV are "better" than the median for the whole sample. (Note that "better" means higher %DV values and lower SRI values.)

The methods developed for this study are not entirely new, but they are refined and defined more completely than in previous studies and were applied consistently across many different exhibitions.

V. FINDINGS

The first section of this chapter describes some of the general features of the 110 exhibitions in the sample, starting with the types of museums and exhibitions studied. It is followed by a summary of the ranges, means or medians, and distributions of the study's four variables: size of exhibition, number of elements, total time spent by visitors, and the number of stops visitors made. The third section compares pairs of the variables for correlations. The fourth section analyzes the data in a summarized form of two indexes that indicate thorough use. In the final section, the data are compared by type of exhibition (e.g., science vs. art, diorama vs. nondiorama) and type of museum.

TYPES OF EXHIBITIONS IN THE SAMPLE

The sample consisted of 110 exhibitions in 62 different museums with a combined total of 8,507 visitors. The 110 exhibitions were divided by topic into two major subcategories: science-related and nonscience-related:
- 81 of the 110 exhibitions (74%) had primarily science-related topics, such as chemistry, ecology, geology, animal species, and natural history;
- 29 (26%) were exhibitions primarily concerned with art (e.g., paintings, sculpture) or cultural history (e.g., civil rights, postal service, families).

In the science-related category, the exhibitions were subclassified by three different types of museums where they were held:
- 34 exhibitions were at science museums (e.g., Science Museum of Minnesota, California Museum of Science and Industry, Boston Museum of Science);
- 29 exhibitions were at natural history museums (e.g., Field Museum, Denver Museum of Natural History, American Museum of Natural History);
- 14 exhibitions were at zoos and aquariums (e.g., Brookfield Zoo, Shedd Aquarium, National Aquarium in Baltimore).

The remaining four of the 81 science-related exhibitions were studied while they were housed in cultural history museums.

Nonscience-related exhibitions were subclassified by two different types of museums where they were held:
- 16 at history museums (e.g., San Diego Historical Society, Minnesota History Center, Colonial Michilimackinac)
- 13 were art museum exhibitions (e.g., Walker Art Center, the J. Paul Getty Museum of Art, San Francisco Museum of Modern Art).

The categories above for types of exhibitions and types of museums (e.g., science or nonscience, history or art) were sometimes unclear because there are museums and exhibitions that combine topics, such as history and art, art and science, science and history.

Exhibitions were also defined and analyzed according to the following characteristics:
- "Old" exhibitions prior to renovations and additions of interpretive materials (e.g., narrative labels, interactive devices) (N = 6);
- "Dioramalike" exhibitions, where the exhibit elements' footprints took up more than half of the available and visible square footage (N = 20);
- Two subgroups of science museums: those with object/artifact collections (N = 20); and "science centers" (noncollection-based exhibits) (N = 14).

Originally the diorama subgroup of exhibitions included only those existing in natural history museums, but closer examination of exhibition layouts and elements showed that other museums have similar designs. Therefore, the definition of diorama has been broadened to include any exhibition that has exceptionally large exhibit elements, that is, in which a large proportion (40% or more) of the floor space of the exhibition is taken up by the elements' footprints. Thus, some zoo and aquarium exhibitions fell into this subgroup (e.g., Brookfield Zoo's "Habitat Africa!") as did one sample from a history exhibition ("A Tribute to Survival" at the Milwaukee Public Museum).

Exhibitions were designated as temporary (special or traveling) or permanent (no established closing date), although these designations were not always as easy to determine or as useful as might be expected. Sometimes a special exhibition stays up for years, and a newly opened permanent exhibition has some of the same exciting appeal as a temporary show.

The vast majority of the exhibitions were free, that is, there was no extra charge beyond regular museum entrance fees. In four cases, visitors paid additional admission fees, but none of the exhibitions were exceedingly popular blockbusters with long lines or timed-ticketed entry.

The sample of 110 exhibitions achieved the study's goal of a large sample that represents a broad range of exhibition types and that includes a majority of science-related topics. The exhibitions represent common fare across the board, although no one exhibition can be called typical for the whole sample.

DESCRIPTIVE STATISTICS OF THE FOUR VARIABLES

Below is a summary of the ranges, means or medians, and distributions of the four main variables: size of exhibition, number of elements, total time spent by visitors, and the number of stops visitors made.

SIZE: SQUARE FEET OF EXHIBITION SPACE
Exhibition sizes ranged from very small to very large (see Figure 1). The smallest was 384 square feet, and the largest was 14,000 square feet. Seventy-five percent (83 out of 110) of the exhibition spaces were more than 2,000 square feet and less than 9,000 square feet. The average size was 4,630 square feet. The median size was 3,500 square feet.

ELEMENTS: NUMBER OF COMPONENTS
Exhibit elements or components included a variety of sensory and media experiences (e.g., static, mechanical, and electronic elements, with things to look at, listen to, or touch, as well as text and graphics). Among exhibitions in this sample, the number of elements ranged from a low of 4 to a high of 179. The average was 37, and the median number of elements was 32. The highest number (179 elements in "Families") was an unusual outlier—a number much larger than the bulk of the rest of the sample (see Figure 2). (For brevity, exhibition titles are shortened in the text. All titles are listed in full in Appendix D. Appendix E lists institution names, and Appendix F has a table of all the summary data.)

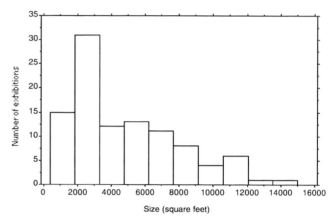

Figure 1. Exhibition Sizes (in square feet). N=110 exhbitions.

Each bar represents the number of exhbitions, with the corresponding square footage shown on the horizontal axis. The most common sizes were between 2,000 and 4,000 square feet.

TIME: MINUTES SPENT BY VISITORS IN EXHIBITIONS
Out of 8,507 visitors to all 110 exhibitions combined, the longest time anyone spent was 128 minutes. The shortest total time was 1 minute. (Times under 1 minute were not defined as visits and were therefore not included in the sample.) Less than 1% of all visitors' total times exceeded 60 minutes. In more than three-quarters of the exhibitions sampled, no one spent more than 60 minutes.

Each exhibition's time data were summarized as frequency distribution—the number of visitors who spent similar total times were grouped. Most of the 110 distributions of visitors total time spent within a single exhibition showed that the densest concentration of times were on the left side (lower times) of the graph, as seen in Figure 3. (Histograms of total times for visitors in all exhibitions in this study are in Appendix G.)

Roughly 90% of the frequency distributions for time data in this study had roughly this shape of a curve, called a right-skewed pattern (Figure 3). Only one frequency distribution of time ("Judith Leyster: A Dutch Master and Her World") out of 110 had a left-skewed pattern.

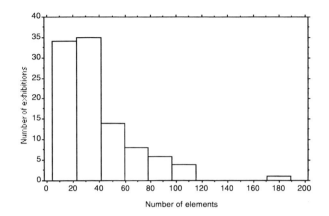

Figure 2. Number of elements. N=110 exhbitions.

Each bar is the number of exhibitions, with the corresponding number of elements shown on the horizontal axis. The majority of exhibitions (62%) had between 10 and 40 elements, and all but three had fewer than 100.

AVERAGE (MEAN) AND MEDIAN TOTAL TIME

The data shown in Figure 3 can be summarized, for comparison purposes, by converting the total times to an average total time spent for the whole sample. This average time is not meant to characterize the "average visitor" but is simply a statistic for comparing observations from different samples. The average total time for the data from the single exhibition shown in Figure 3 is 11 minutes. The median is 8 minutes. In almost all of the 110 cases in this study, the median time was 1 to 4 minutes less than the average time, due to the typically right-skewed distribution.

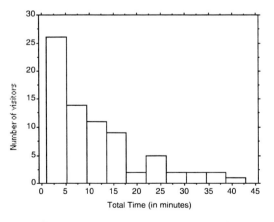

Figure 3. Example of museum time data as a bar graph for the exhibition. N=52 visitors.

Each bar represents the number of visitors in the exhibition's sample who spent the corresponding total time shown on the horizontal axis. In this case, three-quarters of the visitors spent less than 15 minutes, and seven visitors spent more than 30 mintures.

For strongly skewed distributions, it is often recommended that the median be used rather than the average, because the median in some ways captures the central tendency better when the data are not normally distributed (as a bell-shaped curve). Nonetheless, the mean is a more widely understood way to summarize data, and since total time distributions contained only a few outliers (individual data points that were unusually high or low), the mean was used to summarize and compare time data.

In the sample of 110 exhibitions (Figure 4 below), the average total time spent by visitors ranged from 1 to 45 minutes. In 82% of the exhibitions (90 of 110), regardless of the size or the topic, the average total time was less than 20 minutes.

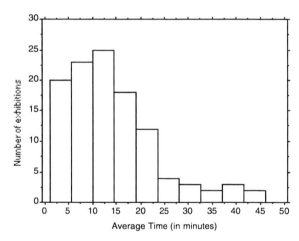

Figure 4. Average total time. N=110 exhibitions.

Each bar represents the number of exhbitions with the corresponding average time spent by visitors shown on the horizontal axis.

STOPS AT EXHIBITION ELEMENTS

The total number of stops visitors made at available elements were graphed for each exhibition. Frequency distributions of stops showed a greater variety of patterns than the distribution of time data. Right-skewed patterns, similar to time data, were the most common, occurring in roughly 58% of the cases. An example is shown in Figure 4 above, and on Figure 5A on the next page. "Normal" distributions (5B) and left-skewed (5C) were less common, occurring roughly 30% and 11% of the time respectively. Only one frequency distribution

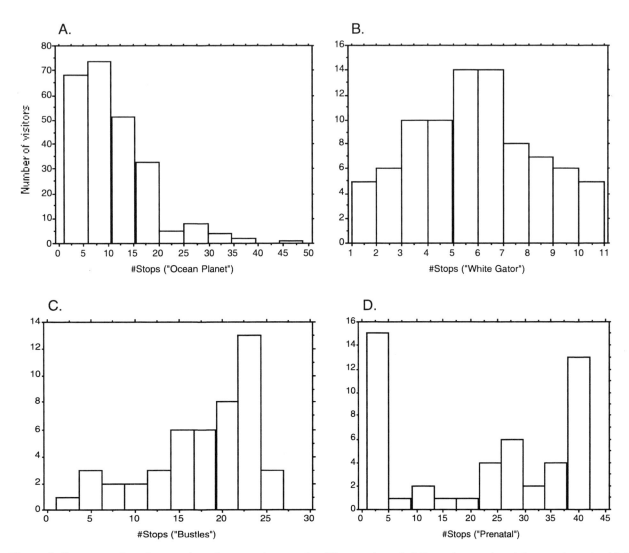

Figure 5. Four examples of stops data shown as bar graphs. (The number of visitors observed and the number of exhibit elements in each exhibition varied.)

Each bar represents the number of visitors in the exhbition's sample who stopped at the corresponding number of stops shown on the horizontal axis. The patterns vary: A. "Ocean Planet" is right-skewed; B. "White Gator" is a bell-shaped distribution; C. "Bustles" is skewed left; D. "Prenatal" is bimodal. Right-skewed was the most common.

of stops had a clearly bimodal pattern (5D), defined as having two clear "peaks," where the tallest bars were over the lowest and the highest numbers.

Out of the total sample of 8,507 visitors, less than 1% stopped at all of the elements, regardless of the number of elements available. The highest number of stops made by any visitor was 77 (in "Artist as Activist" with 77 elements).

PERCENTAGE OF STOPS AT ELEMENTS

The absolute number of stops in any exhibition is determined by the number of elements available. (Returning to visit an element, i.e., stopping at the same element more than once, does not count as an additional stop.) To compare exhibitions that have different numbers of elements, the number of stops each visitor made was converted into the percentage of stops. For example, in an exhibition with 25 elements, a visitor who stopped at 10 elements stopped at 40% of the elements. Figure 6 contains the same data as Figure 5C, but here the horizontal axis shows the percentage of stops instead of the raw numbers. The frequency distribution of each set of observations (raw number of stops and percent of possible stops) reveals the same pattern.

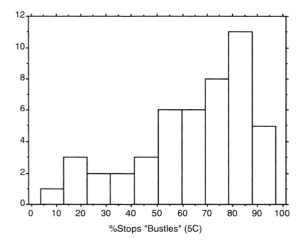

Figure 6. Example of stops data shown as percentage of stops. N=47 visitors.

The horizontal axis shows the percentage of possible stops instead of the raw numbers of stops, as shown on 5C above.

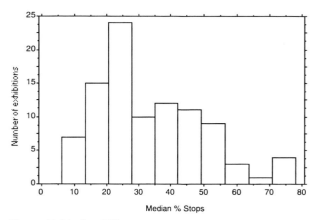

Figure 7. Median %Stops. N=104 exhibitions (missing data for 6).

Each bar represents the number of exhibitions with the corresponding median %Stops shown on the horizontal axis. The frequency distribution of median %Stops shows that visitors typically stop at between 20% and 40% of an exhibition.

MEDIAN PERCENTAGE OF STOPS

In this study the distribution of data for percentage of stops made by visitors in one exhibition was summarized using the median rather than the mean or average. The median percentage of stops (%Stops) was chosen for descriptive and comparative purposes because the patterns of data for stops in different exhibitions were more varied than the patterns of time data.

The %Stops ranged from 6% to 76% and was less than 50% in three-quarters of the exhibitions. The mean of the median %Stops was 34%. See Figure 7.

All of the findings and analysis so far have been by single variables (size, number of elements, total time, or stops) within exhibitions and across exhibitions. The following section will present simple correlations between pairs of variables, shown as scattergrams.

CORRELATIONS BETWEEN VARIABLES

Time and stops variables were correlated within individual exhibitions, and pairs of the four variables were examined for correlations among exhibitions.

ANALYSIS OF TIME SPENT AND STOPS WITHIN INDIVIDUAL EXHIBITIONS

For data within each exhibition, a scattergram was plotted to show visitors' total times against the number of stops they made, with each point on the scattergram representing one visitor. Scattergrams of individual exhibitions showed that there was a direct relationship or correlation between the amount of time people stayed and the percentage of stops they made. In all 110 cases, as time increased, so did the number of stops, as shown in Figure 8 below.

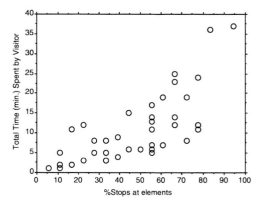

Figure 8. Example of a time-and-stops scattergram for one exhibition. N=40 visitors.

Each dot represents one visitor. As visitors spent more time, they made more stops. The slope of the regression line is from lower left to upper right. This pattern occurred in all 110 time-and-stops data from museum exhibitions in this study.

In Figure 8, the regression value is r² = .56, indicating a fairly strong relationship between the two variables. In roughly 60% of the 110 exhibitions, the value for the regression line was greater than r² = .5. In the other 40% of the cases, the relationship between time and stops was still positive, but less strong (r² = between .4 and .2). The lack of points in the upper-left quadrant of most of the scattergrams showed that relatively few visitors spent a relatively long time at only a few elements.

In addition to the relationship between the points, the locations of the points on the scattergram can indicate another pattern. If there are more points in the upper right (a higher the percentage of visitors staying longer and stopping more), more people used the exhibition more thoroughly (refer to Figure 8).

ANALYSIS OF VARIABLES AMONG EXHIBITIONS

Scattergrams discussed previously indicated the strong positive relationship between two variables—visitors' time and stops in individual exhibitions—where each point on the scattergram represented one visitor. Next, the four exhibition variables will be analyzed in six pairs to show other relationships of size, number of elements, average time, and median %Stops. In the scattergrams that follow, each point represents one exhibition.

Three of the six pairs of variables show a positive correlation with time spent. Average total time spent in an exhibition is related to the size of the exhibition, the number of elements in it, and the median percentage of stops visitors made.

Figure 9 shows that as the size of an exhibition increases, the average total time spent by visitors also increases. For every increase of 1,000 square feet, however, the average time goes up only 1.76 minutes indicating that people do not spend proportionally more time in larger exhibitions. (We are not able to say whether we would observe a similar relationship in the total population of museum exhibitions because these exhibitions were chosen using nonrandom methods.)

The other two relationships—time and number of elements and time and %Stops—while positive, are weaker (see Figures 10 and 11).

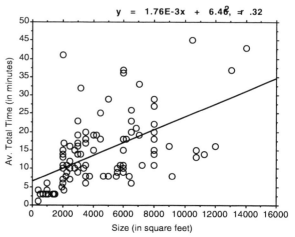

Figure 9. Scattergram of average total time and exhibition size. N=104 exhibitions (excludes 6 "old" exhibitions)

Each dot represents one exhibition.

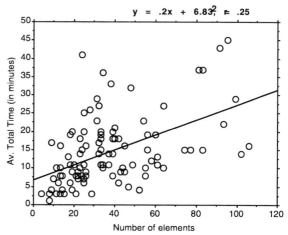

Figure 10. Scattergram of average total time and number of elements. N=103 exhibitions (excludes 6 "old" exhibitions and an outlier with 179 elements)

Each dot represents one exhibition.

Exhibition size and number of elements are also positively correlated. When the unusual outlier mentioned before ("Families," a 2,100-square-foot exhibition with 179 elements) is excluded from the scattergram, the r² value becomes .37, as shown in Figure 12.

The two remaining pairs of variables in this study's sample did not show positive correlations. As the number of elements in an exhibition increased, the median %Stops did not increase (see Figure 13). The relationship was slightly negative, that is, as the number of elements increased, the %Stops decreased.

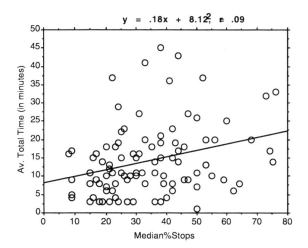

Figure 11. Scattergram of average total time and median %Stops. N=98 exhibitions (excludes 6 "old" exhibitions and 6 exhibitions for which data were missing)

Each dot represents one exhibition.

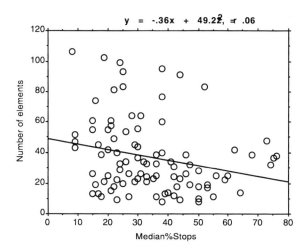

Figure 13. Elements and median %Stops. N=103 (excludes outlier and 6 exhibitions for which data were missing)

Each point represents one exhibition. The scattergram shows a weak inverse relationship between the number of elements in an exhibition and the median %Stops that visitors made.

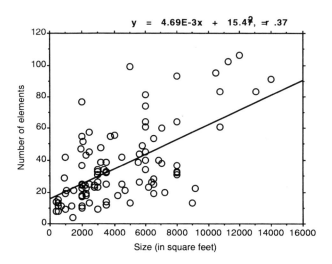

Figure 12. Scattergram of sizes and number of elements. N=103 exhibitions (excludes 6 "old" exhibitions, and outlier)

Each point is one exhibition, and the two variables of exhibition size and number of elements show a positive relationship.

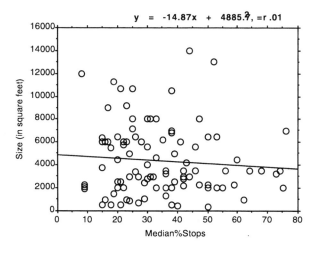

Figure 14. Scattergram of size and median %Stops. N=104 exhibitions (excludes 6 exhibitions for which data were missing)

Each point represents one exhibition. There was no correlation between size and median %Stops.

Figure 14 shows that the size of the exhibition was not correlated with the median %Stops.

MULTIVARIATE FINDINGS AMONG EXHIBITIONS
Even though there was clearly a lot of variability among exhibitions for sizes, times, elements, and stops, and while bivariate analysis revealed small or weak correlations between pairs of independent variables (r^2 values of less than .4), relationships, nevertheless, exist.

Multiple regression can reveal a stronger pattern, as it does in this study. The rationale for using several independent variables in a statistical model is that while each may have a unique effect upon the dependent variable, collectively they predict more than each can predict alone. In a statistical analysis that combines the influence of size, number of elements, and median percentage of stops, their impact together on average time is more dramatic. The r-squared value increases to .54 (p = .0001), meaning 54% of the variance of visitors' average total time in an exhibition is related to the exhibition's size (square feet), the number of elements, and the percentage of stops visitors made. Multivariate analysis reveals a clear relationship: Together, size of the exhibition, number of elements, and median %Stops were strong predictors of the amount of time that visitors spent in an exhibition.

This finding validates the purpose of this study in that it shows a statistically significant relationship between time and these three variables over a broad range of exhibitions. (Again, however, we must use caution in interpreting these results because random sampling methods were not used. Nonetheless, if another study were to be undertaken using a wide variety of educational exhibitions, it would likely reveal similar general trends and patterns.)

As we have seen, exhibitions containing different numbers of elements can be compared to each other by computing the percentage of stops. To compare the data of time and size in a more relative way, the amount of space per unit of time needs to be computed.

FINDINGS OF EXHIBITION INDEXES FOR THOROUGHNESS OF USE

Below, the data are summarized in the form of two indexes that indicate thorough use (longer time spent by visitors, more stops made in exhibition).

SWEEP RATE INDEX (SRI)

To briefly recap the description in Chapter IV, "Methods," sweep rate is an index that allows comparisons of visitors' use of exhibitions between exhibitions of different sizes. SRI is an abstraction that uses two real numbers, exhibition size and average total time, to determine relative amount of time spent by a sample of visitors in a given area. To compute SRI, the square footage of an exhibition is divided by the average total time. As average time goes up, sweep rates go down. Stated another way, the more time visitors spend, the lower the exhibition's sweep rate index will be. Spending more time in a given area is considered for the pur-

poses of this study as a positive indication of thorough use. Numbers for SRIs given below are in square feet per minute.

For the sample of 110 exhibitions, the SRIs ranged from a low of 49 to a high of 3,600. The mean was 432, and the standard deviation was 445, indicating a high degree of variability within the sample. The median SRI was 296, and the mode was 200 to 300. The high variability of the SRIs was primarily due to the wide range of sizes of exhibitions.

Among 110 exhibitions, 103 had SRI values below 900. Of the seven with values greater than 900, six of them were "old" exhibitions. To limit the universe of this study to exhibitions that were not about to undergo or in need of renovation, observations from the six "old" exhibitions were dropped from the sample for the remaining data analyses involving SRIs (thus, N = 104 instead of 110). See Figure 15.

For the remaining 104 exhibitions, the SRIs ranged from a low of 49 to a high of 1147. The mean was 351, and the standard deviation was 211. The median SRI was 284, and the mode was still 200 to 300.

ANALYSIS OF VARIABLES (ELEMENTS AND STOPS) AND SRI

Scattergrams were made to investigate correlations between SRIs and two variables: number of elements and %Stops. The scattergrams show no correlation between SRIs and number of elements (r^2 = .004). There was an inverse relationship between SRIs and %Stops (r^2 = .15). That is, lower (slower) sweep rates were related to higher percentages of stops in exhibitions. See Figure 16.

This scattergram (Figure 16) shows that exhibitions with visits consisting of low percentages of stops might have low or high sweep rates, but that exhibitions with visits consisting of a relatively high percentages of stops consistently have lower sweep rates.

PERCENTAGE OF DILIGENT VISITORS (%DV)

The second index that allows exhibitions of different sizes to be compared is a variable developed for this study called percentage of diligent visitors, or %DV. It is

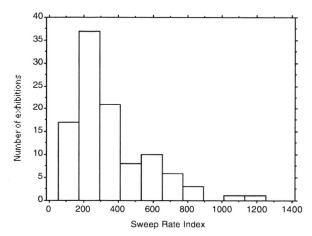

Figure 15. Sweep rate indexes. N=104 (excludes 6 "old" exhibitions)

The frequency distribution of SRIs is shown as a bar graph. (with"old" exhibitions eliminated, the range is reduced, but the mode stayed the same.)

defined as the percentage of visitors who stopped at more than half of the exhibition's elements.

The variable of %DV is based on visitors' stops and is computed by taking the percentages for all visitors' stops, or %Stops (the number of stops they made divided by the number of available elements, times 100), then counting the number of people in the sample who had values of greater than 50%, and dividing that number by the total number of visitors in the sample. The

%DV is different than %Stops because %DV relates to percent of visitors who made a certain percentage of stops instead of the percentage of stops made by certain number of visitors.

DESCRIPTIVE STATISTICS OF %DV

The distribution of the variable %DV will be reviewed in the same way the previous variables have been described. For all 110 exhibitions, the %DV ranged from a low of zero (no one used more than half of the elements) to a high of 86% (most people stopped at more than half of the elements). The mean %DV was 26%, and the median %DV was 24%. See Figure 17 below.

The frequency distribution of %DV data in Figure 17 shows a right-skewed pattern: the vast majority of the exhibitions did not have more than 45%DV.

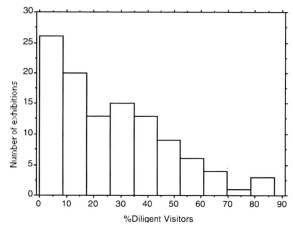

Figure 17. Percentage of diligent visitors (%DV) in 110 exhibitions

The frequency distribution of %DV is shown as a bar graph, ranging from zero to 86%. Most exhibitions had %DV values between zero and 35%, and the mean was 26%.

THE SRI-%DV MODEL FOR RELATIVE THOROUGH USE

The most comprehensive tool for identifying thoroughly used exhibitions is the SRI-%DV scattergram. It is a graph that combines and compares the samples' values from the four original variables—size, elements, time, and stops—which have been converted into the two indexes to show visitors' duration of time (SRI) and allocation of stops (%DV) in each exhibition.

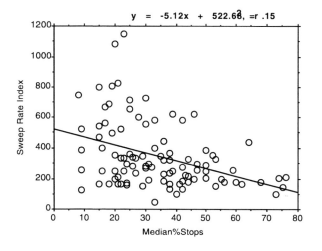

$$y = -5.12x + 522.68, = r .15$$

Figure 16. Scattergram of SRI and median %Stops. N=98 (excludes 6 "old" exhibitions and 6 for which data were missing)

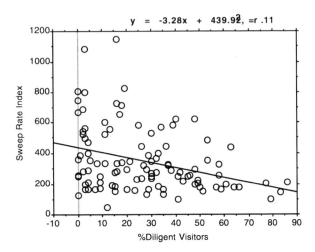

Figure 18. SRI and %DV scattegram. N=104 (excludes 6 "old" exhibitions)

Each point represents one exhibition. The regression line shows the slightly inverse relationship between SRI and %DV.

On the scattergram at left, Figure 18, each point represents one exhibition (N = 104, "old" exhibitions excluded). A regression line shows a slope with a slight inverse relationship between SRI and %DV, with an r^2 value of 0.12. The scattergram reveals exhibitions with low %DV and low or high SRI, but there are no exhibitions with high %DV and high SRI because it is illogical: when visitors make more stops, they cannot do so without spending more time.

Incidentally, the same 14 exhibitions occur at the high end of this model (Figure 18) as fall at the high end of the scattergram in Figure 16, which is based on median %Stops (although the points are in slightly different positions). This coincidence is because when the median %Stops for an exhibition exceeds 50%, it then matches the definition of %DV.

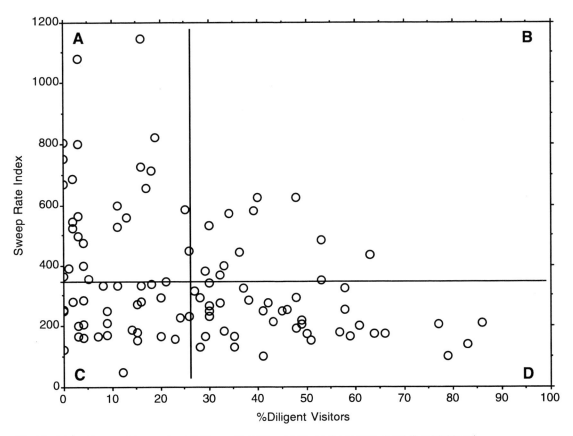

Figure 19. Model for thoroughly used exhibitions. N=104 exhibitions (excludes 6 "old" exhibitions)

Each point represents one exhibition. The solid lines represent the average values for SRI and %DV, forming four quadrants. The most thoroughly used exhibitions are in D quadrant, on the lower right.

Solid lines in Figure 19 divide the scattergram into four quadrants, showing the mean values of both variables. In this model, thoroughly used exhibitions are defined as being above average % DV and below the mean for SRI, in quadrant D.

Some differences occur in the types of exhibitions found in some areas of the model (although no conclusions should be drawn about whether these would hold in the population of museum exhibitions at large):

• Quadrant A: Upper-left quadrant (SRI of more than 352, % DV less than 26): The least thoroughly used exhibitions included all types: zoos and aquariums, science, and natural history museums in numbers that are proportional to the overall sample. There are, however, more large exhibitions here, and they tend to have more elements than those exhibitions in D.

• Quadrant B: In the upper-right quadrant, with above-average % DV and higher-than-average (faster) sweep rates, there are proportionally more dioramas represented.

• Quadrant C: The lower-left quadrant (under 352 SRI, under 26 % DV) contains proportionately fewer natural history exhibitions and more science museum exhibitions than quadrant D.

• Quadrant D. The lower-right quadrant has higher-than-average % DV and slower-than-average sweep rates (SRI), indicating more thorough use. There are proportionately fewer science museum exhibitions, fewer natural history exhibitions, more art and history exhibitions, and only three of the 16 dioramalike exhibitions.

Points in the far right area of quadrant D of the model are the exhibitions that were exceptionally thoroughly used, defined by the criterion references of having a % DV greater than 51 % and an SRI below 300. These 11 exhibitions were found in all five types of institutions—in an aquarium, and in science, natural history, history, and art museums. In the data from these exhibitions, the frequency distribution of visitors' total times were more often bell-shaped curves; the distribution of the percentage of stops was more often left skewed; and 10 of the r^2 values for the exhibitions' scattergrams of time and stops data were above .5. Eight of the 11 are discussed in the various case studies in Chapter VI.

The SRI-% DV model presents descriptive statistics that summarize and compare a large sample of very diverse exhibitions for the quality of being thoroughly used by

	N	SQUARE FEET	NUMBER OF ELEMENTS	AVERAGE TIME	MEDIAN %STOPS	SRI	%DV
Total Sample	110	4629.9 (3117.6)	37.3 (27.0)	13.8 (9.5)	33.9 (16.4)	435.7 (448.6)	26.4 (21.1)
excluding 6 "old" exhibtions	104	4462.6 (3047.1)	36.5 (23.6)	14.3 (9.5)	34.1 (16.1)	351.5 (211.2)	26.9 (21.5)
Dioramas (no "old" exhibitions)	16	7316.5 (3342.4)	36.3 (29.3)	13.7 (11.1)	31.2 (13.0)	638.5 (236.7)	23.3 (19.8)
Nondioramas (no "old" exhibitions)	88	3943.8 (2701.1)	38.2 (27.1)	14.2 (9.0)	35.2 (17.2)	300.6 (160.1)	27.4 (22.0)
Large nondiorama exhibitions (>3,900 square feet)	33	6884.8 (1991.6)	53 (24.4)	20.6 (8.7)	31.4 (14.6)	400.5 (191.5)	23.4 (20.4)
Small nondiorama exhibitions (=<3,900 square feet)	55	2179.2 (973.1)	29.9 (25.6)	10.7 (7.5)	37.2 (18.2)	244.3 (104.8)	29.7 (22.8)
Exceptionally thoroughly used exhibitions (far right side of D quadrant, figure 19.)	11	3165 (1550.2)	29.2 (11.9)	17.3 (9.1)	64.7 (2.6)	200.2 (83.8)	68 (11.0)

Figure 20. Means for four exhibition variables and two indexes by types of exhibitions and for exceptionally thoroughly used exhibitions.(standard deviations in parentheses)

visitors. Another way to summarize and compare the data from different exhibitions is by subgroup types of exhibitions and by types of museums, but this analysis is less reliable due to the convenience-sampling method and the small sizes of the subgroups (e.g., fewer than 30 in each group).

FINDINGS BY TYPE OF EXHIBITION AND TYPE OF MUSEUM

As might be anticipated, differences existed between the four variables (exhibition size, number of elements, average time, median percentage of stops) and the two indexes (SRI and %DV) by types of exhibitions. However, because the observations in the samples cannot be considered truly representative and the number of museums or exhibitions in each group is small, these findings should be considered speculative.

The table in Figures 20 on the previous page shows a summary and a breakdown of the data by diorama and nondiorama exhibitions, large and small exhibitions, and exceptionally thoroughly used exhibitions.

DIORAMA AND NONDIORAMA EXHIBITIONS
Diorama exhibitions tended to be larger in size than nondioramas, but the average times spent by visitors were not greater. The average sweep rate for dioramas was twice the average of nondioramas, suggesting that visitors tend to spend less time per unit area in diorama exhibitions than in nondioramas. The mean number of elements was not different between the two groups, nor was the %Stops.

Given the differences in size and sweep rate, the 16 dioramalike exhibitions will not be included in the following calculations that compare other types of exhibitions and museums. The six "old" exhibitions—those that had tracking data taken prior to renovations—have also been dropped from the analysis that follows in this section, leaving a sample size of N = 88.

LARGE AND SMALL EXHIBITIONS
Significant differences exist between large (greater than 3,900 square feet) and small (less than 3,900 square feet) exhibitions in the number of elements and the average total time spent by visitors. Large exhibitions had longer average times and contained more elements. But visitors did not stay in large exhibitions proportionately longer, as might be expected. The sweep rates are significantly different. Visitors seem to use big exhibitions faster (more square feet per minute) than small ones.

Although visitors tend to use smaller exhibitions more slowly, in general visitors do not appear to use small exhibitions more thoroughly than large ones. The %Stops and %DV are not significantly different in large and small exhibitions.

PERMANENT AND TEMPORARY EXHIBITIONS
There were no significant differences between permanent and temporary exhibitions for any of the variables studied. In this study's sample, temporary exhibitions are not smaller or more thoroughly used. The variability among both types was high.

DIFFERENCES AMONG SUBCATEGORIES BY MUSEUM TYPES
As described at the beginning of this chapter, the sample of 110 exhibitions came from five different museum types: zoos and aquariums, natural history museums, science museums, history museums, and art museums. It should be noted, again, that because these subcategories are small and are not truly representative samples, they cannot be compared with confidence.

Figure 21 shows a breakdown of the data by science-related and nonscience-related exhibitions, five different museum types (zoos and aquariums, natural history, science, history, and art), and science centers versus science museums.

Science-related and nonscience-related exhibitions were not distinguished in terms of the physical variables of size and number of elements or of the visitor-use variables of average time and sweep rates. Two variables did show a slight difference: Science exhibitions had lower median %Stops and %DV than nonscience exhibitions.

When the subcategory of science museums is split into two groups, museumlike (having object and artifact collections) and science-centerlike (noncollection-based exhibitions), the sample sizes are too small to draw firm conclusions, but there is a suggestion that exhibitions at science centers are the least thoroughly used. As a group they had the lowest %DV scores.

In the next chapter, the findings will be discussed and the limitations to the methods will be reviewed. Considerations for future use of these methods also will be discussed.

	N	SQUARE FEET	NUMBER OF ELEMENTS	AVERAGE TIME	MEDIAN %STOPS	SRI	%DV
Total Sample	110	4629.9 (3117.6)	37.3 (27.0)	13.8 (9.5)	33.9 (16.4)	435.7 (448.6)	26.4 (21.1)
Science related	81	4157.4 (2732.6)	37.4 (23.4)	14.9 (9.8)	33.4 (16.5)	300 (156.7)	25.8 (22.4)
Non science related	29	3486 (2621.8)	39.8 (34.1)	13.4 (8.1)	39.2 (18.2)	297.8 (166.2)	31.4 (20.5)
Zoos/Aquariums	14	2643.8 (1659.5)	16.8 (6.1)	9.7 (5.8)	42.6 (15.1)	274.3 (85.3)	41 (18.7)
Natural History	29	6128.1 (2490.0)	48.6 (23.6)	21.3 (11.0)	35.5 (15.6)	335.8 (156.1)	27.4 (22.5)
Science	34	3398.3 (2248.7)	34.7 (18.8)	12.6 (8.3)	28.8 (14.4)	287.1 (156.8)	19.6 (19.1)
History	20	3857.1 (2696.6)	45.9 (41.0)	15.1 (8.6)	38.9 (21.5)	286.4 (151.0)	29.9 (24.3)
Art	13	3582.7 (3348.0)	37.2 (23.9)	12.8 (8.7)	39.3 (16.7)	319.8 (220.1)	34.5 (21.0)
Science Museum	20	4221.7 (2834.9)	38.7 (25.6)	15.8 (10.6)	34.9 (17.4)	285.1 (142.4)	28.9 (23.4)
Science Center	14	3900 (2370.7)	32.3 (10.2)	11.5 (5.0)	26.2 (9.1)	359.9 (200.5)	13.5 (12.0)

Figure 21. Means for four exhibition variables and two indexes by types of museums (standard deviations in parentheses)

VI. DISCUSSION OF METHODS AND FINDINGS

In this chapter, the first section is devoted to discussing the problems encountered with definitions and analysis. Recommendations for using the methods and interpreting the results are covered in the second section. A brief discussion of the common "what-if" questions concludes the chapter.

THE PRACTICALITY OF THE METHODS

The methods developed for this study proved to make sense to most museum practitioners, were easy to learn by people with little or no experience in visitor studies, were not costly, did not use invasive procedures, and worked in a variety of settings.

To create a research methodology that can be widely shared meant defining the parameters and procedures in ways that are clear and consistent in as broad a universe of museum exhibitions as possible. The aim was to be as inclusive as possible, but the methodology was never intended to be applicable to all types of exhibitions. Throughout this study, our universe has shrunk and changed shape to accommodate as many different types of exhibitions as possible, but also to eliminate ones that were not consistent with the basic definitions and variables selected for measurement. Some tracking data contributed to the study were not usable, such as in cases where stops or elements were defined in ways that were not compatible with this study's definitions, or data were missing or were not recorded on the data sheets in a decipherable way. In other cases, a set of observations did not satisfy all of the requirements (i.e., definitions, assumptions) set for the study, such as having a sample size of at least 40 visitor trackings, or sampling across different days of the week. If there were reasons to assume that the deviations would cause a sample not to be compared fairly, that sample was dropped.

Some of the practical problems encountered are discussed below.

DEFINING EDUCATIONAL EXHIBITIONS

This study was limited to exhibitions that had didactic goals and contained interpretive materials. Some clearly contained more interpretive devices than others. The researcher did not visit all the exhibitions but examined floor plans, all of which included physical evidence of interpretive devices (e.g., introductory labels, videos, interactive devices).

The methods and findings in this study are probably most applicable to exhibitions in which communication goals have been stated and exhibit developers have a vested interest in the degree to which their objectives are achieved and a willingness to share that information with other museum practitioners.

An important issue throughout the study was the difference between an exhibition's intent (as defined by the exhibit developer's goals) and how visitors actually experienced it. Can an exhibition be considered educational simply because it exists, without any measurable evidence that it is capable of communicating something? The discrepancy between intent and realization remains an issue.

Another problem encountered was the unclear distinction between an exhibition and a resource room, library, play area, or activity center. "Discovery centers" or "learning labs" are often conceived as places where family groups can engage in longer explorations (White and Barry 1984). Sometimes these areas are not developed with a main theme or "big idea" (Serrell 1994), as an exhibition with a story line would be. The research tools developed for this study are meant for exhibitions and are less appropriate for loosely themed activity centers.

For example, "Hands-On Science" at the California Academy of Sciences, as defined by this study, was not really an exhibition. The %DV was zero. No one would be expected to investigate a discovery area or library-type space fully in one trip, but the median time was only about 4 minutes (Mackinney 1994). There is some anecdotal evidence that discovery areas are perceived as places for children and are avoided by adult groups.

Should they be? If the distinctions between exhibitions and discovery centers are not clear to museum practitioners, the differences in purpose are probably not clear to visitors.

QUESTIONS ABOUT EXHIBITION SIZE

Size was measured in square feet from wall to wall, including the interiors of cases and dioramas. It was most often available from the exhibit designer or from architectural drawings. Sometimes measurements had to be determined as a best guess, because, surprisingly, the information on size was not available.

To keep the methods easy to use, the whole area was included, not just the open spaces where visitors could move and stand. Measuring around cases and objects would require considerably more effort and detail. Another consideration was that if museum floor space was dedicated to an exhibition, it could not at the same time be dedicated to another purpose (e.g., office, storage). The exhibition occupied the "real estate" whether visitors could walk on it or not. An exception to this was made for space where visitors could look into an area behind-the-scenes and see or interact with museum staff at work, such as an animal hospital or archaeologist's lab. In these cases, the sweep rate index might be figured in two ways, one including the off-site-but-visible space, and one not including it.

Some other questions about size that arose were:
• When is an exhibition too small to be called an exhibition?
• Can a section of an exhibition be isolated and measured using the methods of this study?
• Can an exhibition be too big?

In retrospect, the methods and findings in this study are probably most applicable to exhibitions that are larger than 1,000 square feet and smaller than 15,000 square feet for several reasons. Exhibit spaces that are only 500 square feet probably cannot compete for visitors' attention in the same way a larger exhibition can. The conceptual implications of "an exhibition" imply an integrity of concept, environment, and users, which cannot be fulfilled by only a portion of an exhibition. A very large exhibition (e.g., cavernous or multi-roomed) can be indistinguishable to visitors as an exhibition unto itself.

THE DEFINITION OF ELEMENTS AND HOW TO COUNT THEM

Elements were defined as all the places where visitors could stop to do something, such as read a label, interact with a device, watch an audiovisual, or look more closely at an object, artifact, work of art, or phenomenon. Sometimes two elements were so close together that the data collector could not tell which one a visitor was examining. In these cases, two different elements were sometimes called one. But lumping too many disparate exhibits or modes of presentation together can also can distort the findings. When defining elements, we had to make logical judgments in accordance with the definitions given here.

The exhibition with the fewest elements ("History by the Seat of Your Pants") was in a history museum (Minnesota Historical Society) and contained four large interactive units for children to explore. As most exhibitions have 10 or more elements, "Pants" should probably have been dropped from the sample.

The exhibition with the largest number of elements ("Families" with 179 elements) was clearly an outlier in terms of the number of different places planned for visitor activities within one exhibition (refer to Figure 2). For analysis among exhibitions involving number of elements, such as average number of elements or the correlation of number of elements and average time, "Families" was not included. (See Chapter VII, "Selected Case Studies" for more discussion about this exhibition.)

Elements could be defined in all types of museum exhibitions, even though they were unique for each. The definitions were contextual, but not whimsical. Similar elements occurred across exhibitions, including: introductory panels, stand-alone video spaces, and multiple, identical units of the same activity. The number of elements within one exhibition, once defined and identified, did not change, but their nature did if they were installed differently when the exhibition traveled to another site. (See Chapter VII, "Selected Case Studies" for examples.)

Defining elements was a prerequisite to describing and measuring thoroughness of use. Knowing the number of elements is a useful piece of information for exhibit planners and evaluators as well as for visitors. It might be worth investigating, at some time in the future, the correlation between how clearly exhibition elements are defined by the planners and how clearly the elements are recognized as conceptually distinct experiences by visitors. If visitors are aware of where one element stops and another begins, they might be able to budget their time more consciously. We might see more visitors making active choices, rather than drifting aimlessly from place to place (adults) or bouncing like pinballs around the exhibits (children).

TOTAL TIME SPENT BY A VISITOR IN AN EXHIBITION, MEASURED IN MINUTES

Measuring the total duration of a visitor's time spent in minutes posed a few problems. One, if the exhibition was small (e.g., less than 1,000 square feet), a person could spend less than a minute in it and see all he or she wanted to see. Visitors' time in small exhibitions was, in some cases, measured in seconds. In this study visitors must spend at least 1 minute in the exhibition to be counted as having completed a visit. This guideline presents another argument for not including exhibitions of less than 1,000 square feet in the study.

In very few cases, visitors exited and returned later to the same exhibition, a situation that raises the question of cumulative time versus a single visit. If the data collector had not started tracking another person, he or she usually just tacked on the additional time to the earlier observation. Data collectors noted when visitors returned. Fortunately, it did not happen often enough to be a problem.

Other researchers have pointed out that not all of a visitor's time is spent paying attention to exhibits. This is especially true of a visitor's time in the whole museum (including bathrooms, benches, and food services), but it is less of an issue within a single exhibition, where most people do spend most of their time looking at exhibits. As instructed in the Workbook for this study, when more than 1 minute was spent involved in something other than paying attention to exhibits, or walking and glancing, that was noted on the data sheet for possible exclusion from total time. This situation happened only a few times. (Twice visitors sat down and fell asleep.)

In several instances, an exhibit-themed store was part of the exhibition, and the store was counted as one element. It was interesting to note what percentage of the visitors stopped at the store and how much time they spent there compared to other elements in the exhibition. Stores can serve as excellent orientation and concluding, summary activities.

DEFINING STOPS

A stop at an element was counted when both of the visitor's feet were planted on the floor, head or eyes pointing in the direction of the element for 2 to 3 seconds or more. A person returning to a previously visited element did not count as an additional stop. Amounts of time spent at individual elements were not measured in most cases and are not reported in this study (although the information is obviously valuable for the museum where the data were collected.) Thus, a stop of 3 seconds was not counted differently from a stop that lasted 3 minutes. This guideline disturbs some museum practitioners because they believe the value of a long stop is quantitatively and qualitatively different from a short stop. But their concern is more relevant in studies of single exhibit elements than whole exhibitions. The time spent at stops is less relevant for an overall look at visitors' time spent in a whole exhibition, which is the purpose of this study.

Timing visitors at every stop makes tracking more complicated and harder, and it accumulates much larger quantities of data. The concept of exhibit holding power—the amount of time spent divided by the amount of time necessary to "do" an exhibit—is not a practical index for whole exhibitions. Who gets to decide how much time it should take to "do" an exhibition? As informal learners, visitors are under no obligation to do anything. The purpose of this research was simply to look at the total time visitors actually spent and to compare exhibitions according to the patterns presented by the data itself.

Stop has been defined in other studies as less than 2 to 3 seconds, more than 2 to 3 seconds, or not defined as a quantity of time. When a stop is less than 2 to 3 seconds, it becomes difficult to distinguish between a glance (looking briefly without both feet stopped) and a stop. Data recording may be less accurate with stops defined as less than 2 to 3 seconds, because data collectors can easily miss seeing briefer stops. When a stop is defined as more than 2 to 3 seconds, such as 5 seconds or 10 seconds, many brief stops go unrecorded. Museum visitors normally make lots of brief stops as they search for personally meaningful, intrinsically rewarding connections with exhibits. These moments are counted as paying attention, albeit briefly. Many exhibit experiences can reinforce what visitors already know; in those cases, visitors do not need or want to spend more than a few seconds at an element.

SAMPLING METHODS

This study did not have a probabilistic, random sample of exhibitions. It was a sample of convenience. Moreover, for the sample of visitors observed, no record was kept of the number of visitors who crossed the line into exhibitions during the observation periods. This statistically important detail would have required having twice as many data collectors, thereby doubling the labor hours and costs. We cannot, therefore, claim that this study is truly representative. However, given the normal constraints and limitations of most museum budgets for evaluations, it allowed us to establish a database that permits a reasonable set of findings. As a first effort to amass a multi-site database of tracking studies, it is a place to start.

SAMPLE SIZE

The recommended sample size for this study was 40 or more people per exhibition, and the majority (69%) of the trackings included sample sizes of more than 50 visitors each. The average was 72, but one exhibition ("A Tribute to Survival") had a whopping 458 observations. A sample of 40 visitors is sufficient for information about general patterns (e.g., average time, most popular and least popular elements). Usually by the time 30 visitors have been tracked in an exhibition containing 20 to 40 elements, almost all elements will have been used by at least one visitor, and the patterns of most and least popular elements and average time will have emerged.

Within tracking samples of more than 80 visitors, a split-half test was done to check the validity of the patterns of total time and number of stops that emerged in a sample size of 40. To do this, samples with more than 80 visitors were split in half. The first 40 were analyzed and compared to the second 40 as long as both halves were representative of a cross-section of a museum's whole audience. In all these cases, there were no significant differences between average time and % Stops. That is, when the sample of 40 was collected over a variety of days of the week and included diverse types of visiting groups, the trends produced by that sample were the same as the trends collected on the other 40 visitors under the same conditions. This step helped validate our procedure. Since the goal was simply to get an overview of total times and number of stops in one exhibition, a tracking sample of more than 100 is probably overkill. While it is always desirable to have the largest practical sample, a smaller one will suffice for finding general trends, as it did in this study.

A sample size of 40 or less was not sufficient for an analysis of subgroups within the samples, such as male versus female, or adult-only groups versus groups with children. While it might be interesting to know about these differences, if any exist, the questions posed by this study are meant to include all types of visitors in the diverse audiences.

TRAINING DATA COLLECTORS

Many data collectors were trained by reading the workbook (see Appendix B) and discussing the first few tracking samples over the phone with the research director. If everything seemed clear and consistent, data collection proceeded, and the results (either raw sheets or summaries) were mailed to the researcher. Many of the participants were collecting data for the first time, but with minimal assistance they accomplished the task without any problems and often found the job an interesting and rewarding experience.

EXHIBITION TYPES

The sample of 110 exhibitions in this study was large and diverse, but when broken down into subcategories, three problems are apparent: The number within subcategory becomes very small, only 13 to 34 samples per group; the exhibitions are not always a good cross-section; and the definitions of the subcategories are not always as tight as one might expect. For example:

- In the museum type subcategory of zoo/aquarium, seven of the 14 exhibitions were from one institution (Shedd Aquarium), and five of the seven were temporary exhibitions. Three of the five did not contain any live animals—rather atypical for an aquarium or zoo exhibition.

- Within the museum type subcategory of science museums, all of the exhibitions contained some interactive elements, but there were different ratios of collections-based exhibits, static displays, and phenomena-based exhibits.
- The distinction between "science center" and "science museum" was not clear. Using the name of the institution was not consistently the clue: Is the California Academy of Sciences a science museum or a natural history museum or a science center? Is the Museum of Science and Industry in Chicago a science museum or a science center? (During the course of this study, the California Museum of Science and Industry actually changed its name to the California Science Center.)
- Subgrouping science versus natural history museums, in some cases, seemed arbitrary, especially when the same exhibition was traveling to different types of institutions, as was the case with "Hunters of the Sky," "Global Warming," "Hidden Kingdoms," and "Whodunit." These special situations are discussed in Chapter VII, "Selected Case Studies."
- Some exhibitions were difficult to categorize as "science" or "nonscience" because they combined art and science or cultural history and science.
- Three exhibitions at children's museums were included because they had targeted family audiences, not just young children. Because they were too few to form a subgroup, these exhibitions have been included in the five main categories according to their topics (one art, one science, and one history).

For all the reasons stated above, there clearly is no typical art museum exhibition, for example, or a typical science museum exhibition. It makes most sense to look at the findings of this study as a whole. The importance of this study is in seeing the ranges, the extremes, the clusters, or patterns of the full sample, instead of trying to tease out subcategories when and where the variability is too high and the sample sizes are too small.

DISCUSSION OF THE DATABASE

In this section, the problems and implications of the findings are discussed. Why is it useful to know total time, time and stops, and time per unit area?

TOTAL TIME

By and large, visitors did not spend much time in the exhibitions in this study. The average and median time spent by visitors to 82% of the 110 exhibitions, regardless of size, was less than 20 minutes. Although the sample of exhibitions was not selected to be truly representative, this finding deserves careful consideration because of the sample's size and diversity.

No single common factor stood out among the 18 exhibitions that broke the 20-minute barrier. This group included exhibitions that charged a fee, were new and big, had extremely captivating elements, or attracted an audience that was very intentional. "Amber: Window to the Past," the most thoroughly used exhibition in this study, apparently had all four of these factors working for it when it opened at the American Museum of Natural History. When it was shown at the California Academy of Sciences, no fee was charged, and the average time was still over 20 minutes.

The following three exhibitions had the longest average times (but not the most diligent visitors):

- "Spiders!" at the Field Museum, a temporary exhibition covering more than 10,000 square feet and charging an admission fee, had an average time of 45 minutes.
- "Prehistoric Journey" at Denver Museum of Natural History, a newly opened, 14,000-square-foot permanent exhibition, held visitors for an average of 43 minutes.
- "Hidden Kingdoms: The World of Microbes" had a 41-minute average time for its 2,000-square-foot installation when it traveled to the Louisiana Nature Center, where most visitors came, stopped, sat down at microscopes with live microbes, and were engaged for extended times.

The above cases are exceptional. Most exhibitions do not, on average, hold visitors' attention for such long times. Many museum practitioners seem out of touch with this fact. These (anonymous) quotes illustrate:

- From an art critic's review in a newspaper: "The artist's works are densely layered with both ideas and images, so viewers should not expect to breeze through the show in less than two hours."
- From a summative evaluation at a science center: "Visitors cannot hope to digest these complicated, abstract, surprising thematic concepts in less than 30 minutes. They are well worth the effort."
- From an exhibit team member: "The exhibition planning team expects that the average visitor will spend one to one-and-a-half hours in this space."

Even though the notion of average time spent by visitors in an exhibition has been eschewed and called an invalid or uninteresting statistic, it is, nevertheless, an easily measured and useful number. While the number itself is revealing, the process one has to go through to obtain it is equally interesting because it forces museum practitioners to take a careful look at what visitors are really doing in the galleries. To determine an average time, a sample of more than 30 observations (of 30 different people) needs to be collected, and among those 30 randomly selected visitors, the typically unequal distribution of more short-time versus long-time visitors is likely to become apparent. Seeing for themselves that 10 to 15 minutes or less is typical for average time, and knowing that right-skewed patterns are common among time data, can help museum practitioners appreciate and adapt their exhibition designs to the typically brief visitors' responses to exhibitions.

PATTERNS OF TOTAL TIME DISTRIBUTIONS
The most common pattern of visitors' time was a skewed-right distribution (refer to Figure 3). Only one distribution of time in this study was clearly bimodal: In the exceptionally thoroughly used exhibition "Prenatal Development" most visitors were fascinated with looking at real fetuses in jars but others were clearly not (refer to Figure 5D). Visitors rarely seemed to have such a clear-cut like-or-dislike reaction to an exhibition topic. Instead, a more continuous distribution typically existed, from lots of people who spent a little time, to fewer people who spent more time, to very few people who spent a lot of time. Thus, while it is often said that "some visitors spend a little time, some spend a lot"—a general observation implying a "two hump" bimodal pattern—the results of this study indicate that it is more

precise and descriptive to say, "Few museum visitors spend a relatively long time in exhibitions."

The pattern of time distribution among the most thoroughly used exhibitions was more commonly a bell-shaped curve than in the less thoroughly used exhibitions. This pattern suggests that the audiences in these places may have been more "intentional" than in exhibitions where many visitors drop in casually and then drop out again after only a few minutes. The single instance of a skewed-left pattern of time (for "Judith Leyster") suggests a very intentional audience. The self-selected visitors who made that exhibition a specific destination within the museum were probably in the majority due to, among other things, good marketing techniques by the museum. While good marketing of an exhibition can help get visitors in the door, it takes other factors to keep them inside. The vast majority of visitors evidently found the Leyster experience very engaging.

TIME PATTERNS OF INTENTIONAL VISITORS
The original plans for this research included collecting data from visitors face to face through questionnaires, but the logistics and costs were prohibitive on a large, multi-site scale. In the dozen or so cases where exit questionnaires were administered—in addition to the unobtrusive tracking and timing (but not involving the same visitors)—the total time data for cued visitors (visitors who agreed to fill out a questionnaire after viewing the exhibition) were consistently more bell-shaped. Visitors became more intentional viewers when they knew they were going to be interviewed afterward, and, as a result, fewer people stayed shorter times. (These data will be reviewed in a separate report.) This finding raises the question of how to encourage more visitors to be intentional on their own once inside the museum and while discovering exhibitions there.

PATTERNS OF TIME AND STOPS WITHIN EXHIBITIONS
Within exhibitions, total time spent by visitors was positively related to the number of stops made, and scattergrams showed points spread from the lower-left part of the graph moving up toward the upper right. This pattern was created by the whole sample of visitors. If there was validity to the notion that "visitors browse around until they find something interesting and then they spend lots of time there," the data would not have

the strong correlation between the number of stops and the amount of time. Instead, the data suggest that, in general, visitors browse and spend similar amounts of time at different elements. This pattern does not preclude the occasional visitor who spends more time with a few elements, but nevertheless, overall, in thoroughly used exhibitions, more visitors used more elements.

The scattergrams below (Figure 22, A and B) plot the data for samples of visitors from two different exhibitions of similar square footage and number of elements with a resulting contrast in patterns.

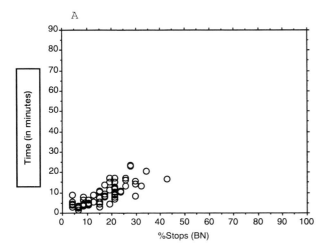

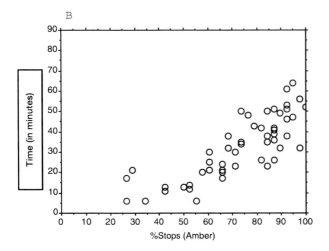

Figure 22. comparison of two scattergrams of total time and %Stops of visitors in two different exhibitions of similar size. A (top) was not thoroughly used by visitors; B (bottom) was thoroughly used.

The difference in the patterns is clear between the one that is more thoroughly used (B) and the other (A), which is not thoroughly used, documented by the points bunched down at low times and low percentages of stops.

When visitors stop at a lot of elements, there is probably a good match between the visitors' expectations and abilities and the intentions of the exhibit developers to provide appealing, engaging things to see and do. Whether visitors came intentionally to see one exhibition (and perhaps even paid a fee) or stumbled upon it, they found it interesting, spent time, and paid attention.

Data on time and number of stops, while a simple and limited measure, go well beyond anecdotes or assumptions about popularity. Data provide evidence to support, question, or deny our assumptions. What does it mean when exhibit developers and their peers think an exhibition is really good but data showed that visitors did not use it thoroughly? For example, "The Swamp: Wonders of Our Wetlands" at Brookfield Zoo is, in my opinion, one of the best multi-modal interpretive museum exhibitions on conservation I've seen, but it's at a zoo—where visitors are focused on looking at animals, not reading labels and using interactives.

The possible reasons for visitors' not staying a long time and not using exhibitions thoroughly are many. They had another personal agenda that did not include spending a lot of time in that space; other interesting things to do competed with it; the exhibition was not interesting; too much was offered. Maybe just doing part of the exhibition was enough (i.e., visitors reached satisfaction or satiation after a short time). Maybe the visitors didn't realize there was more to see and do. The exhibition might have been in a hallway, where visitors passed through on their way to somewhere else. Or it might have been a resource room, more like a library, where a visitor would not be expected to use many of the elements at one visit.

Did the exhibit planners think about these reasons and issues and attempt to avoid the avoidable problems? If the visitors who left after spending 10 minutes and seeing 15% of the elements were bored, confused or frustrated, how would the exhibit developers even be aware of their responses?

In a less than thoroughly used exhibition, if the visitors who left after spending 10 minutes and seeing 15% of the elements were satisfied and generally understood the exhibition's message, that outcome is probably fine with many museum practitioners. But if that was the case, maybe the exhibition could have been smaller.

PATTERNS OF USE AMONG EXHIBITIONS

There were positive correlations between average time and exhibition size and number of elements, findings that stand to reason because, in general, it takes longer to walk through a larger exhibition, and larger exhibitions have room for and contain more elements.

There is not the same strong correlation between SRI and %DV among exhibitions as there was between average time and number or percentage of stops within exhibitions. This is most likely due to the large variability among types of exhibitions (e.g., large and small exhibitions, large and small elements, different degrees of interest among visitors, different intrinsic values of elements, etc.). Therefore, the variables of SRI and %DV should be considered as independent variables. A lower sweep rates is good because it means visitors are spending more time per unit area; a higher percentage of diligent visitors is good because it means visitors have paid some attention to more elements. But the two variables do not automatically correlate with each other. In addition, neither one nor both together guarantees that visitors have learned the intended messsage. For example, in "Molecules in Motion" at the California Museum of Science and Industry, visitors used the exhibition exceptionally thoroughly, but interviews revealed that few of them got the exhibit developer's intended messages about chemistry. Many people, nevertheless, said they enjoyed the exhibition.

Spending time and paying attention are, in general, simply the observable behaviors that can be prerequisites for and good indicators of the potential for learning. Thorough use (lower SRIs, higher %DVs) is, in and of itself, a positive characteristic for an exhibition to have.

DIFFERENCES BETWEEN SCIENCE-RELATED AND NONSCIENCE EXHIBITIONS

Science exhibitions overall had lower %DV than nonscience exhibitions. Some museum practitioners accept that their exhibitions may be less than thoroughly used. Science center staff often argue that it is not a matter of how many elements visitors use, but how deeply visitors experience any one of them. This argument may work for exhibitions that have no pretensions about sequencing, narrative, construction of generalizations through multiple examples, or layouts and conceptual designs with contrasting points of view to be explored.

There were six exhibitions in which no one stopped at more than half of the exhibit elements. Zero diligent visitors raises important questions about "bang for the buck," communication objectives, and visitor satisfaction. Many exhibitions (of all types) are conceived, planned, and executed with intended themes to be communicated in a logical structure (e.g., clusters of exhibits, sequences, zones) that supports them. If visitors do not explore the places in the exhibition where those themes are presented, how can they be expected to understand the overall point of the exhibition? If the thematic areas are not clear, how can visitors be expected to get the point of the exhibition? In some cases, even the data collectors—who spent hours tracking visitors in the exhibition—failed to notice or grasp the conceptual layout!

SWEEP RATE INDEXES AS AN INDICATOR OF VISITOR ATTENTION

Knowing the size of an exhibition allows museum practitioners to estimate the average amount of time that visitors are likely to spend in the space. Across all types of nondiorama exhibitions, visitors commonly use exhibits at sweep rates of between 200 and 400 square feet per minute. The sweep rates are usually higher for larger exhibitions and dioramalike exhibitions. In only one case was the sweep rate under 100 square feet per minute; in this case the majority of visitors stopped and sat down to interact with exhibit elements for extended periods of time. For nondiorama exhibitions, 300 square feet per minute is a good ballpark figure.

Dioramalike exhibitions (containing exhibit elements with very large footprints) had significantly higher sweep rates (SRI = 621.2) than nondioramas

(SRI = 318, Mann-Whitney U, p = 0.000). In general, the rates are about twice as high. Unless something engages and prolongs their attention, visitors visually sweep large areas of diorama scenes very rapidly. For the amount of time and money spent on amazing re-creations of natural environments, these data are probably disappointing to many natural history museums. For the amount of real estate that immersion environments take up on the exhibition floor, visitors' time is often not spent accordingly.

There were exceptions to the tendency for dioramas to have high sweep rates. In the case of the newly created glassless dioramas with extensive interpretation and interactive opportunities at the Grand Rapids Public Museum's "Habitats," the sweep rate (SRI = 335) was closer to the average for nondioramas. The new, large "Prehistoric Journey" exhibition at Denver Museum of Natural History (Marino 1996) had a sweep rate of 326, which was close to the median for nondiorama exhibitions.

Another way to look at the diorama data is to consider an alternative analysis. Sweep rates for dioramas can be divided by a factor of 2 to compensate for the large amounts of space occupied by the elements. With this calculation, the median and mode of the whole database stay roughly the same (around 300) but the range and variance are reduced considerably. This SRI conversion by a factor of 2 for dioramalike exhibitions could make all the data more comparable, which can increase the usefulness of SRI as an easily measured, empirical piece of data. A larger sample of dioramas is needed to test this idea.

PERCENTAGE OF STOPS (MEDIAN %STOPS) VERSUS PERCENTAGE OF VISITORS (%DV)

As pointed out in Chapter V, "Findings," the same exhibitions occurred at the high end (lower right quadrant) of the SRI-%DV scattergram (refer to Figure 18) as at the high end of Figure 16, which is based on median %Stops (although the points are in slightly different positions).

Astute readers might be asking themselves at this point, "Well then, why not just use median %Stops instead of %DV?" One of the objectives of doing this research was to give museum practitioners some tools to measure and report on the effectiveness of exhibitions. If median %Stops is the measure, the number will always only represent where the midpoint of the data is. Median %Stops can never be zero, because visitors who don't make at least one stop in the exhibit are not included in the data, and the median can never reach 100% because in real life everybody would never look at everything. (Remember that we are talking about exhibitions, groups of exhibit elements, not single exhibits.) On the other hand, measuring %DV is more versatile and descriptive from a criterion point of view, that is, the desirable objective of being more thoroughly used, because %DV can vary from zero to 100%. Zero means that no one in the sample looked at more than half of the exhibits; 100% means that all of the visitors looked at more than half of the exhibits. A goal of 100% diligent visitors is ambitious but achievable.

CONCERNS ABOUT "WHAT IF. . . ?"

Using one method across many different types of exhibitions and generalizing between exhibitions raised questions in many museum practitioners' minds because of the enormous variations among and between exhibitions. "What if you have an exhibition that . . . ?" "What if one visitor did . . . ?" But most of the "what ifs" were problems that arose in museum practitioners' imaginations rather than in reality. For example:

- "What if the exhibition contained only one large element?" We never encountered that situation. If we had, it probably would not fit the study's definition of an exhibition: a group of elements, planned as a cohesive unit, under a specified theme or topic.
- "What if one museum defined elements as every single different component and another museum lumped them all together?" That would not be consistent with the definition of "element" for this study, and that situation was never encountered. To be consistent across multiple sites, definitions must be adhered to.
- "What if the visitor just came in to 'case the joint' and then came back later for a longer look?" Visitors who did not stop or stay at least 1 minute were not included in the data analysis. If a visitor returned soon, dur-

ing the same observation period, the data collector
noted it and resumed timing, but this situation happened only a few times.

Even though exhibitions vary in multiple ways across
museums and between sites, it was possible to compare
them according to a few broadly defined variables that
gave important information to museum practitioners
about the relative success of an exhibition as measured
by how thoroughly visitors used it. What if? What if the
majority of museums put these methods into regular
practice?

VII. SELECTED CASE STUDIES

This chapter elaborates on findings from the data and adds information about some of the study exhibitions that was gathered in the course of the project from site visits and staff involved with the exhibitions and the affiliated institutions. A few of the brief discussions of case studies go beyond the systematically collected data and are not conclusions based on the findings; therefore, they are to be considered anecdotal. Where available, reports or documents that provide additional data and discussion are referenced.

In all these case studies, the indexes of sweep rate (SRI) and the percentage of diligent visitors (%DV) provide snapshots of visitor behavior that allow the relative success of the exhibition, based on how thoroughly it was used, to be gauged and compared. The case studies include four of the most thoroughly used exhibitions, seven traveling exhibitions studied at different sites, two exhibitions measured before and after renovations, two examples of multiple exhibition studies at the same institution, and three of the least thoroughly used exhibitions. While the stories illustrate the often relative nature of the data and the influence of context on the measures, the indexes help give museum practitioners a handle on judging effectiveness and making decisions.

FOUR OF THE MOST THOROUGHLY USED EXHIBITIONS

There was one clear factor in common for this group. The four exhibitions in which visitors stayed the longest times per unit area and used the highest percentage of the available elements were all object based: amber in "Amber"; beach fashions and fabrics in "From Bustles to Bikinis"; paintings in "Judith Leyster"; and archaeological materials in "Treasures from the Sand." Some of the unusual reasons that these exhibitions apparently met visitors' expectations are given below.

"AMBER: WINDOW TO THE PAST" AT THE AMERICAN MUSEUM OF NATURAL HISTORY

Of the 110 exhibitions in this study, "Amber: Window to the Past" had the highest %DV: 86%. Many factors appear to have contributed to the exceptional data for this exhibition, including good press, an exhibition entrance fee, and high intrinsic appeal. No one factor alone was responsible.

The good press included an article in *Time* magazine. An unusually high percentage of visitors came to the American Museum of Natural History specifically to see this exhibition (Giusti and Thau 1996). The fee screened out visitors who were not motivated enough to pay for the ticket. Visitors who paid were likely to stay long enough to get their money's worth. Thus, the self-selected visitors who made up the audience were highly intentional; they were not there by chance.

More important, "Amber" appealed to a broad range of audience interests. As a natural artifact, as jewelry and other aesthetic artifacts, and as an artifact in popular culture (from the book and movie Jurassic Park), amber was the single subject, and the exhibition was about one thing. It was a conceptually coherent, and positive redundancy—multiple examples of similar topics—helped keep the exhibition from being overwhelming (i.e., there were not too many different topics, dissimilar ideas, varied content). The exhibition was multi-modal. A combination of real objects, re-created environments, video, live demonstrations, text, and even some blank walls helped make the exhibition appealing and varied. This variety prevented early visitor burnout from seeing too many of the same things. Finally, many of the objects were small and needed to be examined up close and carefully. Slow, careful looking was rewarded by seeing more interesting details. The sweep rate index (SRI) was 212.

"FROM BUSTLES TO BIKINIS: A CENTURY OF CHANGING BEACH FASHIONS" AT SAN DIEGO HISTORICAL SOCIETY

"From Bustles to Bikinis" had 77% DV and an SRI of 206. Amy Simon, Curator for Costumes and Textiles at the San Diego Historical Society, commented about the tracking and timing in their thoroughly used exhibition:

> These results confirm the efforts of the exhibition design team to create a cohesive, concise, and read-

ily understood exhibition about costume and social history. Darcie Fohrman, Exhibition Developer, and Ava Ferguson, Label Editor, stressed the need for every graphic, costume, artifact, and text panel to tie into the exhibition theme and subthemes. By stressing the development process so thoroughly, the design of the exhibition elements and floor plan seemed to fall into place naturally.

"JUDITH LEYSTER: A DUTCH MASTER AND HER WORLD" AT THE WORCESTER ART MUSEUM

The characteristics of appropriate objectives, clear labels, and logical design have often been stressed as guidelines for good exhibition design (e.g., Hicks 1986; Bitgood 1994; McLean 1993; Serrell 1996a). What is unusual about the Leyster example is that the Worcester Art Museum's intent was corroborated by visitor data: 79% DV and SRI 100. That is, the experiences the exhibit developers planned for visitors to engage in and what visitors chose to do were in fact very similar. George Hein, who evaluated this exhibition, reported that it had beautiful pictures and interesting labels, resulting in unusually high visitor time data compared to other exhibitions. The person hired to collect the tracking data said she got really tired while watching one person at a time inching his or her way along past the paintings, reading almost every label carefully, looking back and forth between the label and the painting. Evidently, careful looking rewarded and reinforced visitors as they saw more interesting details in the paintings.

Because "Leyster" was a temporary show, one might suppose that visitors had a special interest in Dutch master paintings and so were predisposed to spend a lot of time, but exit interviews did not confirm this. Instead, exhibit developer Honee Hess attributed the exhibition's success largely to the nature of the exhibition rather than just the audience. Exhibit developers had taken care with developing appropriate communication objectives, writing clear and visually based exhibit labels, and laying out an installation that was not crowded, either conceptually or physically. The main messages of "Leyster" not only appeared in the labels; they were expressed and reinforced in the total design of the art and interpretive components. In addition, every area of the exhibition contained elements that exhibit developers intended to be attractive to the

majority of visitors, not targeted at Dutch master painting specialists (Hess, personal communication).

"TREASURES FROM THE SAND" AT COLONIAL MICHILIMACKINAC

Randi Korn evaluated this exhibition for Colonial Michilimackinac and presented information about it at the 1995 Visitor Studies Conference. In her talk (unpublished), "It's the Exhibit! Not the Visitors," she said, "I have thought about this exhibition a lot because of the unusual data and have tried to come up with reasons why visitors behaved in this way. Simply, 'Treasures' is a good exhibit." She showed slides of examples of the changes that were made during remedial evaluation that, in the end, enhanced visitors' experiences and understanding of the history of Fort Michilimackinac. She believed that the graphic and physical layout, well-written text, and repetition of the big ideas contributed to the exhibit's success. "Treasures" had 83% DV and an SRI of 143.

SOME OBSERVATIONS

The above four exceptionally thoroughly used exhibitions were all object-based, and many visitors apparently found their careful attention to the objects and other multi-modal interpretive experiences rewarding. Visitors' time-consuming behaviors in these exhibitions are indicative of learning and enjoyment.

In addition to the similar tracking and timing studies conducted, "Amber," "Leyster," and "Treasures" also were evaluated using dissimilar methods of visitor interview or questionnaire strategies. Thus, each exhibition's impact on visitors as revealed through personal feedback cannot be compared in the same way that the measures of SRI and %DV can be compared among exhibitions. Unfortunately, until we develop an instrument that can be administered universally to collect comparable data, we cannot draw conclusions across exhibitions about visitors' level of satisfaction or the appropriateness of their perceptions of exhibition messages and how those correlate with time or thoroughness of use.

SEVEN TRAVELING EXHIBITIONS

Seven exhibitions were studied as they traveled and were installed at different institutions. "Global Warming" was tracked in six different sites; the rest have data from two sites to compare. More studies are planned for multiple-site exhibitions in the future. Some museum practitioners find these cases particularly interesting because studying the same exhibitions in different locations can help control many of the exhibit variables that make comparisons among exhibitions seem invalid or unreliable.

"GLOBAL WARMING: UNDERSTANDING THE FORECAST"

"Global Warming" was on the road for several years, and Ellen Giusti evaluated it at six different sites. At five of the six sites, the summary data were similar (%DV = 33, 36, 30, 34, and 42) and above average for %DV compared to the database as a whole. At the Denver Museum of Natural History, 48% of the visitors used it more thoroughly. Interestingly, staff at Denver noted that "Global Warming" was not very popular; that is, it was not crowded, especially compared to the other traveling exhibition on site at the time, "Backyard Monsters." The visitors who sought "Global Warming" out, however, appeared very engaged with it.

In her report, Giusti (1997) points out that some elements were popular across all sites, and alternate layouts at different sites contributed to some differences. She concluded that the site was the strongest factor, and "Global Warming" was less thoroughly used at science centers than it was at natural history museums. The next case study contains aspects of the same pattern.

"BEYOND NUMBERS"

"Beyond Numbers" was much less thoroughly used at the Maryland Science Center in Baltimore than when it traveled to the New York Hall of Science in Corona, Queens. There, good reviews in the *New York Times* were believed to have contributed, as some visitors were seen entering the hall with the newspaper article in hand, or they asked for the exhibition by name. In addition, MSC exhibition staff made extensive changes in the layout of the exhibits, in response to the first tracking study in Baltimore—which revealed 0% DV—to encourage visitors to use the exhibition more thoroughly. At the Hall of Science, the percentage of diligent visitors was 35%.

In both venues, "Beyond Numbers" was located on the third floor of the museum, but in Corona, the Hall of Science is the only large public institution, making it a destination site for visitors who come to spend half a day. At the Maryland Science Center, the exhibitions have heavy local competition from the Baltimore Aquarium, a technology museum, an art museum, and the harbor-front mall where the science museum is located.

"DARKENED WATERS: PROFILE OF AN OIL SPILL"

Data were collected for "Darkened Waters" while it was at the Oakland Museum in 1993 and at the Anchorage Museum of History and Art in 1996. The %DV figures were very similar in both sites: 51% DV at Oakland; 49% DV at Anchorage. The 1993 data helped create the "thorough-use" concept that started this study, and it was interesting to find that the data were very close to being the same three years later at a different site—still better than average compared to others. The exhibition had not been changed. With a SRI of 154, "Darkened Waters," while at Oakland, ranked as one of the 11 exceptionally thoroughly used exhibitions out of the sample of 110.

"HIDDEN KINGDOMS: THE WORLD OF MICROBES"

Visits to the 2,000-square-foot "Hidden Kingdoms" averaged a very long time (41 minutes) at Louisiana Nature Center but a much shorter time (11 minutes) when it was at the California Museum of Science and Industry. The nature center director, Robert N. Marye, said:

> The unusually high rate of time spent in the exhibit does not surprise me. I believe that the primary reason is that this was the only major exhibit at the Louisiana Nature Center. This means, of course, an absence of competition for the visitor's time. Also, a visit to the Nature Center is a deliberate choice and not an impulse decision. Given that and the approximately 50% level of repeat visitation, I believe that visitors come willing and expecting to invest time in their experience. Finally, I think the quality of the exhibit had a lot to do with holding the interest of our visitors.

In both places, however, the figures for %DV were similar (15% and 12%), and the most popular elements were the microscopes with live microbes. Visitors in Louisiana used the elements for significantly longer times, but they did not become engaged with proportionately more of them. In both locations, vague delineation of the exhibit's boundaries may have encouraged visitors not to conceive all the parts as belonging to one exhibition.

"HUNTERS OF THE SKY"

This large, nonlinear, multi-modal traveling exhibition with more than 90 elements had low %DV at both sites where studies were done. The Denver audience was less engaged with this exhibition about raptors than the visitors to that exhibit's home base in Minneapolis at the Minnesota Science Center, where the %DV was higher (9% vs. 0%) and the SRI was lower (172 vs. 364) than at Denver, a reverse of the pattern noted by Giusti above. The difference may have been due to the presence of a live-animal demonstration in Minneapolis that was not included in the Denver installation. Live animals are often among the most attractive elements in all types of museum exhibitions.

"SPIDERS!"

At the Field Museum in Chicago, visitors to the large temporary exhibition "Spiders!" spent an average time of 45 minutes, much higher than usual for many permanent exhibitions at Field (typically around 10 minutes). Field Museum visitors paid a special fee to see this traveling exhibition. While "Spiders" was at the Smithsonian's National Museum of Natural History, the average time was 15 minutes, and admission was free. The percentage of diligent visitors was 4% in Washington, D.C., and 26% in Chicago.

"WHODUNIT: THE SCIENCE OF SOLVING CRIME"

An evaluation of the traveling exhibition "Whodunit" while it was at the Museum of Science and Industry in Chicago led exhibit developers to modify the layout and number of elements for its next installation at Fort Worth Museum of Science and History. Developers eliminated elements that had low attracting power with visitors and were not essential to communicating the main ideas of the exhibition. In the streamlined 1996 installation, visitors spent significantly more time and stopped at more elements. In Chicago, the %DV was

16%; in Fort Worth the %DV increased to 57%, and with an SRI of 180 it ranks as exceptionally thoroughly used.

SOME OBSERVATIONS

Some museum practitioners believe that the only way to compare exhibitions is by studying the same exhibitions in different locations so that many of the variables are controlled. From the case studies above, however, we see that often the same exhibition is not really the same when the context, cost, audience, layout, size, and media response differ from site to site. For some traveling exhibitions the number of uncontrolled variables is so great that, for purposes of comparison, they might as well be considered different exhibitions. On the other hand, exhibit developers can intentionally make changes to a traveling exhibition to improve its ability to engage visitors' attention, and %DV and SRI provide comparable data for evaluating whether the changes contributed to more thorough use.

TWO EXHIBITIONS BEFORE AND AFTER RENOVATIONS

Many museums are making renovations to large, old exhibitions. In-house evaluations can allow staff to track progress and improvements in visitors' satisfaction as indicated by their spending more time and not leaving through the nearest available exit—especially in large halls with multiple doorways.

ADLER PLANETARIUM & ASTRONOMY MUSEUM

The Adler Planetarium renovated its exhibits of historical astronomical instruments, opening "The Universe in Your Hands" in 1995. Old hall data showed high sweep rates, which lowered considerably as visitors to the renovated hall slowed down to stop longer at the new cases and interactives. Visitors who used the two advance-organizer elements spent more time in the exhibition. They used more of the total exhibit elements, and they participated in more reading, more looking at objects, and greater use of interactive elements. Exit interviews confirmed that the majority of visitors could understand the exhibition's main messages. A summary (Raphling 1997a) and a complete evaluation report by Britt Raphling are available from the Adler.

DENVER MUSEUM OF NATURAL HISTORY

Boettcher Hall, a room with eight large dioramas at the Denver Museum of Natural History, was renovated into the new "Explore Colorado" hall with more graphics, interactives, and a central orientation element. Prior to renovations, data had shown a very high sweep rate, the highest seen in this study (SRI 3,600). Visits in the old hall averaged only 2 minutes. Visitors stopped longer at the renovated dioramas, improved labels, and new interactives, and the sweep rate dropped to 655. Average time went up to 11 minutes. Techniques used in the updated exhibits are described in *Curator* by Dyer (1992).

SOME OBSERVATIONS

In the two cases above, as well as in others in the study, the new exhibition had more elements compared to the old one, and while visitors did slow down and spend more time in the renovated exhibition, indicated by lower SRI values, the percentage of elements stopped at did not increase as much as was expected or desired by exhibit developers. When an exhibition is renovated and many new elements are added, the median percentage of stops and %DV can actually decrease if the new elements are not sufficiently attractive to the majority of visitors. These data tend to be unwelcome and depressing for museums and museum professionals who have just made a major financial investment and staff effort in a hall's overhaul. Low %DV does not mean a priori the exhibition is not good, but the figure provides a useful reality check on overall patterns of actual visitor use.

DIFFERENT EXHIBITIONS IN THE SAME INSTITUTION

The variables of city, location, and audience characteristics are more consistent, for comparison purposes, among the following two case studies of different exhibitions mounted at the same institution. In-house evaluations and comparisons among exhibitions can allow staff to plan new exhibitions that are in line with the past patterns of time and stops for their institution's audiences.

FIELD MUSEUM

Eight different exhibitions have been studied at the Field Museum in Chicago using the strategies of this research protocol, starting with a brief tracking study of the old Hall of Birds in 1990, in the renovations of the animal halls (birds, mammals) and in the traveling special exhibition "Spiders!" in 1996.

The exhibit developers' main behavioral goal for visitors in the renovated bird hall was to "slow people down," and they were successful (Serrell and Becker 1990). The sweep rate went from 778 to 560. When exhibit developers worked on renovating two other permanent exhibitions, "Messages from the Wilderness" and "What Is An Animal?," they made conscious efforts to increase opportunities for visitors to become engaged in interpretive elements that were gauged to visitors' typically brief stops. In "Messages" these efforts were most effective, as 48% of the visitors were diligent and the SRI was 622 (compared to a similar diorama hall without much interpretation that had an SRI of 1,750).

JOHN G. SHEDD AQUARIUM

Over the past six years, Shedd Aquarium in Chicago has developed several temporary exhibitions in its 3,500-square-foot special exhibit gallery. Measurements of average time in the gallery space had shown that visitors spent less than 10 minutes in two earlier shows ("On Arctic Ice" about Inuit culture, and "Classic Craft" about model boat building). With this information in mind while planning the 2,500-square-foot exhibition called "Silent Witness" (an interactive exhibition about wildlife forensic science), exhibit developers consciously structured the 10 activity stations so that visitors could experience and comprehend each in less than 1 minute and to "get it" by visiting 5 or 6 stations. This goal was honed during formative evaluation of each station. After opening, exhibit developers were pleased that visitors spent more time with the interactives and used more of them than had been expected. The average time in the exhibition was 9 minutes, making the sweep rate 256 square feet per minute, and 58% of the visitors were diligent about visiting more than half of the elements.

The aquarium's next special exhibit, "White Alligator: Secret of the Swamp," had large dioramalike elements that immersed visitors in a southern cypress swamp and featured a large white alligator. Visitors used it at a higher sweep rate and lower percentage of use than the three earlier shows, which inspired designers to lay out the next exhibition, "Frogs!," to encourage visitors not to miss or skip elements, as they seemed to do in "White Alligator." "Frogs!" turned out to have the highest percentage of stops and the lowest sweep rate to date of Shedd's exhibitions, making it one of the most thoroughly used exhibitions of all (64 % DV; SRI 174). Visitors took their time at the small tanks, helping each other find the often well-camouflaged frogs. Exit questionnaires showed that visitors could understand the exhibition's messages about the diversity of frog species, their adaptations, and the need for conserving frog habitats. The exhibition's run was extended a year.

SOME OBSERVATIONS

When museum staff conduct their own in-house evaluations, use consistent methods, and make comparisons among exhibitions over the years, staff can apply what they have learned in planning new exhibitions. By keeping records, sharing reports, and discussing the usefulness of the findings, an "institutional memory" can be created and preserved, even if there are changes in the staff. Too often, evaluations are conducted by outside experts who use different methods and draw conclusions in different ways; reports are filed away on a shelf, and the few staff members who were involved in the evaluation and learned from it leave for greener pastures, taking their experience with them.

THREE OF THE LEAST THOROUGHLY USED EXHIBITIONS

No single variable measured by this study accounted for extremely low values for % DV. Looking at each exhibition individually reveals a unique combination of factors that might account for low use and raises some challenging questions about museums' intentions and visitors' orientation, expectations, and perceptions.

"FAMILIES" AT THE MINNESOTA HISTORY CENTER

The 2,100-square-foot "Families" exhibition in Saint Paul at the Minnesota History Center contained the largest number of elements of any exhibition in this study. The elements were presented in a wide variety of formats, including cases, drawers, stories, photograph albums, flip cards, video clips, and an object theater. No visitors, however, were diligent enough to penetrate this dense display to any degree approaching 50 %. "Not a single visitor attended to 92 or more of the 180 components" (Cutting and Litwak 1997, 67). The average number of stops was 18, and the highest was 56. The evaluators reported that no single format of element predominated visitor use; visitors sampled the range, and the frequency of use roughly paralleled the availability of each type of component. A lack of thorough use of "Families" did not negatively affect adult visitors' enjoyment of the exhibition. In exit interviews, the average enjoyment rating was 8.6 on a scale of 1 to 10. Could the exhibition have been considerably less dense without negatively affecting visitors' enjoyment?

"JURASSIC!" AT THE CALIFORNIA ACADEMY OF SCIENCES

"Jurassic!" was located in one of the Academy's hallways. "Many visitors walked through it quickly and only stopped to look at the largest exhibit elements. Some observation subjects appeared to read large text panels at a distance, and some questionnaire respondents reported new ideas that contradicted the interpretive content of the exhibit" (Mackinney 1994, 12). The sweep rate index for the 1,950-square-foot exhibition, not including the store, was 800 square feet per minute, whereas the SRI for the store was 182. Shopping speed was considerably slower and more engaging than exhibit viewing! Exhibitions that include special retail areas should, I believe, treat them as part of the total thematic exhibition experience. It makes sense to include the store experience in the intended communication objectives for visitors.

"SCIENCE IN AMERICAN LIFE" AT THE NATIONAL MUSEUM OF AMERICAN HISTORY

"Science in American Life" was a very large exhibition (12,000 square feet) with many elements (106). Few visitors to this Smithsonian exhibition chose to spend much time with it or investigate it fully. The majority of the exhibits in "Science in American Life" were attended to by less than 15% of the exhibition's visitors, and only 10 of the 106 elements were cited by more than 5% of visitors as being interesting, informative, or communicative. "Interestingly, the popularity of a stop and the time it held visitors could not be used to predict visitor responses" (Pekarik, et al. 1995).

Was the lack of correlation between visitor stops and time at exhibits and recall of them during exit interviews due to the overall very low level of engagement? Visitor response may have been below the threshold where the usual positive correlation between time spent and recall exists.

Perhaps more Smithsonian exhibitions should be smaller and geared more for visitors who are making whirlwind tours of our nation's capital.

SOME OBSERVATIONS

Are jam-packed exhibitions really a good idea? I believe not. Too many objects, labels, elements, and so forth, can be overwhelming and do not help visitors feel competent. What is the point of including many elements that rarely get used? The notion that visitors will come back to see the things they missed the first time—commonly used to justify large, layered, dense exhibitions—has yet to be tested.

In exhibitions with low thorough use, instead of focusing on the explanation that visitors had personal agendas other than the desire to pay attention to the exhibits at hand, museum practitioners might think more carefully about the degree to which relative thorough use of their exhibitions could be changed by making improvements to the exhibit elements or by orienting visitors better so that they can make more informed decisions about which exhibitions they choose to spend their precious time in.

IT'S ALL RELATIVE

These case studies, especially the ones that compared the same exhibition at different sites, show the way that all SRI and %DV values for exhibitions in this study are relative. They simply are what they are, at that time, given all the variables present at that moment, and are subject to change as variables change. The question then becomes which variables can be changed by exhibit developers to increase the likelihood that self-selected visitors will be attracted to the exhibition, spend more time and have more positive and meaningful experiences. For example, why not, whenever possible, improve visitor orientation to enable visitors to make intelligent choices? Why not modify or delete elements that fail to attract people or hold their attention until the majority of elements are attractive to a broad range of visitors? "Engaged visitors are our model (though not typical) visitors. They spend a long time in the exhibit and use many of the components available" (Cutting and Litwak 1997, 66). How can more museums create educational exhibitions in which engaged visitors are the model not the exception? Can the current patterns revealed in this diverse sample of 110 exhibitions be changed and the percentage of diligent visitors be raised over time or is an average of 26% diligent visitors the most that we can reasonably expect?

VIII.   CONCLUSIONS AND IMPLICATIONS FOR MUSEUM PRACTITIONERS

Eighty years of museum visitor studies have contributed greatly to our understanding of how visitors use exhibitions and which exhibit strategies are likely to engage the museum-going public's attention. Pulling these studies together into a coherent body of knowledge and systematically adding to the literature of museum visitor studies can improve the usefulness of this information for museum professionals. The results of this study build upon previous studies and lay a groundwork for future studies that can contribute to improving the educational value of museum exhibitions for more visitors.

The conclusions and implications in this chapter are presented in three sections: the first addresses the conclusions about the methods developed for this study and their usefulness; the second recaps the major findings from the data and the model that is generated from it; and the final section speculates on how the model can be used by museum practitioners to gauge the effectiveness of their exhibitions using thorough use as a criterion for success.

CONCLUSIONS ABOUT THE METHODS

- When using the relatively quick and simple summative evaluation technique of tracking and timing, a sample of 40 visitors is sufficient for gathering information about general trends. Tracking and timing can be used to check differences in visitors' responses before and after remedial evaluation of whole exhibitions or to set objectives during exhibition planning phases for visitors' use of new exhibitions. Museum practitioners who follow the directions and protocol used in this study can compare their own findings to this database.
- Elements can be defined in all types of museum exhibitions, even though elements are unique for each. Distinct elements allow for better conceptual and spatial orientation for exhibit planners and evaluators as well as for visitors.
- This study revealed general patterns, but it was not large enough for analysis by subgroups. The sample of 110 exhibitions was diverse enough to suggest broad

conclusions, but randomly selected samples of at least 30 per subcategory of museum type are necessary to draw any reliable conclusions about differences by type of museum. Additional studies are needed. More statistically reliable and valid methods are desirable, but such studies are often beyond the capability of museums with small staffs and minimal budgets for evaluation and research on visitor behavior. This study's methods can provide museum staff with an inexpensive alternative to the anecdotal observations that have often represented the only type of "informal evaluation" a museum could undertake.

THE MAJOR FINDINGS AND THEIR IMPLICATIONS

- Visitors do not spend much time in exhibitions. Twenty minutes or less is a common duration for a single exhibition experience in a museum. Regardless of the size or topic of the exhibition, visitors seem unwilling to devote the hours of attention fantasized by some exhibit planners. We need to have more realistic expectations for visitors' time.
- It was typical for an exhibition to be explored partially, not fully. On average, visitors stop at roughly one-third of the available exhibition elements. Fewer visitors paid attention to more than half the elements. The average percentage of diligent visitors (those who stopped at more than half of the available elements) was 26%. These findings may have serious implications for successfully communicating a exhibition's educational objectives, especially in large, complex, or thematic exhibitions.
- The more elements visitors stop at, the longer time they spend in an exhibition. This was the case for all types of museums and exhibitions. There were positive correlations between the amount of time spent and the percentage of stops made in thoroughly used exhibitions and in exhibitions where visitors used few elements. In general, visitors do not spend a relatively long time at relatively few places. While it is true that a few individual visitors can and will deviate from this pattern, the overall tendency is for total time and stops to increase in a direct correlation. Exhibit developers can take advantage of this normal visitor behavior by

creating elements that are similar, complementary and reinforcing, and they can encourage visitors to use exhibitions more thoroughly by allowing for immediate applications of what is learned.

• A sweep rate index (SRI) of roughly 300 square feet per minute is typical "museum-visitor speed" for non-diorama exhibitions. (To get an idea of what a sweep rate of 300 square feet per minute looks like, mark out a 15-by-20-foot area, or 300 square feet, in a large room and spend 60 seconds strolling around, pretending to look at exhibits and stopping at the imaginary elements.) Sweep rates are usually higher for dioramas and for larger exhibitions (more than 4,000 square feet). An unusually low sweep rate of under 100 square feet per minute occurs only when the majority of visitors interact with some exhibits for exceptionally long periods of time.

APPLICATIONS FOR MUSEUM PRACTITIONERS

• The SRI/%DV scattergram in Figure 19 shows how a diverse selection of exhibitions compare for values that indicate thorough use. While time and stops data alone are not sufficient to tell whether the exhibit is "good" or "bad," and a high average time and a high percentage of stops will not say why the exhibition was engaging, the model provides a context for better understanding how visitors use exhibitions.

• A relatively low SRI and a relatively high %DV indicates a thoroughly used exhibition. The original first two criteria for success presented in the "51% Solution" (Serrell 1992)--visitors covering less than 300 square feet per minute combined with more than half of the visitors stopping at more than half of the elements--have proven to be easy to measure and compare. The model revealed that while an SRI of 300 or less is not unusual, exceptionally thoroughly used exhibitions may be few and far between. The norm for diligent visitors was well below 51%. But some exhibitions do achieve these criteria, suggesting that museums can strive for and hope to achieve higher standards in regard to thoroughness of use.

• Eleven exhibitions met both criteria for exceptionally thorough use (less than 300 SRI, more than 51% DV). In these exhibitions (that included all types of museums) visitors spent the most time and used the most elements. As a group, the exceptionally thor-oughly used exhibitions were smaller and had fewer elements than the least thoroughly used exhibitions. Larger, denser exhibitions may be overwhelming to visitors. This information can help planners overcome the urge to show every object and tell every story in one exhibition.

• Knowing the amount of time visitors are likely to spend can help exhibit planners design museum experiences that are manageable for realistic visitor time budgets. Exhibit developers can strive for a better-than-average percentage of stops by making more of the elements appealing to a greater number of visitors. They need to think realistically about the number of activities that a visitor can successfully accomplish in 20 minutes or less.

• Thorough use of an exhibition indicates that visitors are creating many opportunities for themselves to have meaningful experiences. The majority of visitors are spending time at a majority of exhibit elements. This level of success comes when visitors are engaged, and the majority of things to see and do in the exhibition are interesting to them. These visitors apparently find the experiences the exhibition offers sufficiently rewarding to stay longer and stop at more elements. Research results from other studies show that more time leads to more learning. Thus, time and stops--unobtrusively and easily measured--are indicators of learning-related behaviors.

IX. POSSIBLE NEXT STEPS

From 1993 to 1996, approximately 45 samples were collected for this study. In the last year (from 1996 to 1997), a Small Grant for Exploratory Research from the National Science Foundation enabled Serrell & Associates to double the sample size; meet with advisers; travel to several sites for meetings with colleagues and other professionals to present and discuss the study; prepare a summary article for *Curator* magazine; and write, publish, and distribute this report.

Where do we go from here? There are multiple options, such as: continue to gather data on an ad hoc basis; reanalyze the existing database; seek another grant to conduct another large and randomly selected sample; add the questionnaire strategy to subsequent tracking and timing studies; and conduct other, supporting research. Each of these options is discussed briefly below.

CONTINUE TO GATHER DATA ON AN AD HOC BASIS

We could continue in the same way, collecting data as it becomes available from other museum practitioners and from studies conducted by Serrell & Associates for clients around the country. We would like to accumulate data on at least 30 exceptionally thoroughly used exhibitions--those that would fall in the far lower-right quadrant on the scattergram model for SRI and %DV– and then look for common patterns among them. We cannot draw firm conclusions from the small sample of 11 exceptionally thoroughly used exhibitions.

The advantages to proceeding in this way are that no new grant or new strategies would be required. The disadvantage is that it would probably take a long time (more than five years) to gather enough data to obtain 30 thoroughly used exhibitions at the rate we have been finding them. They seem to occur, within a broad sample, about one in every 10. We could specifically recruit those exhibitions that we anticipate will be relatively high in thorough use (e.g., exhibitions that charge a fee, newly opened big exhibitions, exhibitions with extremely captivating elements, or exhibitions that attract very intentional audiences). We could also put out a call for data from museums that believe they have thoroughly used exhibitions. The disadvantage to this strategy, however, would be the creating of an intentionally biased sample of convenience.

Another emphasis could be to continue to gather data on an ad hoc basis but to look for exhibitions that are traveling to different sites so that they could be repeatedly tested as they move around the country. This strategy would help control some of the variables among types of exhibitions. Right now we have seven exhibitions that have been studied at two sites ("Amber," "Beyond Numbers," "Darkened Waters," Hidden Kingdoms," "Hunters of the Sky," "Spiders!," and "Whodunit?") and one that has data for several sites ("Global Warming"). Traveling exhibitions can be natural laboratories for comparing differences in visitor responses that arise from variables such as demographics, cultural context, and media attention.

REANALYZE THE EXISTING DATABASE

We could take the existing data and analyze it in a different way by lumping all the raw data together and using numbers of visitors in each sample instead of summarizing it by exhibition. This approach would give us a database of more than 8,000 visitors to work with instead of 110 exhibitions. Because visitors were selected randomly, statistical tests could be performed and compared among visitors to different types of exhibitions (e.g., science and nonscience, natural history, art). Giusti (1997) used this method in her comparisons of visitors who came to see "Global Warming" in six different museum sites.

The advantage to this process is that no new data would need to be collected. The disadvantage is that the overall selection of exhibitions would still not be a random sample.

SEEK ANOTHER GRANT TO CONDUCT A LARGER AND RANDOMLY SELECTED SAMPLE

One of the main criticisms of the current study is that it used a nonrandom sample. To conduct another study on the same scale or larger would require additional funding. A probabilistic sample of 200 or more exhibitions would be needed to address questions about valid generalizations across all exhibitions and make comparisons of subcategories of exhibition types. Advantages to this approach are that the methods are worked out and can be applied on a larger scale. Disadvantages are, as usual, time and money.

ADD THE QUESTIONNAIRE STRATEGY TO ALL NEW TRACKING AND TIMING STUDIES

Adding the questionnaire strategy to the tracking and timing methods could gather feedback from visitors about outcome measures that might be related to time spent and number of stops made. The problems with this approach revolve primarily around the issue of intentions. It can be difficult to establish the museum's intentions in presenting the exhibition; the visitor's intentions when coming to it; and the match or mismatch between the two.

The original plans for this research included collecting data from visitors face-to-face through questionnaires, but the logistics and costs of such an approach were prohibitive on a large, multi-site scale. Although the questionnaire instrument developed by Raphling and Serrell (Raphling and Serrell 1993) to collect visitors' impressions has been used successfully in a wide variety of exhibitions, a logical way of analyzing the data so that the results can be compared across museum types has yet to be worked out. The primary issue that needs to be resolved is how to analyze the content of open-ended responses in a goal-referenced way when goals and objectives are not set beforehand, are not clear, or are inappropriate (too easy, too difficult, too obscure) for the majority of the visitors.

CONDUCT OTHER, SUPPORTING RESEARCH

We can (and do) plausibly speculate that visitors who spend more time in an exhibition and stop at more of the elements are in some sense getting more out of the exhibition, relative to visitors who do not spend more time and do not stop at elements. This assumption is reasonable, given the voluntary, informal nature of museum visits. Most museum professionals, however, are more interested in knowing more about who is learning from exhibits, what they are learning, and why. While this study sought to understand more about exhibitions and visits than about visitors, we contend that by finding out where visitors are currently spending more time and by looking at those places, we can find out more about learning. The model for defining and recognizing thoroughly used exhibitions created by this study can help address the more challenging questions about the educational value of exhibitions.

X. OTHER POINTS OF VIEW: COLLEAGUES COMMENT

Rarely do museum professionals openly engage in critical reviews of each other's work, and I hope that this example will encourage more people to venture onto the frontier. The comments in this chapter illustrate a sample of different points of view about my research project since it began. The comments were responses to articles I have published and talks I have given over the years, up to a draft of the book you now hold in your hands.

To be fair, this section should not be read before you read the main body of the book. You should understand my colleagues' comments in light of the current report: How many of the issues raised by my colleagues have I addressed? Which ones remain unanswered or controversial? Readers will need that context to reflect on the opinions given below, to form their own points of view, and to continue the dialogue.

Jane Bedno, Design and Exhibition Teacher

Bedno, who teaches exhibition and graphic design and is Director of the Graduate Program in Museum Exhibition Planning and Design at Philadelphia College of Art and Design, has been working recently on the American Association of Museum's guidelines for judging excellence in exhibitions. She responds to Serrell (1997) in Curator.

I welcome this article, the study it documents, and observation focused data it contains, as both necessary information and a tool for exhibition planning.

I might lightly question the list of objections to time as a measure of exhibition impact and the suggestions as to uses to which these observations may be put. As to time as a measure, the observational statistics themselves suggest some other objections: Visitors preallot time to the exploration of subjects in which they have some interest, allotting a sufficient amount to satisfy themselves that they have explored the subject sufficiently. The typical museum visitor is clearly only willing to give a limited amount of time to the interesting, but arcane, subjects often addressed in exhibits. Visitors will spend enough time to make sure that the basics of the presentation have been "checked out" —explaining

the shorter time given to dioramas, as simple "eyeballing" of a diorama will assure visitors that they have noticed the vital elements, and the longer time spent on crowded exhibits, as the presence of many other visitors implies the importance of the exhibit.

The discussion of the potential uses of the data, to my mind, pose some deeper problems. The discussion is how to defeat expected behaviors, not to use them. We must face the possibility that exhibits ought to be designed to be comprehended in the average time given to them, or that the way to change the time figures is either to aim at a narrower ("diligent") audience or to create the kind of aesthetic/spatial experience that makes visitors want to linger. If the visitor is only mildly engaged by the general interpretive concept, there is little reason to spend more time. In a well done exhibit, detail which is potentially interesting can be identified by visitors very quickly. I find it interesting to first go through exhibits at a normal walking pace, at which speed a good exhibit "reveals itself." Such examples as the United States Holocaust Memorial Exhibition and exhibits of popular art movements (impressionism, for example) show that, if current standards for creating good exhibits are maintained, it is content that draws visitors to spend greater time. Another conclusion jumps to mind when reading the data: If visitors spend less time, proportionately, on large exhibits than on small ones, doesn't this suggest that large exhibits should be broken down into small ones? Most of the exhibit planners I talk to know, intuitively, that large exhibits need very defined ending points within them where visitors can stop, reflect, and move on to a different body of material.

In sum, I welcome this article, this approach, and this information, and hope we will see more of it.

Lauren Brownstein, Museum Studies Graduate

These comments are excerpted from "Museum Practitioners Discuss the 51 Percent Solution Research Project," Journal of Museum Education 21, no. 3, (1996): 12. Brownstein responds to Serrell (1996b) in the same issue and the talk on which it was based.

Beverly Serrell's presentation to the Museum Practitioner Seminar on March 15, 1996, was followed by a lively discussion. Participants in the discourse included museum educators, evaluators, researchers, administrators, and students. By discussing ways to evaluate visitors' experiences, seminar participants examined the efficacy of museum exhibitions and their own belief statements about the purpose of cultural institutions. This examination produced insightful and passionate commentary.

The 51% Solution project uses time as an important measurement of quality: data are collected according to the amount of time a visitor spends in an exhibition. Some participants felt that time was not an appropriate measure of quality. They argued that it is more important for museum professionals to know what visitors get out of an exhibition than it is to know how long they spent there. Many symposium participants agreed that data about time can be coupled with exit interviews or other investigative methods to create a complete picture of the visitor experience.

Some discussants raised the issue of thoroughness of use and its effect on the lasting impact of a museum visit. When a "stop" at an exhibition element is very short, perhaps only several seconds, it is possible that an exhibition's didactic goals are not being met. A short stop may merely represent the appeal of an exhibition's design, the draw of some exhibitions' "bells and whistles." With a very short stop at an element, the visitor does not achieve the same thoroughness of use as he or she would with a longer stop.

The research project includes various types of visitors (family and individual), visits (first-time and repeat), and exhibitions. While all these factors are taken into account, some participants wanted to be able to distinguish these factors more clearly when examining Serrell's research results. Some questioned the sample size of the research.

Some practitioners see the 51% Solution as one of several evaluative tools at their disposal. Others believe that it creates a useful and viable standard by which the museum field may evaluate its work in a wide variety of setting and institutions.

Zahava D. Doering, Sociologist, and Andrew J. Pekarik, Museum Program Analyst

Doering and Pekarik, from the Institutional Studies Office, Smithsonian Institution, respond to Serrell (1997).

Serrell claims that SRI and %DV identify "exceptional" exhibitions. We maintain that these indicators cannot be used as measures of exhibition quality.

Exhibition or audience? These numbers measure the interaction between exhibitions and their audiences. Serrell assumes that differences in these measures only reflect differences in exhibitions. They could just as easily represent differences in audiences. Or they could represent some unknown combination of exhibition and audience differences.

For example, we have just calculated the average time spent in "Amber: Window to the Past," at the National Museum of Natural History, for various subgroups. Visitors who came specifically to see "Amber" spent on average one-third more time in the exhibition than those who came to the museum for other reasons. Audience differences in interest and motivation are important.

The most "thoroughly used" exhibition in Serrell's data is the "Leyster" exhibition. The cited report states that it attracted primarily "frequent" museum visitors, many from far away. These visitors could be expected to show high motivation.

It is wrong to assume that "thorough use" is only about differences among exhibitions and not about differences in audiences. By applying these measures to all museums regardless of their audiences, Serrell assumes that all museum audiences are the same. This is simply not true except in special cases.

One could just as easily (and incorrectly) assume that all exhibitions are the same and claim that Serrell's measures indicate the quality of the audience, i.e., the degree to which the audience is the one interested in the exhibition.

What happened to content? Even if differences in audiences could be accounted for, the measurement ignores the effect of content.

The "Leyster" exhibition, for example, contained only 36 paintings and 11 didactic panels. Is it surprising that visitors who had traveled long distances would stop to look at many of these relatively few images? What if there were 150 paintings? What if the paintings had been less attractive? Is it ever possible to compare exhibitions without comparing their content?

Our other difficulties with this study include small sample sizes, lack of data representativeness, poor definition of exhibition "elements," and the use of square footage without reference to the visit path. But even if terms were better defined, and even if data were collected with greater rigor, the resulting measures should not be used to compare exhibitions.

Everyone would like a simple, reliable method of establishing standards for exhibitions. Unfortunately, these measures do not meet that need because they depend on two impossible assumptions: the assumption that all museum audiences are the same, and the assumption that all museum content is the same.

Ava Ferguson, Exhibit Developer and Writer

Ferguson, now on the staff at the Monterey Bay Aquarium, has participated in this research project from the start, contributing data and using the findings. Her comments respond to Serrell (1997).

As an exhibit developer, I find the methods and results described in your report to be extremely useful both for planning new exhibitions and evaluating existing ones.

For example, at the aquarium, I recently used your study to help establish goals for a 6,000-square-foot temporary exhibition we're planning about the deep sea. Your study prompted the exhibit team to estimate the average amount of time visitors might reasonably spend in the exhibition; this figure served as the basis for selecting the type and amount of content the exhibit team would attempt to communicate. We also used this "time-budgeting" process to select and pare down the density of exhibit elements we would present in each area of the exhibition (which we based on the number of potential stops visitors might make and the average amount of time they might spend). Our ultimate goal is to encourage a majority of our visitors to stop at more than half of the exhibit elements we present to them— a lofty goal, to be sure, given the track record of the zoos and aquariums that contributed data to your study!

However, understanding how visitors spend time in our exhibition won't end in the planning phase, since we will be evaluating how closely our time estimates match visitors' real experiences when the exhibition opens in 1999. We plan to use the timing and tracking methods you describe in your report—combined with semi-structured interviews—to assess how visitors spend time in the completed exhibition and what they take away from their experience.

Of course, having access to the database you've amassed will allow us to compare our exhibition to the more than 100 other exhibitions you've studied so far. Being able to compare exhibitions and identify trends among them is perhaps the most powerful aspect of your work. For years, exhibit developers like myself have been reading and conducting individual evaluations, but have been unable to take away any generalizable results that they could apply to all exhibitions. Your study makes great strides in this direction, and I applaud you for your efforts to advance our understanding of visitors and exhibitions.

Having contributed evaluation data to your study in the past, I hope to continue to do so in the future. In this way, I, too, can say that my work has had an impact on the field. Thank you for providing me with that opportunity.

Eric Gyllenhaal, Exhibit Developer

These comments are from a panel discussion of Serrell (1997) at the Visitor Studies Association annual meeting in 1997.

What can Beverly's research do for me? First, it gives me a much needed perspective on evaluation results from exhibits I have worked on. Second, it gives me a new way to look at the numbers that come out of evaluations. And third, it gives me one more tool in my arsenal when I'm in a project meeting, sitting across the table from a content advocate, arguing for things that I know will be more effective at communicating content.

One of the frustrations I've had reading evaluation reports is that I never quite know how numbers like average time spent in the exhibit and attracting power really stand relative to what I could have accomplished. I don't expect perfection -- but what should I expect? Well, now I have a clue -- I can take data from an exhibit I've worked on, plot it on her graph, and say that maybe I could have done better. How much better, and what kind of better, I'm not yet sure. Perhaps I couldn't persuade most visitors to spend more time, but I could have given them fewer, more effective elements to look at. I'll have better perspective when Beverly has enough data from different sizes and types of exhibits that I can know how well the "best" of each size or type has done.

I like to think about the range of things that visitors do in an exhibit, rather than just what an "average" or "typical" visitor does. I can learn from means, medians, and modes -- and take some meaning from the differences among them -- but I'm also interested in the tails of a distribution, or the extremes of visitor behavior. That oddly named numerical index, the percentage of diligent visitors, or % DV, measures how big, or fat, that upper tail is, and if the tail becomes so fat that it holds most of the visitors, that's a good thing. But, do I accept Beverly's judgment that a 51% DV is the measure of success for an exhibit? Well, no and yes. Consciously, I reject it -- it's arbitrary, and it's impossible to achieve for big exhibits and for most exhibits in big museums. It probably even violates visitors own, personal goals for most of the exhibits they visit in most museums. I believe that most visitors don't want to look at half of everything! Unconsciously, however, I'm sure I'll never be able to completely reject Beverly's 51% Solution. It will always be there, gnawing away at my self-esteem when I fail to achieve her goal.

Exhibit developers, and I suppose educators in general, are supposed to be visitor advocates. Curators, and I suppose scientists in general, are the prototypical content advocates -- but in many of my experiences at the Field Museum, educators and even developers are fre-

quently seduced by the fascinating content that we could be putting into an exhibit. The really odd thing to me is that Field Museum content advocates tend to wind up advocating the quantity of content, rather than the effectiveness with which that content is communicated. "I mean, we've got so many cool things to tell our visitors, how could we leave any of them out?" To take on those kinds of arguments in ways that I will feel comfortable with, I need data. I need to be able to say, "Yes, the encyclopedic approach has been tried here and here and here, and this is what happened" I also need to say, "These people set out with more modest goals, but look how much more they accomplished!" So, when I look at Beverly's scattergrams, I dream of a time when the data points will be labeled, or grouped, in ways that I can use to convince both myself and the rest of the exhibit team that it's time to draw the line and stop adding content! I also dream of a time when the data points will be firmly linked to other types of data about what an exhibit has achieved, or failed to achieve with its visitors.

Would I use the 51% solution as a measure of success? To me it's a given that, if I had enough evaluation money, I'd commission a tracking and timing study so I could both better understand the particular exhibit and contribute to the database. But, if I had a typically under-funded exhibit, and I had to make a choice between spending the evaluation time and money on a small tracking and timing study, or on a small study where we talked to visitors about their experience, there's no question in my mind that I would rather talk with visitors, first and foremost. I might sequester some funds until after the first set of interviews, and then decide if there were questions raised that could only be answered by tracking and timing. But I want to know first what visitors were saying about the exhibit, rather than what they were doing -- and, despite the difficulties involved in such a study, I'd prefer to use the words of visitors to measure my success.

Harris Shettel, Exhibit Evaluator

These comments are excerpted from "Should the 51% Solution Have a 'Caution' Label?" Visitor Behavior *10, no. 3, (1995): 10-13. Shettel responds to Serrell (1995) in the same issue.*

There are several "pluses" to the approach that Beverly is investigating. For one thing, it is based upon the three conceptual pillars of summative exhibit evaluation: Attracting power, Holding power, and Communicating power. It has been accepted almost from the very beginning of serious visitors studies that a "good" exhibition (or exhibition element) is one that attracts visitors, holds them long enough to get its messages across, and actually gets those messages across. Unobtrusive visitor tracking studies and pre-post interview/questionnaire data consistently reveal a veritable gold mine of valuable information about these three independent (orthogonal) variables for a specific exhibition or element thereof, including what could be done to reduce any problems or weaknesses that may have been identified in any of these three areas.

If it were possible to simplify the collection of summative time and impact data without compromising their inherent value, and, at the same time, standardize the collection and interpretation of these data so that meaningful effectiveness comparisons could be made across exhibitions of all types and sizes, it would represent a breakthrough of major proportions, both practically and theoretically, for the visitor studies field. Showing that this is indeed possible is the challenge Beverly faces in carrying out her research project.

Beverly uses "total time on task" for the overall exhibition. Most would agree that such a figure has meaning only in the context of other factors such as the size, content, complexity, and density of a particular exhibition. One must take into account at least some of these differences if the total average time in any one exhibition is to be interpretable on a "universal" scale. To achieve this aim, Beverly has selected a single figure as the basic datum--the overall square footage of the exhibit area. This figure, divided by the average time visitors spent in the exhibition area, is the basis upon which the notion of "square feet per minute" is derived. This figure is intended to tell us how quickly (or slowly) the average visitor moves through that space. An upper limit of 300 square feet per minute or less (slower) is considered an "effective" or "acceptable" exhibition in terms of this variable.

It seems to me that while the total time data calculation has achieved a kind of mathematical comparability (6,000 sq. ft. is 6,000 sq. ft. no matter where it is located), it has lost its connection with meaningfulness. The real exhibit being planned for the 6,000 sq. ft. space is a very dense combination of objects, labels, hands-on activities, videos and an introductory orientation film (the latter of which will itself require about 10 minutes to view) and, as such, is very typical of exhibits being produced these days. If a visitor read, looked and did everything there was to do, I would estimate three hours would be required (an unrealistic expectation!).

This has been one of the hardest parts of the 51% approach for me to understand. It is certainly true that a square footage figure is a lot easier to obtain for an exhibition than the linear footage (pathway) that would take the visitors past all the exhibit elements. It would thus be the "figure of choice" if it could be shown to relate to the way exhibits are actually "used" by visitors. I remain skeptical on this point.

Sam Taylor, Editor

Editor of Curator Magazine, *Taylor published Serrell's 1997 article and responds here to a final draft of the book's contents.*

Beverly Serrell's work is important for many museum professions--exhibition development, museum evaluation, museum learning, visitor studies, and, of course, museum management. Here we have an entire book reporting on the behavior of visitors to museum exhibitions. Not opinions, but actual research results in numbers that are truly impressive.

Serrell's two measures (sweep rate and percentage of diligent visitors) must be appreciated for just what they are: numbers attached to two critical factors that can be used to describe visitor behavior in exhibitions. It would be a mistake to think that these factors alone represented complete measures of "effectiveness," but who would argue that having visitors move slowly through an exhibition, paying close attention to a large percentage of the elements in the gallery, is not a goal?

Serrell has initiated a search for comparable measures of effectiveness that suggests that effective communication is THE measure of effectiveness of an exhibition–ahead of great reviews, fund raising success, happy trustees, etc.

Those concerns are real (even necessary), but Serrell's focus is on the issue of communication with the visitor. That alone is significant, and that we have a book of research looking at that issue is commendable.

Charlie Walter, Museum Administrator

Walter, senior vice president of the Fort Worth Museum of Science and History and a member of Serrell's National Science Foundation advisory committee, witnessed many early drafts of this report. These are his comments on the semi-final draft.

It is refreshing that in the highly complex endeavor of exhibition development Beverly Serrell has given us a powerful new model for gauging exhibition effectiveness. It is no longer acceptable to have exhibitions that simply combine accurate content information with attractive design when our true goal is to have an educationally significant exhibit. In these days of ever tighter budgets and competition for dollars, museums must step up and show increasing effectiveness with the resources entrusted to them by the community. This report gives us important tools for studying the effectiveness of educational exhibits, a clearer picture of visitor use of museum exhibitions, and a database of visitor use which can be used as a baseline for future studies.

It should be a wake-up call to museums that in 80% of the 110 exhibitions studied visitors spent less than twenty minutes and interacted with only about one-third of the available elements. The implications to effective use of limited resources, and thus organizational effectiveness, are important and deserve close attention. Not only may we be spending money unwisely in terms of exhibit elements that are not being utilized, we may also be losing revenue as longer visitor stay times generally equate to higher spending in our institutions.

There is no one "best" model for exhibition development just as there is no one "best" approach to exhibition evaluation. Beverly's thorough use data does provide an important comparable link which should be part of our rubric of evaluation parameters. How do your exhibits compare to the thoroughly used exhibitions in this study? When interviewing exhibit design firms, does their résumé include thoroughly used exhibits? What would be the best use of floor space in terms of longer visitor stay times? When developing a themed educational exhibit, will the interpretive approach you are signing fit into a twenty-minute visitor experience?

Paying Attention: Visitors and Museum Exhibitions should not be thought of or used to limit your thinking, rather use it to inform your vision. Museums should step into the exhibition development process with their eyes wide open. If we are truly creating significant educational experiences, as opposed to pretty displays, we must look at thorough use data as important indicators of effectiveness, and we must question our notions of how exhibitions are utilized in light of new data showing how they actually are.

REFERENCES AND OTHER SOURCES   59

REFERENCES AND OTHER SOURCES

Beer, Valerie. 1987. "Great Expectations: Do Museums Know What Visitors Are Doing?" *Curator* 30, no. 3: 200-215.

Bickford, Adam, et al. 1996. *Ocean Views: A Study of Visitors to the "Ocean Planet" Exhibition at the National Museum of Natural History.* Washington, D.C.: Smithsonian Institution, Institutional Studies Office.

Bicknell, Sandra, and Graham Farmelo. 1993. *Museum Visitor Studies in the 90s.* London: Science Museum.

Bicknell, Sandra, and Sally Goodman. 1992. "Science Box–Living With Lasers: Summative Evaluation." Science Museum. London. In-house publication.

Bicknell, Sandra, and Jo Jarrett. 1993. "Science Box–Passive Smoking: Summative Evaluation." Science Museum, London. In-house publication.

Bicknell, Sandra, and Dominique Nivision. 1992. "Science Box–DNA Fingerprinting: Summative Evaluation." Science Museum, London. In-house publication.

Bitgood, Stephen. 1994. "Designing Effective Exhibits: Criteria for Success, Exhibit Design Approaches, and Research Strategies." *Visitor Behavior* 9, no. 4: 4-15.

Bitgood, Stephen, and Amy Cota. 1995. "Principles of Orientation and Circulation Within Exhibitions." *Visitor Behavior* 10, no. 2: 7-8.

Bitgood, Stephen, Joe Hines, Wayne Hamberger, and William Ford. 1991. "Visitor Circulation Through a Changing Exhibits Gallery." *Visitor Studies: Theory, Research, and Practice* 4: 103-114.

Boisvert, Dorothy Lozowski, and Brenda Jochums Slez. 1995. "The Relationship Between Exhibit Characteristics and Learning-Associated Behaviors in a Science Museum Discovery Space." *Science Education* 79, no. 5: 503-18.

Borun, Minda. 1996. "Families Are Learning in Science Museums." *Curator* 39, no. 2: 123-38.

Borun, Minda, Margaret Chambers, and Ann Cleghorn. 1995. "Family Learning in Four Science Museums: Preliminary Results." *Current Trends in Audience Research and Evaluation* 9: 116-24.

Brooks, Joyce, A.M., and Philip E. Vernon. 1956. "A Study of Children's Interests and Comprehension at a Science Museum." *British Journal of Psychology* 47: 175-82.

Crane, Valerie. 1994. *Informal Science Learning.* Dedham, Mass.: Research Communications.

Csikszentmihalyi, Mihaly, and Kim Hermanson. 1995. "Intrinsic Motivation in Museums: What Makes Visitors Want to Learn?" *Museum News* 74, no. 3: 34-37, 59-62.

Cutting, Andrea, and Jane Marie Litwak. 1997. "Minnesota Historical Society 'Families' Exhibit Summative Evaluation." Minnesota Historical Society. In-house publication.

Davidson, Jan. 1996. "Exploring the Outer Bay: Summative Evaluation Report." Monterey Bay Aquarium. In-house publication.

Doering, Zahava D., et al. 1994. *From Reptile Houses to Reptile Discovery Centers: A Study of the Reptile Discovery Centers Project at the National Zoological Park, Zoo Atlanta & the Dallas Zoo.* Washington, D.C.: Smithsonian Institution, Institutional Studies Office.

Dritsas, Jennifer. 1996. "On The Floor." *Exhibitionist,* 15, no. 2: 27-28.

Dyer, Jennifer. 1992. "New Life for an Old Hall." *Curator* 35, no. 4: 268-84.

Eason, Laurie P., and Marcia C. Linn. 1976. "Evaluation of the Effectiveness of Participatory Exhibits." *Curator* 19, no. 1: 45-62.

Falk, John H. 1982. "The Use of Time as a Measure of Visitor Behavior and Exhibit Effectiveness." *Roundtable Reports* 7, no. 4: 10-13.

Falk, John H. 1983. "Time and Behavior as Predictors of Learning." *Science Education* 67, no. 2: 267-276.

Falk, John H. 1984. "The Use of Time as a Measure of Visitor Behavior and Exhibit Effectiveness." In *Museum Education Anthology: 1973-1983,* edited by Susan K. Nichols, 183-90. Washington, D.C.: Museum Education Roundtable.

Falk, John H. 1993. "Assessing the Impact of Exhibit Arrangement on Visitor Behavior and Learning." *Curator* 36, no. 2: 133-46.

Falk, John H., and Lynn Dierking. 1992. *The Museum Experience.* Washington, D.C.: Whalesback Books.

Foster, John Scott. 1992. "The Effects of Visitor Perceptions and Encoding Cues on Learning from Museum Exhibits." Ph.D. diss., University of Florida.

Garfield, Donald. 1992. "Darkened Waters: Profile of a Spill." *Museum News* 71, no. 2: 24-26.

Giusti, Ellen. 1993. "Hall of Human Biology and Evolution Evaluation." American Museum of Natural History, New York. In-house publication.

Giusti, Ellen. 1994. "Visitors Evaluate Evolution Hall." *Exhibitionist,* 13, no. 2: 15-19.

Giusti, Ellen. 1995. "Global Warming: Understanding the Forecast, A Multi-site Exhibition Evaluation." American Museum of Natural History, New York. In-house publication.

Giusti, Ellen. 1997. "Call of the Wild: Are the Visitors Listening? Multi-site Evaluation of 'Global Warming: Understanding the Forecast.'" Paper presented at the annual meeting of the American Association of Museums, Atlanta, Ga.

Giusti, Ellen. 1993. "Hall of Human Biology and Evolution Evaluation." American Museum of Natural History, New York. In-house publication.

Giusti, Ellen, and Allison Thau. 1996. "'Amber: Window to the Past' Summative Evaluation: Analysis of Exit Interviews." American Museum of Natural History, New York. In-house publication.

Gladwell, Malcolm. 1996. "The Science of Shopping." *The New Yorker,* November 4 1996, 66-75.

Graburn, Nelson. 1984. "The Museum and the Visitor Experience." *In Museum Education Anthology: 1973-1983,* edited by Susan K. Nichols, 177-82. Washington, D.C.: Museum Education Roundtable.

Griggs, S., and J. Manning. 1983. "The Predictive Validity of Formative Evaluation of Exhibits." *Museum Studies Journal 1,* no. 2: 31-41.

Harvey, Mark, and Margie Marino. 1995. "Boettcher Summative Evaluation Report 1 (of 2): Observations of Visitor Behavior Before and After Renovation." Colorado State University and Denver Museum of Natural History. In-house publication.

Hein, George E. 1996. "The Dilemma of Constructivism: Do We Focus on the Learner at the Expense of What We Want to Teach?" Paper presented at the annual meeting of the Association of Science and Technology Centers, Pittsburgh, Pa.

Hein, George E., Catherine Hughes, and Robin Mello. 1994. "Evaluation Report 'Judith Leyster: A Dutch Master and Her World': Worcester Art Museum, September 18 -December 5, 1993." Lesley College, Cambridge, Mass. In-house publication.

Hicks, Ellen Cochran, ed. 1986. "An Artful Science: A Conversation About Exhibit Evaluation." *Museum News* 64, no. 3: 32-39.

Horn, Adrienne, and Lisa Hubbell. 1991. "Evaluation Study: Visitor Response to the 'Life Through Time' Exhibition at the California Academy of Sciences." Evaluation Seminar, Center for Museum Studies, John F. Kennedy University. In-house publication.

James, William. [1908] 1969. "Psychology and the Teaching Art." In *Educational Psychology: Selected Readings*, edited by Richard C. Sprinthall and Norman A. Sprinthall, 292-295. New York: Van Nostrand-Reinhold Co.

Klein, Hans-Joachim. 1993. "Tracking Visitor Circulation in Museum Settings." *Environment and Behavior* 25, no. 6: 782-800.

Korenic, Mary. 1994. "Summative Evaluation of the Milwaukee Public Museum Exhibit, 'A Tribute to Survival.'" Milwaukee Public Museum. In-house publication.

Korn, Randi. 1993. "Postinstallation: Visitor Evaluation." In *The Visitor's Voice*, edited by C. Griffith Mann, 62-75. Cleveland: Cleveland Museum of Art.

Korn, Randi. 1995. "An Analysis of Differences Between Visitors at Natural History Museums and Science Centers." *Curator* 38, no. 3: 150-60.

Litwak, Jane Marie, and Andrea Cutting. 1994a. "Remedial Evaluation of 'A Common Ground' for the Minnesota History Center, Saint Paul, Minnesota." In-house publication.

Litwak, Jane Marie, and Andrea Cutting. 1994b. "Summative Evaluation of 'Minnesota Almanac' for the Minnesota History Center, St. Paul, MN." In-house publication.

Mackinney, Lisa Hubbell. 1994. "'Being Able to Touch': A Summative Evaluation Study of the Discovery Room and Three Experimental Exhibits at the California Academy of Sciences." California Academy of Sciences. In-house publication.

Mann, C. Griffith, ed. 1993. *The Visitor's Voice.* Cleveland: Cleveland Museum of Art.

Marcellini, Dale L., and Thomas A. Jenssen. 1988. "Visitor Behavior in the National Zoo's Reptile House." *Zoo Biology* 7: 329-38.

Marino, Margaret. 1996. "'Prehistoric Journey': Summative Evaluation Report." Denver Museum of Natural History. In-house publication.

Marino, Margie, and Mark Harvey. 1995. "Boettcher Summative Evaluation Report 2 (of 2): Visitor Response to 'Edge of the Wild,' Achievement of Educational Objectives, Assessment of Individual Exhibit Components." Colorado State University and Denver Museum of Natural History. In-house publication.

McLean, Kathleen. 1993. *Planning for People in Museum Exhibitions.* Washington, D.C.: Association of Science-Technology Centers.

McManus, Paulette M. 1988. "Good Companions: More on the Social Determination of Learning-Related Behaviour in a Science Museum." *International Journal of Museum Management and Curatorship* 7: 37-44.

Melton, Arthur W. 1933. "Studies of Installation at the Pennsylvania Museum of Art." Museum News 10, no. 14: 5-8.

Melton, Arthur W. 1935. *Problems of Installation in Museums of Art.* Washington, D.C.: American Association of Museums.

Miles, Roger. 1993. "Holding Power: To Choose Time Is to Save Time." In *What Research Says About Learning in Science Museums*, 2: 17-20. Washington, D.C.: Association of Science-Technology Centers.

Pekarik, Andrew J., Zahava D. Doering, and Adam Bickford. 1995. *An Assessment of the "Science in American Life" Exhibition at the National Museum of American History.* Washington, D.C.: Smithsonian Institution, Institutional Studies Office.

Raphling, Britt. 1997a. "Summative Evaluation of 'The Universe in Your Hands.'" *Visitor Behavior* 12, nos. 1-2: 21-23.

Raphling, Britt. 1997b. "A Summative Study of 'The Universe in Your Hands: Early Tools of Astronomy.'" Evaluation Department, Adler Planetarium and Astronomy Museum. In-house publication.

Raphling, Britt, and Beverly Serrell. 1993. "Capturing Affective Learning." *Current Trends in Audience Research and Evaluation* 7: 57-62.

Robinson, E. S. 1928. *The Behavior of the Museum Visitor.* Washington, D.C.: American Association of Museums.

Rubenstein, Rosalyn, Andrea Paradis, and Leslie Munro. 1993. "A Comparative Study of a Traveling Exhibition at Four Public Settings in Canada." *Environment and Behavior* 25, no. 6: 801-20.

Serrell & Associates. 1992. "From Stuffed Birds on Sticks to Vivid Feathers, Gleaming Talons and Sparkling Beaks: A Summative Evaluation of the Bird Halls at Field Museum of Natural History." Serrell & Associates, Chicago, Ill. In-house publication.

Serrell, Beverly. 1992. "The 51% Solution: Defining a Successful Exhibit by Visitor Behavior," *Current Trends in Audience Research and Evaluation* 6: 26-30.

Serrell, Beverly. 1993a. "Animal Kingdom Project: Exhibit Evaluation Studies." Field Museum of Natural History, Chicago, Ill. In-house publication.

Serrell, Beverly. 1993b. "The Question of Visitor Styles." *Visitor Studies: Theory, Research and Practice* 6 48-53.

Serrell, Beverly. 1993c. "Using Behaviour to Define the Effectiveness of Exhibitions." *In Museum Visitor Studies in the 90s,* edited by Sandra Bicknell and Graham Farmelo, London: Science Museum: 140-44

Serrell, Beverly. "What's the Big Idea?" 1994. *Exhibitionist,* 12, no. 3: 16.

Serrell, Beverly. 1995. "The 51% Solution Research Project: A Meta-analysis of Visitor Time/Use in Museum Exhibitions." *Visitor Behavior* 10, no. 3: 5-9.

Serrell, Beverly. 1996a. *Exhibit Labels: An Interpretive Approach.* Walnut Creek, Calif.: Alta Mira Press, a division of Sage Publications, Inc.

Serrell, Beverly. 1996b. "In Search of Generalizability: New Tools for Visitor Studies." *Journal of Museum Education* 21, no. 3: 11-18.

Serrell, Beverly. 1997. "Paying Attention: The Duration and Allocation of Visitors' Time in Museum Exhibitions." *Curator* 40, no. 2: 108-125.

Serrell, Beverly, and Barbara Becker. 1990. "Stuffed Birds on Sticks: Plans to Re-do the Animal Halls at Field Museum." *Visitor Studies: Theory, Research and Practice* 3: 263-69.

Shettel, Harris. 1973. "Exhibits: Art Form or Educational Medium?" *Museum News* 52, no. 1: 32-41.

Shettel, Harris. 1976. "An Evaluation of Visitor Response to 'Man in His Environment.'" Field Museum of Natural History, Chicago, Ill. In-house publication.

Shettel, Harris. 1995. "Should the 51% Solution Have a 'Caution' Label?" *Visitor Behavior* 10, no. 3: 10-13.

Shettel, Harris, et al. 1968. "Strategies for Determining Exhibit-Effectiveness." *Report No. AIR E95-4/68-FR*. Pittsburgh, Pa.: American Institutes for Research.

Taylor, Sam. 1997. "A Note from the Editor." *Curator* 40, no. 2: 85.

White, Judith, and Sharon Barry. 1984. *Families, Frogs, and Fun: Developing a Family Learning Lab in a Zoo*. Washington, D.C.: Smithsonian Institution, National Zoological Park.

HOW TO USE THE APPENDIX

This Appendix provides an overview of the museums and exhibition sites, the detailed methodology, and raw data from the study. The appendices begin with a general overview and conclude with information about each individual exhibition.

Appendix A.   People who helped in the study

Appendix B.   The Methods Workbook used in the study, discussion of the 51% solution, definitions of terms, tools for collecting and analyzing data, cued interviews, and instructions for tracking and timing

Appendix C.   Sample data sheets and floor plans used by museums in the study

Appendix D.   List of exhibitions studied by name of exhibition, followed by the location at which the exhibition was studied, and exhibition code number (the same number used in Appendix F.)

Appendix E.   List of institutions followed by name of the exhibition studied at that institution and exhibition code number

Appendix F.   Summary table of the 110 exhibitions in the study. Read this table vertically to compare data from one exhibition or site to another.

Appendix G.   Each page describes a single exhibition. Graphs of specific exhibitions are arranged in numerical order by exhibition code number. For example, "001-Outer Bay", 001 is the exhibition code number. The bar graphs compare the single variables of time and stops or the number of visitors and the time spent in each exhibit. The scattergrams plot time and percentage of stops, or the number of stops made in each exhibit.

USING THE APPENDIXES:

1. To find data for a specific **exhibition**:

   In Appendix D, look up the name of the exhibition, get the exhibition code number and use that number to find the specific data in Appendices F and G.

2. To find data for a specific **institution**:

   In Appendix E., look up the name of the institution, get the exhibition code number and use that number in Appendices F and G to find the page(s) for the institution.

APPENDIX A.

LIST OF PARTICIPATING MUSEUM PROFESSIONALS

These are the names of many of the people who helped by collecting data, sharing data, commenting on early drafts of the report, processing the data, and sharing techniques, photos, advice, and stories.

PEOPLE WHO HELPED

Sharon Abbott
Susan Ades
Wendy Aibel-weiss
Rick Ainsworth
Erik Alexander
Barry Aprison
Jacqueline Arendse
Barbara Becker
Jane Bedno
Louise Belmont-Skinner
Sandra Bicknell
Stephen Bitgood
Colleen Blair
Dorothy M. Boisvert
Minda Borun
Florence Bramley
Adam Bickford
Ann Brubaker
Suzanne Bubic
Kristen Buchner
Hillary Churchill
Robert Cohon
David Combs
Amy Cota
Lisa Craig
Emily Curran
Jan Davidson
Zahava D. Doering
Letitia Doggett
Emily Easton
Robyn Einhorn

Valerie Eisenberg
Carol Enseki
John Falk
Ava Ferguson
Christine Fitzgerald
John Scott Foster
Diana Galindo
Ben Gammon
Veronica Garcia-Luis
Ellen Giusti
Kenneth C. Gold
Anne B. Gurnee
Eric Gyllenhaal
George Hein
D. D. Hilke
Kim Hunter
Dawn Huntwork
Jessica de Jesus
Mary Korenic
Randi Korn
Vicky Kruckeberg
Jane Marie Litwak
Ross Loomis
Diane Manuel
Margie Marino
Lisa Mackinney
Kathleen McLean
Patty McNamara
Margaret Menninger
Roger Miles
Ed Miller
Debbie Moskovitz
Francie Muraski-Stotz

Martha Nichols
Maureen Otwell
Ann F. Peabody
Paul Pearson
Andrew J. Pekarik
Deborah Perry
David Phillips
Carolyn Pirnat
Christine Randall
Britt Raphling
Stephanie Ratcliffe
Rachel Reklau
Lisa Roberts
Cody Sandifer
Carol Saunders
Vicki Schirado
Paula Schaedlich
Harris Shettel
Cathy Shiga-Gatullo
Amy Simon
Jeanne Sousa
Larry Stone
Katherine Street
Susan Sudbury
Helen Valdez
Pat Villeneuve
Charlie Walter
Martin Weiss
Kristine Westerberg
Marjorie Williams
Linda Wilson
Adrienne Wiseman
Donald P. Zuris

APPENDIX B.

METHODS WORKBOOK

The methods workbook was developed by the author of *Paying Attention* over the years of the research study from 1993 to 1997 with input from its users. Its purpose is to guide data collectors in sharing explicit strategies. It is a work in progress.

THE METHODS WORKBOOK

This workbook will instruct you in the methods that will help you discover interesting and useful information about how well your exhibition is working. The easily applied techniques will inform you about how much time visitors spend, which elements in the exhibition are most popular, how thoroughly visitors use the exhibition, if they can understand the main ideas of the exhibition, and what parts of the exhibition they find most memorable.

We collected time and stops data from a broad range of exhibition types and sizes during the research project, "A Search for Generalizability: Visitor Time/Use in Museum Exhibitions," funded by the National Science Foundation. The goal of collecting data from 100 different exhibitions was achieved. If you follow the directions and definitions in this workbook, you will be able to see where your exhibition fits into the model of thoroughly used exhibitions, as described in the body of the report, *Paying Attention: Visitors and Museum Exhibitions.*

For data to be comparable, participants must share–to the best of their abilities–explicit definitions of terms and strategies. Thus, this workbook will concentrate largely on defining and providing rationales for the chosen terminology. Also included are directions for specific protocols. Sample data collection sheets can be found in Appendix B.

When the project first started, it was called the "51% Solution."

WHAT IS THE 51% SOLUTION?

The 51% Solution is a methodology that combines a systematic, summative evaluation strategy for assessing and comparing the effectiveness of a broad range of educational exhibitions. The factors being described and the measures being compared are visitors' time, the percentage of the exhibition they paid attention to, and the degree to which they were able to find meanings that matched the exhibition developers' intentions. Quantitative guidelines for success are offered.

WHAT ARE THE CRITERIA OF THE 51% SOLUTION?

The 51% Solution has three criteria, or guidelines, for measuring and comparing the effectiveness of an exhibition:

1. Do 51% of the visitors move through the exhibition at a rate of less than 300 square feet per minute (size of exhibit divided by total average time)?
2. Do 51% of the visitors stop at 51% or more of the exhibit elements?

3. Can 51% of a random sample of cued visitors, immediately after viewing the exhibition, express general and specific attitudes or concepts that are related to the exhibition's objectives, thereby providing evidence that they understood what the exhibition was about?

Fifty-one percent, while arbitrary, represents a simple democratic majority as well as a realistic standard that many exhibitions can strive for, considering the diversity of visitors' demographic and psychographic characteristics. Fifty-one percent provides a reference point, e.g., is the data below 51%, or does it exceed 51%? By how much? It is not an end point. The three criteria prescribe desirable yet flexible benchmarks within which we can choose to focus our attention to make the most expedient choices when planning exhibits.

WHAT THE 51% SOLUTION PROVIDES

The model provides tools (methods and criteria) for a goal-related investigation, based on visitor feedback, to determine how well the exhibition is working. To do this, it includes ways to answer the following specific questions:

- How much time do visitors spend in this exhibition? (duration)
- What percentage of the visitors pay at least some attention to the different parts of the exhibition? At how many of the elements or stations do they stop? (time allocation, utilization)
- What experiences do visitors have that they find meaningful and memorable in this exhibition? Could they get the main ideas? Can they remember any specifics? Can they make personal connections? (impact)
- How does visitor use of this exhibition compare with use of other exhibitions? What is the impact on visitors relative to other exhibitions? (comparisons)

The performance of the exhibition is measured by looking at a variety of visitor behaviors involving time (duration and allocation), observable overt actions, and self-reported impacts and outcomes. This feedback can then be compared with the exhibition's stated communication objectives. In addition, the exhibition's time/behavior potential (size of exhibit, number of elements, modalities of elements, type and location of the host institution, etc.) can be compared with the data from other exhibitions, where similar evaluation methods have been used.

The methods and model provide a simple yet rigorous approach to defining, collecting, and analyzing data, but at the same time, this process lets visitors act naturally and normally. This approach dictates the researcher's behavior, not the visitor's.

The 51% Solution is unique because it provides a relatively uncomplicated and inexpensive methodology that can be used across disciplines, and it allows us to gather a large database to share and compare. To be more creative and innovative about what might be, we have to understand better what is. We are looking for broad trends and patterns that provide useful information for making decisions about exhibition development and evaluation. The goal that is aided by the 51% Solution is the goal of improving the educational effectiveness of exhibitions.

WHAT THE 51% SOLUTION IS NOT

The 51% Solution is not the ultimate or only way to look at what visitors get out of an exhibition. It does not measure long-term learning, but it does assess the potential and prerequisites for it. It is not based on a pre- or post-knowledge gain model. The 51% Solution is not focused on understanding how different kinds of people learn from exhibitions (that is, looking at differences among special audiences, e.g., gender, social group, educational characteristics), but it does look at some exhibition variables that may contribute to visitor learning (size, density, modalities present). It is not anecdotal, and it does not seek to predict what any one person will get out of any one exhibition. The 51% Solution is not a methodology meant for doing formative evaluation or for evaluating single exhibit elements; it is designed for whole exhibitions. It is not a formula that limits the creativity or innovativeness of the exhibition development process.

DEFINITIONS OF TERMS

Within the context of this systematic summative evaluation strategy for educational exhibitions, each term has a particular meaning:

- **Systematic** means using the same definitions and techniques in consistent ways in a variety of museum settings so that the data will be comparable.
- **Summative evaluation** means evaluating the whole exhibition (all of its parts in context) after the exhibition is open to the public.
- **Strategy** consists of a combination of two techniques–unobtrusive observations of visitor behavior and an exit interview/questionnaire with open-ended questions–and a variety of ways to analyze the data (e.g., simple statistical analysis, content analysis, qualitative review).
- **Assessing** means gathering data and comparing it to the criteria.
- **Comparing** means that the data gathered can be shared across exhibition types, sizes, and disciplines. We are looking for norms, ranges, and exceptional data.
- **Effectiveness**, or success, is defined by the degree to which the exhibition achieves its stated objectives with its intended audience and is thoroughly used.
- **Broad range** means a diversity of museum sizes, disciplines, and budgets.

- **Educational** implies that the exhibition has stated specific communication objectives, where "learning" is defined very broadly, e.g., "Visitors will find out about or realize something new about X"; "Visitors will make a personal connection with Y"; "Visitors will be inspired to wonder 'what if . . . ,' about Z"; etc., as a result of experiencing this exhibition.
- **Exhibition** means a defined room or space of known square footage with a given title, containing elements that together make up a conceptually coherent entity recognizable as an exhibition of objects, interactives, and/or phenomena. Some form of interpretation is present (text labels, graphics, videos, interactive devices), beyond mere identification of objects.
- **Visitors** are people who enter the exhibition and appear to be in it because they are using it (not lost, not using it as a hallway). Only adults (ages 16+) are the subjects; only individuals are tracked (regardless of the number of other people they are with); similarly, only casual visitors are observed, not people in tour groups. For each study, the recommended minimum sample size is 40; the suggested maximum is 100.
- **Randomly selected** means adult casual visitors selected by a specified mechanism (e.g., every nth visitor) without bias for gender, age, race, or social group. Subjects are selected over representative days of the week and times of day.
- **Exhibition objectives** are the educational objectives (see "educational" defined earlier) that the exhibition's developers have clearly identified.
- **Exhibit elements** are defined as discrete, conceptual units, experiences, or components within the exhibition layout. They may vary widely in size and type, e.g., a panel, a case, a diorama, a set of artifacts, a video theater, a computer, an interactive device, etc. They should be defined by the in-house staff, who are familiar with the exhibition.
- **Stop** equals both feet of the visitor coming to a full halt for 2 to 3 seconds while the person's body and/or head is oriented toward the exhibit element. Counting stops provides evaluators with the number of exhibit elements "used" by each visitor (a very simple and admittedly generous interpretation). Multiple stops at a single element are counted as only one stop. A stop at every element would mean that total stops and number of elements are the same.
- **Total time** is the time elapsed as the visitor entered the exhibition, looked around, made stops, and left. (Time at individual elements need not be recorded unless the element has a clearly definable amount of time to be used completely, such as a 3-minute video.)
- **Average time** is the sum of the total times for all visitors in the sample, divided by the number of visitors in the sample.
- **Square feet per minute** is a figure derived by dividing the total square footage of the exhibition by the average time. This measure allows exhibitions of different sizes to be compared against each other. Previously referred to as "speed," now called **sweep rate** (because as visitors stroll through the exhibit, they look around, visually sweeping the area), this figure is an abstract index for comparison purposes.

WHAT METHODS DOES THE 51% SOLUTION USE?

The 51% Solution uses two methodologies: unobtrusive observations of visitor behavior, called tracking and timing, and feedback from individual visitors in an open-ended exit interview, called here the cued questionnaire.

INSTRUCTIONS FOR TRACKING AND TIMING

A randomly selected, representative sample of visitors (n = 40 or more) is tracked and timed on weekends and weekdays. The data collector notes visitors' gender, approximate age, social-group make-up, where they go in the exhibition, and how long they stay. The demographic information helps determine if the sample was representative of the museum's "normal" visitor profile. Pathways through the exhibit and stops at elements are noted on the map (usually a floor plan of the exhibition). Data are tallied on a spreadsheet listing each individual, total time, total stops (and other behaviors, if systematically recorded). These unobtrusive, objective measures, which focus on time and attention, are valuable indicators of the exhibit's attractiveness and interest to visitors, and these factors have been found to correlate positively with learning and enjoyment.

The procedures for tracking and timing are:

1. Choose as your subject the first adult casual visitor who crosses an imaginary line as he or she enters the exhibition. If more than one person crosses the line, choose the person closest to you. (You are picking among visitors who have self-selected to enter the exhibition.) Collect the sample of 40 or more visitors over different days of the week.

2. Follow the subject unobtrusively throughout the time he/she is in the exhibit. Even if the subject leaves the gallery right away, or runs right through it without stopping, that data sheet is still counted. We want a random sample of what visitors do–even if they do not really interact much with the exhibits.

3. Mark each stop with an X on the floor plan. If the visitor is inching along an area, you don't have to record an X for every few steps. A stop is defined as both feet planted on the floor with the head facing in the direction of an exhibit element for 2 to 3 seconds or more. Mark the X on the floor plan close enough to the element so that you can tell at which element the visitor stopped.

4. Connect each X with a line that denotes the path the visitor took through the gallery. If he or she doubles back a lot, or circles around, put arrows on the path line, so you can tell which way the visitor went.

5. If desired, note the various behaviors you see at each exhibit element. The data sheet has definitions of the behavior codes. If a visitor does a behavior more than once at an exhibit element, you only need to circle or mark the behavior once.

Commonly used codes on tracking sheets are listed below:

- **Sheet #**: Number your samples consecutively, do not start over each day.

- **TOD**: Time of day when you begin each sheet; this also can be in blocks of time (e.g., noon-2pm) to indicate the period during which you were timing.

- **TT**: Total time. Put down the exact duration of the person's visit. It is also helpful if you put that actual finish time at the end of the visit, where the subject exits the space. All times should be in minutes and seconds. Use a stopwatch if you have one.

- **Exhibit stops**: Count the exhibit elements visited. There may be more than one X at each element, but one or more Xs count as one stop at that element. The greatest number of stops you will ever count will be the total number of elements in the exhibit.

- **Exit**: Make sure it is clear where the visitor exited the exhibition. Circle the door through which he or she leaves if there is more than one exit.

- **Gender**: Circle the sex of the subject.

- **Age**: Circle estimated age of subject.

- **# in Group**: Determine how many other people the subject is with by watching who is moving around together.

- **Group Type**: Circle whether the subject's group is made up of adults only (A only) or adult with children (A + K). Write in ages of kids, if desired.

- **Video and computer times**: If desired, keep track of and total up exact subtimes for each video or computer that people use (minutes and seconds). Use running time on the stopwatch as you track, then compute video times after visitor leaves and before starting another tracking.

6. Note in the comments any interactions you think are significant-including lack of attention or time (such as standing around, sitting down, waiting for parents or friends, etc.). Also note in comments any unusual variables in the environment (such as construction in the exhibit area, areas blocked off, things broken, tour groups in the way). If a visitor spends an unusually long time at one element, make a note of it. Resist the temptation to make subjective value judgments about the level of visitor involvement or interest. For example, say "visitor is smiling" instead of "visitor is happy."

7. If the subject walks slowly past an exhibit element and looks at it but doesn't stop, put an arrow on the path that indicates which way he or she was looking. Although we would not count it as a stop, it can tell us that they were "taking in" the exhibits. An exception to this is a very large element that can be thoroughly looked at while walking by or around without stopping. Note a "G" for glance.

If visitors try to talk to data collectors during observation periods, it is a good idea to say, "I don't work here" or "I'm a student." Although this may not be true, it can keep you from being interrupted and distracted from the person you are watching. Also you can just ignore people who try to catch your eye to see what you are doing. You do not have to be unfriendly, but sometimes it is easier to just avoid people than to try to answer their questions while you are tracking and timing someone else.

Try to remain unobtrusive. Look out of the corner of your eyes, or in reflections through the glass. If someone becomes aware that you are following them and it seems to bother them, abort the tracking session--note what happened on the sheet, and begin again with someone else. It is important to let the museum staff know the exact times when you will be in the halls doing the observations. Let the guards know. If a visitor becomes uncomfortable about being watched (this does happen occasionally) and complains to a guard, you will want the guard to know to reply, "We are conducting some very important research today..." instead of throwing you out of the museum.

A generic tracking and timing sheet is below.

INSTRUCTIONS FOR CUED INTERVIEWS

The second data-collecting method employed for this type of summative evaluation is an exit interview/questionnaire with cued visitors. Feedback from cued visitors who answer five open-ended questions provides information about what visitors remember and find meaningful in the exhibition, and about how much they under-stand the educational concepts and communication goals of the exhibition.

The advantage of letting people answer open-ended questions in writing is that the evaluator does not put words into their mouths, pressure them for a quick answer, or create categories that limit or direct visitors' responses. On the other hand, this form of data is more difficult to score and summarize, which is why the evaluation report should include several different ways of looking at the questionnaire feedback as well as copies of all the original forms or transcriptions for interested staff and reviewers to examine for themselves.

The procedures for the cued exit questionnaire are as follows:
1. Recruit visitors as they enter the exhibition. The sample of 30 to 50 should consist of a representative group of adult casual visitors who have self-selected to be there. They should not be the same people that will be unobtrusively timed and tracked. Sample the cued visitors on at least three different days.
2. Choose the sample randomly by selecting the fifth person to cross an imaginary line when you are ready to start (or the next

---

Tracking & Timing for _____

Day _____   TOD _____   Date _____   Sheet # _____

Gender: M F

TT _____Exhibit Stops _____Age: < 20s 30s 40s 50s 60s +

Group Size: 1   2   3   4   5 +   Group Type: A only   A + K

X = stopped   R = read   ROL = read out loud   P = point   T = talk I = touch, manipulate

LOS = looked over shoulder   CO = call over to look   G = glance

Read main label

Use touch screen computer

Watched a video

Used an interactive

(exhibit floor plan map goes here)

                                                              data collector _____

person, after you've finished with the first). Do not avoid approaching someone because they "look like they might not want to" or any other reason (bias).

3. Your recruiting statement might sound like this: "Hello. Excuse me, the museum is conducting a special survey about this exhibit today, and we would like to talk to visitors after they have visited this exhibition. Would you be willing to spend a few minutes answering a brief questionnaire when you are done?—You will receive this free gift [show it to them] for doing it." The gift should be valued at $2 to $5. It should not be a free pass to come back, although one could be given out in addition to the gift.

4. When visitors say no, thank them anyway. Do not ask why, although they may offer a reason, which you should write down (e.g., small children impatient; in a hurry; don't speak the language; not interested). Keep track of how many people refuse.

5. When a visitor says yes, give him or her a slip of paper with a number and the current time, and ask them to show it to the survey person at the end of the exhibit or after they finish. Make sure the visitor understands to come back to you after finishing this exhibition, not the whole museum. Keep track of the number of "escapees," or visitors that never come back.

6. When the visitor has finished looking at the exhibition and comes to the survey table or desk (outside the exit), take the paper and note the elapsed time and number on that person's survey sheet.

7. When the visitor arrives at the desk, observe and/or ask for demographic characteristics, e.g., "How many people are with you today? Any children?" and circle the appropriate codes on the sheet.

8. Then ask the visitor the next two questions: "Is this your first visit?" and "Do you have any special interest?" and write what he or she says, verbatim. Visitors will often say "no, it's not my first visit, but I haven't been here for a long time." If they say they do have special interest, knowledge, or training in the topic, look curious, and get them to explain briefly. Write what they say verbatim.

9. Give the questionnaire sheet and a pencil to the visitor and show him or her to a table where he or she can sit and write uninterrupted. Tell the visitor to take as much time as needed. It is a good idea to have some extra paper and colored pencils, crayons or washable markers so children can amuse themselves while adults fill out the form.

10. The prompts (e.g., "I never realized") on the sheets are derived from visitors' language in previous questionnaire data and help them get writing.

11. When the visitor finishes and brings the sheet to you, immediately put it aside (do not examine the answers), give the visitor the gift, and thank him or her.

12. If you are doing this as a contract study, be sure to get permission and show the data collection schedule to the contact person at the museum well in advance. You will need this person's assistance to obtain a desk or table at which to work during the questionnaire times.

A generic cued questionnaire form is on the next page.

WHAT CUED INTERVIEWS TELL US

Visitors in the sample (n = 30 to 50, not the same people that were timed and tracked) are asked to fill out the questionnaire after a very brief interview about their visit and prior interest. The visitors' responses are summarized by content analysis–looking at the words used and how those words relate to the individual exhibit elements, the ideas communicated, and how visitors related to the stated goals of the exhibition. Even if a visitor's comment is extremely terse (e.g., one word), that word, if specific enough, can be matched with the exhibit or area goal to which it is closest. Individual questionnaires also can be rated or sorted according to how appropriate the person's reactions are compared to the exhibit developer's hopes or intentions (e.g., "low–not related," "medium low–partially related," "medium high–related to essentials," "high–extensively related"). For a good example of how this has been used, see Raphling 1997.

In summative evaluation studies, cued testing normally is not recommended because cuing increases people's level of motivation and attention. It can be argued, however, that cuing is useful in museum settings. Visitors' recall levels are likely to be very low, due in part to the typically brief, incomplete, and informal visits people make to exhibitions and, in some cases, confusing or unclear exhibits. In addition, visitors to the exhibition are under no obligation to learn anything. The summative question about learning reflects not whether they did learn, but whether they could learn. The cued questionnaire measures the exhibition's potential to communicate.

Cuing provides a "best-case scenario." Thus, if cued visitors cannot grasp the main idea, or if they fail to notice, understand, or remember parts of an exhibition, one can assume that it is very likely that uncued visitors are not relating to them either. Missing data (no response, no recall, no meaningfulness) or a lack of patterns in the data where one might expect to find them provides insightful information.

On the other hand, if cued visitors to an exhibition do have a high rate of learning, that level of response cannot be assumed to be typical for a population of "normal" visitors to the exhibition, i.e. those people who are less motivated and spend less time. Cued visitors provide empirical evidence that visitors can learn from the exhibit, but they do not prove how many actually do. Among exhibitions, however, cued visitors' learning can be compared for the achievement of the learning criteria (i.e., the communication goals) as a dichotomous variable (yes/no) rather than a rate.

Cued Exit Questionnaire for _____

Date _____ Time _____ Sheet # _____

Sex: M   F   Age: # Group   A only
                      < 20s   1   A + K
                       20s   2
                       30s   3
                       40s   4
                       50s   5 +
                       60s

Is this your first visit to the _____ Museum?   Yes _____   No _____

Do you have any special interest, knowledge or training

in_____?

No _____   Yes

_____

1. What would you say is the main purpose of the displays in these galleries?

To show...

_____
_____

To make people...

_____
_____

2. What is one new idea you are taking away with you?

I didn't know, or I never realized that...

_____
_____

and/or

It reminded me that...

_____
_____

Anything else? (use other side if necessary)

Data collector_____

MISUNDERSTANDINGS ABOUT CUED VISITORS

Five common misunderstandings persist regarding the use of cued visitors for answering exit questionnaires in exhibition evaluation, as follows:

Misconception #1.

Cuing visitors causes them to act unnaturally.

While it is true that visitors who have been cued will, as a group, spend more time in the exhibition, cuing does not make them smarter or more knowledgeable about the exhibition topic than they were before.

Misconception #2.

The questionnaire is a test for how many facts visitors learned.

The questionnaire has three open-ended questions that ask for visitors' impressions and interpretations. Visitors' answers show exhibit developers what parts of the exhibition visitors found meaningful and memorable. When visitors are recruited, they are told that they will answer some questions about their opinions. The word "test" is inappropriate and is carefully avoided by recruiters.

Misconception #3.

Cuing visitors will inflate the success rate and make any exhibition rank highly.

Cuing does not enable visitors to understand what is not understandable to them or make them interested in something that is not interesting to them.

Misconception #4.

The data from the questionnaire is an end in itself to prove if the exhibit was successful.

The cued-questionnaire data is most useful for showing what has not worked and for making decisions about what should be improved. Ideally, after analyzing the data and making changes in the exhibition, another sample should be taken to see if there has been an improvement in the exhibit's ability to communicate its messages.

Misconception #5.

Ultimately, the goal should be to use an exit questionnaire with uncued visitors and compare their answers to those of the cued visitors.

The evaluation question is not, "Do cued visitors understand the exhibit messages and find them more meaningful than uncued visitors?" Since all visitors are under no obligation to learn anything, the question is not what did they learn, but what could they learn? Using cued visitors provides a best-case scenario for answering the question, "What is it possible for motivated visitors to get from this exhibition, and is that related to what the exhibit developers hoped they would get?"

ANALYSIS OF THE QUESTIONNAIRE DATA

The methods for goal-related content analysis of open-ended visitor feedback on the 51% Solution cued questionnaire are not as simple or well developed as the methods for analyzing and comparing tracking and timing data. What follows are some suggestions that have been useful in a variety of settings. Visitors' responses to the first two open-ended questions can be analyzed in three ways: 1) by looking at visitors' answers and noting how many were specific (goal-related or exhibit element-related) or general (not related to a goal or exhibit element); 2) by looking at each visitors' questionnaire responses as a whole and ranking them for the relative number of goal-related comments; and 3) by looking at each of the main message goals or key words and counting the number of visitors who mentioned them.

Analysis by Communication Goals and the Number of Related Responses

For example, in the "White Alligator" exhibition, there were six main messages. The percentage of the 38 visitors who mentioned them in their feedback (from any of the questions) is as follows:

1. that white alligators exist—42%
2. what white means—how the alligator got that way (genetics)—47%
3. the impact whiteness has on the animal in its habitat, and the role of alligators in the swamp environment—42%
4. the role of wetlands—13%
5. the need for conservation of wetland habitats—29%
6. the difference between alligators and crocodiles—13%

Messages number two and three are more specific and conceptually complicated than number one. Messages number four and five are less specific overall, but are related to number three. Message number six is very specific, and not closely related to all the others. The more different, unrelated messages in an exhibition, the less likely this questionnaire will be to capture evidence for them all.

Analysis by All Visitors' Responses to Each Question

For example, when asked to describe in their own words what the "White Alligator" exhibition was meant "to show," and what it was "to make people (do)," visitors' responses to the questions were fairly specific, and those answers that related to the objectives of the exhibition outnumbered the more general ones. An example of a specific answer is, "To show why we need to protect swamps." An example of a general answer is, "How animals are adapted to the environment." There were more specific than general answers to the question about learning from the exhibition as well. An example of a specific answer is, "The alligator is white because of its genes."

Analysis by All of the Total Responses on Each Person's Questionnaire

Looking at each questionnaire, one finds that some people were more thorough in their answers overall than other people were. The 38 questionnaires for "White Alligator" fell roughly into four categories according to how thoroughly and specifically visitors related to the exhibition's goals, with the highs outnumbering the lows:

- Forty-seven percent of the cued visitors made general or only a few specific comments. Nine people's questionnaires were ranked "low–not related" (i.e., contained only general comments); nine ranked "medium low–partially related" (contained general and one or two specific comments about white alligators existing and/or habitat).

- Fifty-three percent made more specific, goal-related comments. Fifteen people's questionnaires ranked "medium high–related to essentials" (i.e., contained two or three specific, goal-related comments about whiteness, adaptations, and habitat), and five people ranked "high–extensively related" (contained four or five of the six intended messages).

Cued visitors often spend significantly more time in an exhibition than uncued visitors. While cued visitors' responses to open-ended questions cannot tell you what most uncued visitors are learning from the exhibition, they do show evidence for learning by visitors who are motivated to pay more attention than average to the exhibits.

Among uncued visitors, people self-select where and how much attention they pay, but they are under no constraints to pay any attention at all. Exit interviews with randomly selected uncued visitors will include visitors who did not try to learn anything. However, this is not a negative reflection on the exhibition's ability to communicate to someone who is paying attention and is attempting, at least minimally, to see what the exhibition is about.

APPENDIX C.

EXAMPLES OF DATA SHEETS AND FLOOR PLANS

Data sheets are in-house tools based on floor plans and used for collecting information in a systematic manner. They are typically hand-drawn and not to scale. Since these sketches were not designed for publication, they may be difficult to read. However, they are included here to illustrate how some institutions organized data collection. Most of the examples here were sketched by the person who collected the tracking and timing data.

OLD SOUTH MEETING HOUSE

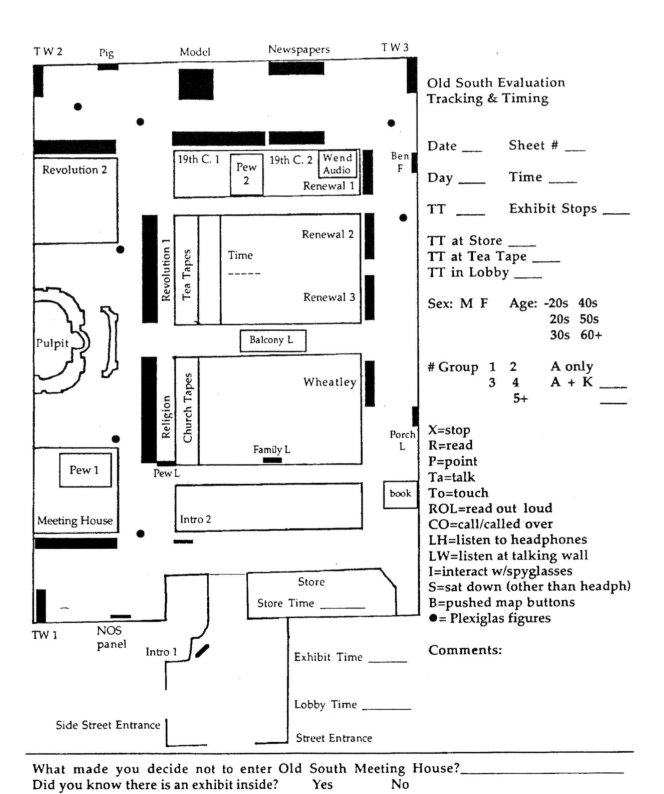

What made you decide not to enter Old South Meeting House?_____
Did you know there is an exhibit inside?   Yes   No

Figure 2. Tracking and timing data sheet

SAN DIEGO HISTORICAL SOCIETY

Tracking & Timing for San Diego Historical Society 1996

Visitor #: 29   Day: Fr   Date: 8/30   Enter: Exit: TT: Stops:

Gender: M F   **Age:** <20s   20s   30s   40s   50s   60s+

Group Size: 1   2   3   4   5+   **Group Type:** A only   A+K

Key: **X**= stopped   **I**= touch, manipulate **R**=read

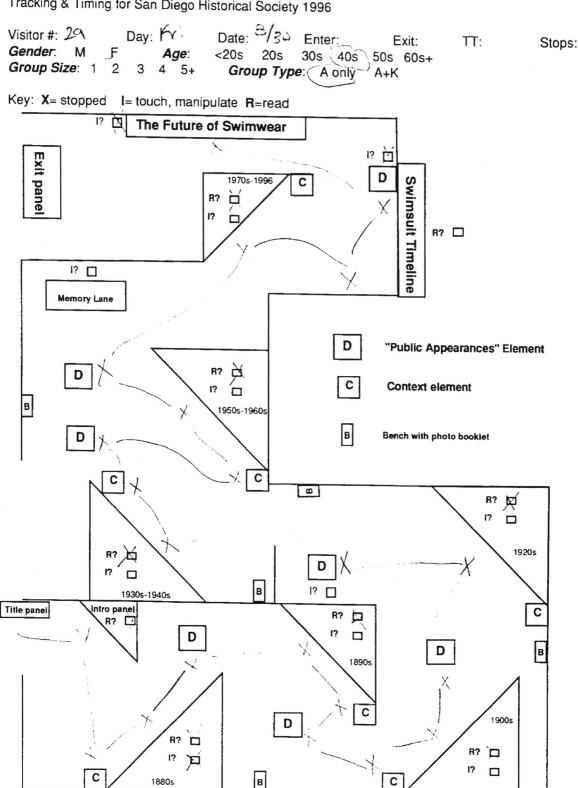

FIELD MUSEUM OF NATURAL HISTORY

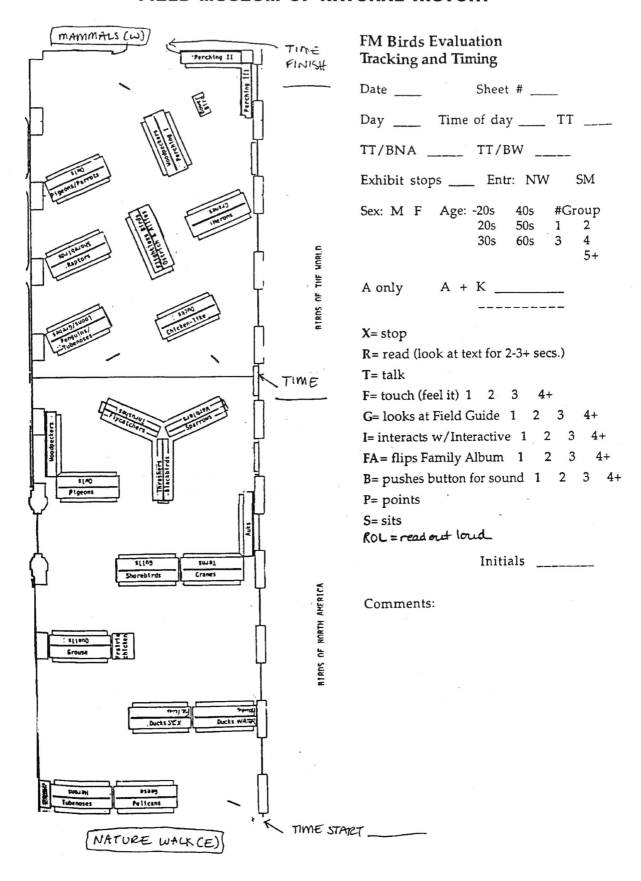

FM Birds Evaluation
Tracking and Timing

Date ____   Sheet # ____

Day ____   Time of day ____   TT ____

TT/BNA _____   TT/BW _____

Exhibit stops ____   Entr: NW   SM

Sex: M F	Age: -20s	40s	#Group	
	20s	50s	1	2
	30s	60s	3	4
				5+

A only   A + K _____

X= stop
R= read (look at text for 2-3+ secs.)
T= talk
F= touch (feel it) 1   2   3   4+
G= looks at Field Guide 1   2   3   4+
I= interacts w/Interactive 1   2   3   4+
FA= flips Family Album 1   2   3   4+
B= pushes button for sound 1   2   3   4+
P= points
S= sits
ROL = read out loud

                    Initials _____

Comments:

AMERICAN MUSEUM OF NATURAL HISTORY

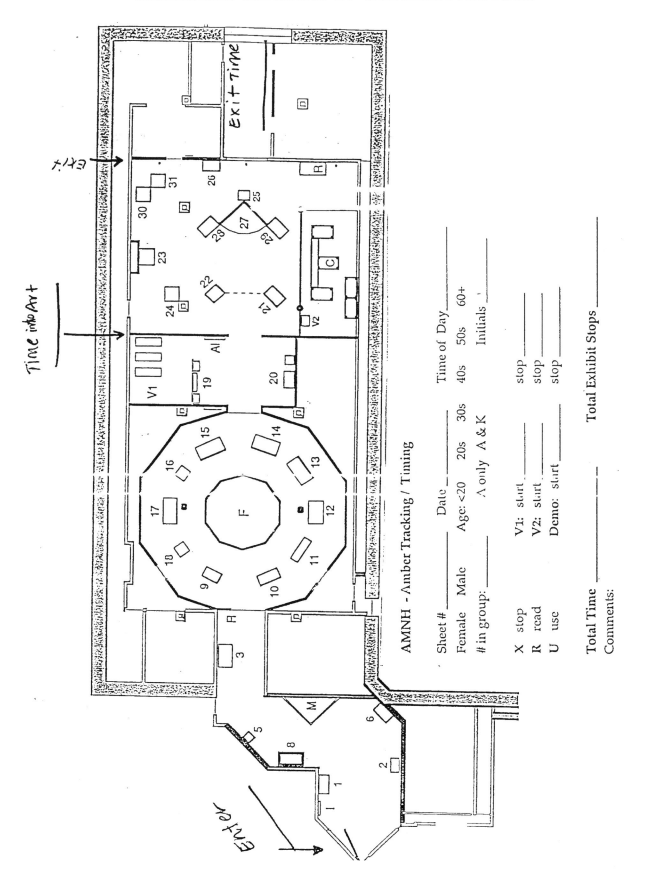

AMNH - Amber Tracking / Timing

Sheet # _____ Date _____ Time of Day _____

Female Male Age: <20 20s 30s 40s 50s 60+

in group: _____ A only A & K Initials _____

X stop
R read
U use

V1: start _____ stop _____
V2: start _____ stop _____
Demo: start _____ stop _____

Total Time _____ Total Exhibit Stops _____

Comments:

OAKLAND MUSEUM OF CALIFORNIA

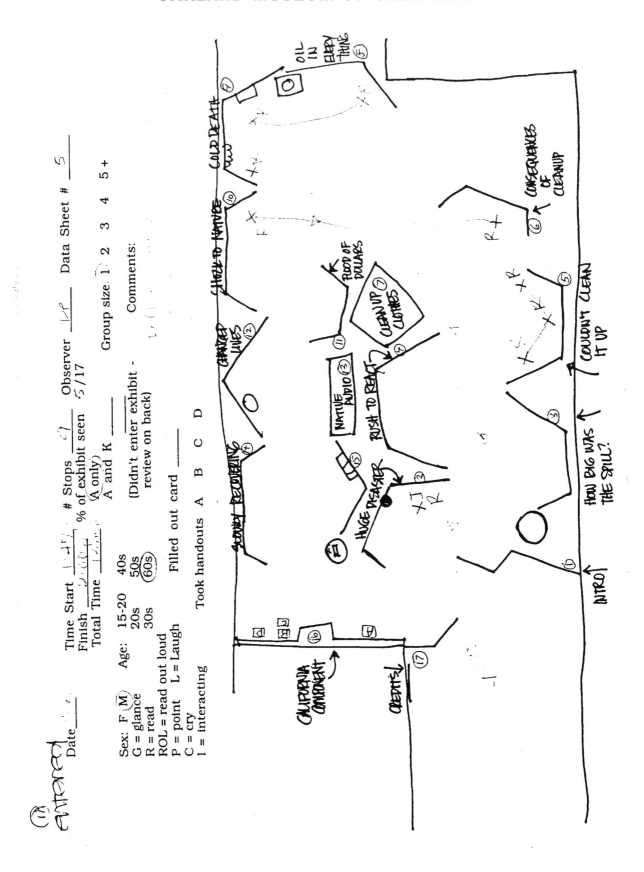

CALIFORNIA MUSEUM OF SCIENCE AND INDUSTRY

Appendix B. Sample data sheet

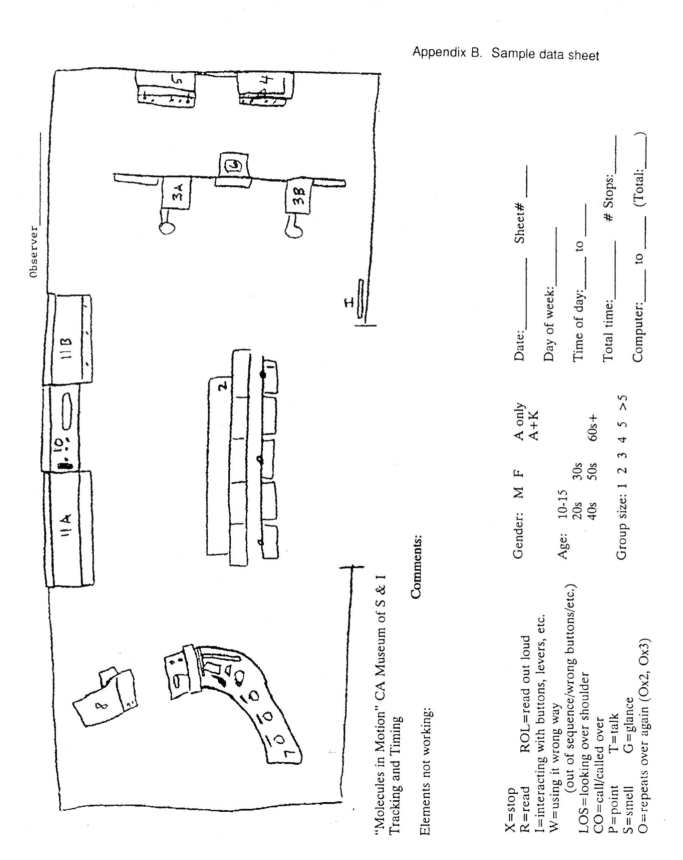

"Molecules in Motion" CA Museum of S & I
Tracking and Timing

Comments:

Elements not working:

X=stop
R=read   ROL=read out loud
I=interacting with buttons, levers, etc.
W=using it wrong way
       (out of sequence/wrong buttons/etc.)
LOS=looking over shoulder
CO=call/called over
P=point   T=talk
S=smell   G=glance
O=repeats over again (Ox2, Ox3)

Date: _____   Sheet# _____

Day of week: _____

Time of day: _____ to _____

Total time: _____   # Stops: _____

Computer: _____ to _____ (Total: _____)

Gender: M F   A only
                  A+K

Age: 10-15
      20s   30s
      40s   50s
            60s+

Group size: 1 2 3 4 5 >5

MEXICAN FINE ARTS MUSEUM

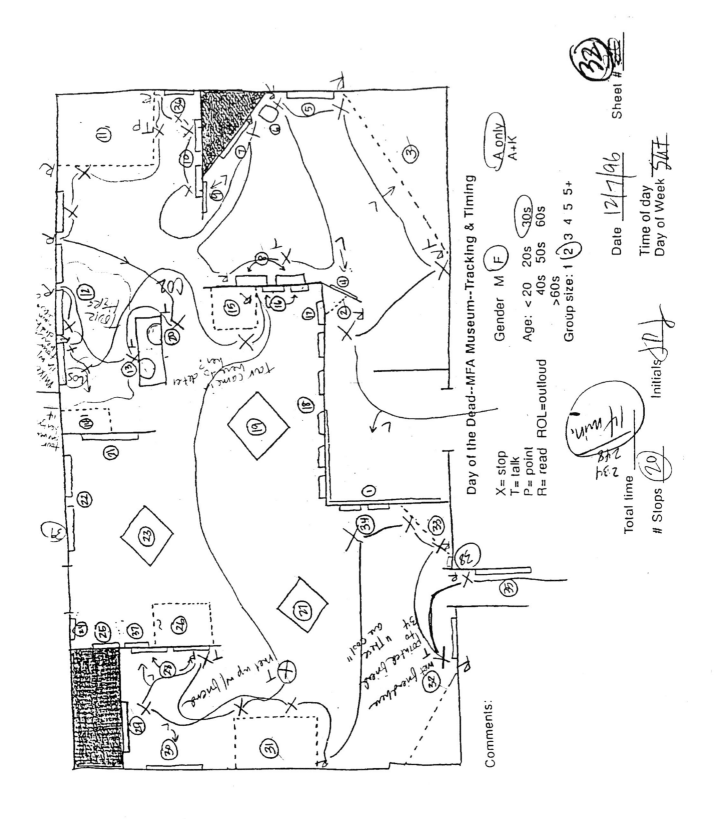

SHEDD AQUARIUM

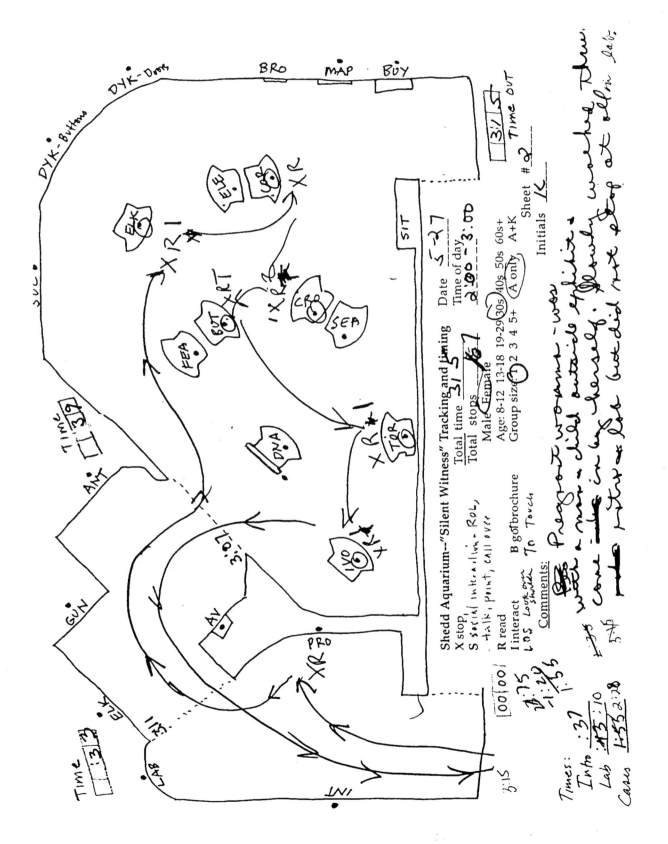

APPENDIX D.

LIST OF EXHIBITIONS

This appendix alphabetically lists the titles of all the exhibitions in the study. Also are included are the names of the museums at which the exhibitions were studied. Some exhibitions were studied at more than one site.

Code numbers (001-110), assigned during the study, allow you to find each exhibition's summary data in Appendix F.

Exhibition Name	Institution Name	Code #
ABCs of Sailor Language	Mystic Seaport	088
African Hall	California Academy of Sciences	110
Amber: Window to the Past (1)	American Museum of Natural History	016
Amber: Window to the Past (2)	California Academy of Sciences	053
American Encounters	National Museum of American History	081
Anatomical Sections	Museum of Science and Industry	055
Art as Activist	International Gallery, Smithsonian Institution	093
Art That Works	The Art Institute of Chicago	102
Asian Mammals	Field Museum of Natural History	107
Astronomical Instruments	Adler Planetarium	109
Behind the Seams	Discovery Place Inc.	069
Beyond Numbers (1)	Maryland Science Center	056
Beyond Numbers (2)	New York Hall of Science	054
Binding the Nation	National Postal Museum, Smithsonian Institution	082
Birds of a Feather	California Academy of Sciences	073
Birds of the World	Field Museum of Natural History	027
Boettcher Hall	Denver Museum of Natural History	108
Calaveras Pa Todos	Mexican Fine Arts Center Museum	103
Classic Craft	John G. Shedd Aquarium	006
Common Ground	Minnesota Historical Society	083
Confrontation Gallery	Birmingham Civil Rights Institute	078
Customers & Communities	National Postal Museum, Smithsonian Institution	084
Cycladic Art	The J. Paul Getty Museum	094
Darkened Waters: Profile of an Oil Spill (1)	Oakland Museum of California	022
Darkened Waters: Profile of an Oil Spill (2)	Anchorage Museum of History and Art	042
Dia de los Muertos: Where Past and Present Meet	Mexican Fine Arts Center Museum	096
Discovery and Deceit	The Nelson-Atkins Museum of Art	095
DNA Fingerprinting	The Science Museum (London)	049
Edge of the Wild	Denver Museum of Natural History	035
Explore Colorado	Denver Museum of Natural History	033
Exploring the Outer Bay	Monterey Bay Aquarium	001
Families	Minnesota Historical Society	089
Frogs!	John G. Shedd Aquarium	003
From Bustles to Bikinis: A Century of Changing Beach Fashion	San Diego Historical Society	076
Gallery 218	The Cleveland Museum of Art	097
Gallery 5	San Francisco Museum of Modern Art	104
Geographica	National Geographic Society	043
Global Warming: Understanding the Forecast (1)	American Museum of Natural History	026
Global Warming: Understanding the Forecast (2)	San Diego Natural History Museum	025
Global Warming: Understanding the Forecast (3)	Denver Museum of Natural History	017
Global Warming: Understanding the Forecast (4)	Carnegie Science Center	047
Global Warming: Understanding the Forecast (5)	St. Louis Science Center	060
Global Warming: Understanding the Forecast (6)	Oakland Museum of California	019
Habitat Africa!	Chicago Zoological Society	014
Habitats	Public Museum of Grand Rapids	031
Hall of Birds	Field Museum of Natural History	105
Hall of Human Biology & Evolution	American Museum of Natural History	018
Hands-On Science	California Academy of Sciences	074
Harvesting the Sun	Science Museum of Virginia	063
Hidden Kingdoms: The World of Microbes (1)	California Museum of Science and Industry	070
Hidden Kingdoms: The World of Microbes (2)	Louisiana Nature Center	030
History by the Seat of Your Pants	Minnesota Historical Society	090
History in a Box	National Postal Museum of Canada	086
Human Body Discovery Zone	Museum of Science (Boston)Science Museum of	045
Hunters of the Sky (1)	Minnesota	057

Exhibition Name	Institution Name	Code #
Hunters of the Sky (2)	Denver Museum of Natural History	029
In the Tomb of Nefertari	The J. Paul Getty Museum	098
Inventing Lab	Chicago Children's Museum	048
Judith Leyster: A Dutch Master and Her World	Worcester Art Museum	101
Jurassic Hall	New Mexico Museum of Natural History & Science	039
Jurassic!	California Academy of Sciences	050
Kelp Lab	Monterey Bay Aquarium	008
Kopje	Chicago Zoological Society	005
Landforms/Lifeforms	Museum of the Rockies	020
Life Through Time	California Academy of Sciences	068
Living with Lasers	The Science Museum (London)	058
Lower Gallery	Royal Saskatchewan Museum	037
Mammals of the World	Field Museum of Natural History	015
Messages from the Wilderness	Field Museum of Natural History	036
Molecules in Motion	California Museum of Science and Industry	065
Monarca	California Academy of Sciences	044
Motor City	Detroit Historical Museum	087
Mystery of Things	The Brooklyn Children's Museum	085
Nature Walk	Field Museum of Natural History	034
Next Stop Westchester!	The Hudson River Museum of Westchester	079
North American Mammals Hall	American Museum of Natural History	106
North American Wildlife Hall	Carnegie Museum of Natural History	038
Ocean Planet	National Museum of Natural History	021
Old South Meeting House	Old South Meeting House	077
On Arctic Ice	John G. Shedd Aquarium	009
On the Trail of History	Kalamazoo Valley Museum	080
Otters & Oil	John G. Shedd Aquarium	002
P.G.A. Gallery	Roswell Museum and Art Center	100
Passive Smoking	The Science Museum (London)	062
Permanent Collection (1)	Walker Art Center	092
Permanent Collection (2)	Walker Art Center	099
Prehistoric Journey	Denver Museum of Natural History	032
Prenatal Development	Museum of Science and Industry	052
Question of Size	The Exploratorium	071
Rites of Passage: Celebration of Life	Corpus Christi Museum of Science and History	064
Science in American Life	National Museum of American History	041
Signals	Ruben Fleet Science Center	072
Silent Witness	John G. Shedd Aquarium	004
South American Tropical Rainforest	National Aquarium in Baltimore	011
Spiders! (1)	National Museum of Natural History	023
Spiders! (2)	Field Museum of Natural History	028
Swamp: Wonders of Our Wetlands	Chicago Zoological Society	010
Symmetry	Ruben Fleet Science Center	066
Treasures from the Sand	Colonial Michilimackinac	040
Tribute to Survival	Milwaukee Public Museum	091
Tunnel of Discovery	Orlando Science Center, Inc.	061
Turbulent Landscapes	The Exploratorium	067
Underwater Viewing Gallery	John G. Shedd Aquarium	007
Universe in Your Hands	Adler Planetarium	046
Wetland Aviary	Bergen County Zoological Park	013
What is an Animal?	Field Museum of Natural History	024
White Alligator: Secret of the Swamp	John G. Shedd Aquarium	012
Whodunit? The Science of Solving Crime (1)	Fort Worth Museum of Science and History	051
Whodunit? The Science of Solving Crime (2)	Museum of Science and Industry	059
Wild California	California Academy of Sciences	075

APPENDIX E.

LIST OF PARTICIPATING INSTITUTIONS

This appendix lists all the institutions with exhibitions studied in this project alphabetically by museum name. Also are included are the names of the exhibitions studied at that site. Some exhibitions were studied at more than one site.

Code numbers (001-110), assigned during the study, allow you to find each exhibition's summary data in Appendix F.

Institution Name	Exhibition Name	Code #
Adler Planetarium	Astronomical Instruments	109
	Universe in Your Hands, The	046
American Museum of Natural History	Hall of Human Biology & Evolution	018
	Amber: Window to the Past (1)	016
	Global Warming: Understanding the Forecast (1)	026
	North American Mammals Hall	106
Anchorage Museum of History and Art	Darkened Waters: Profile of an Oil Spill (2)	042
Art Institute of Chicago, The	Art That Works	102
Bergen County Zoological Park	Wetland Aviary	013
Birmingham Civil Rights Institute	Confrontation Gallery	078
Brooklyn Children's Museum, The	Mystery of Things	085
California Academy of Sciences	Life Through Time	068
	Monarca	044
	Birds of a Feather	073
	Wild California	075
	Jurassic!	050
	Hands-On Science	074
	Amber: Window to the Past (2)	053
	African Hall	110
California Museum of Science and Industry	Molecules in Motion	065
	Hidden Kingdoms: The World of Microbes (1)	070
Carnegie Museum of Natural History	North American Wildlife Hall	038
Carnegie Science Center	Global Warming: Understanding the Forecast (4)	047
Chicago Children's Museum	Inventing Lab	048
Chicago Zoological Society	Swamp: Wonders of our Wetlands, The	010
	Kopje	005
	Habitat Africa!	014
Cleveland Museum of Art, The	Gallery 218	097
Colonial Michilimackinac	Treasures from the Sand	040
Corpus Christi Museum of Science and History	Rites of Passage: Celebration of Life	064
Denver Museum of Natural History	Explore Colorado	033
	Edge of the Wild	035
	Boettcher Hall	108
	Global Warming: Understanding the Forecast (3)	017
	Prehistoric Journey	032
	Hunters of the Sky (2)	029
Detroit Historical Museum	Motor City	087
Discovery Place Inc.	Behind the Seams	069
Exploratorium, The	Question of Size, A	071
	Turbulent Landscapes	067
Field Museum of Natural History	Nature Walk	034
	What is an Animal?	024
	Birds of the World	027
	Spiders! (2)	028
	Asian Mammals	107
	Mammals of the World	015
	Messages from the Wilderness	036
	Hall of Birds	105
Fort Worth Museum of Science and History	Whodunit? The Science of Solving Crime (1)	051
Hudson River Museum of Westchester, The	Next Stop Westchester!	079
International Gallery (Smithsonian Institution)	Art as Activist	093
J. Paul Getty Museum, The	Cycladic Art	094
	In the Tomb of Nefertari	098
John G. Shedd Aquarium	Frogs!	003
	Otters & Oil	002
	White Alligator: Secret of the Swamp	012

Institution Name	Exhibition Name	Code #
	Classic Craft	006
	Silent Witness	004
	On Arctic Ice	009
	Underwater Viewing Gallery	007
Kalamazoo Valley Museum	On the Trail of History	080
Louisiana Nature Center	Hidden Kingdoms: The World of Microbes (2)	030
Maryland Science Center	Beyond Numbers (1)	056
Mexican Fine Arts Center Museum	Calaveras Pa Todos	103
	Dia de los Muertos: Where Past and Present Meet	096
Milwaukee Public Museum	Tribute to Survival, A	091
Minnesota Historical Society	History by the Seat of Your Pants	090
	Common Ground, A	083
	Families	089
Monterey Bay Aquarium	Kelp Lab	008
	Exploring the Outer Bay	001
Museum of Science (Boston)	Human Body Discovery Zone	045
Museum of Science and Industry	Whodunit? The Science of Solving Crime (2)	059
	Anatomical Sections	055
	Prenatal Development	052
Museum of the Rockies	Landforms/Lifeforms	020
Mystic Seaport	ABCs of Sailor Language	088
National Aquarium in Baltimore	South American Tropical Rainforest	011
National Geographic Society	Geographica	043
National Museum of American History	Science in American Life	041
	American Encounters	081
National Museum of Natural History	Ocean Planet	021
	Spiders! (1)	023
National Postal Museum of Canada	History in a Box	086
National Postal Museum, Smithsonian Institution	Binding the Nation	082
	Customers & Communities	084
Nelson-Atkins Museum of Art, The	Discovery and Deceit	095
New Mexico Museum of Natural History & Science	Jurassic Hall	039
New York Hall of Science	Beyond Numbers (2)	054
Oakland Museum of California	Darkened Waters: Profile of an Oil Spill (1)	022
	Global Warming: Understanding the Forecast (6)	019
Old South Meeting House	Old South Meeting House	077
Orlando Science Center, Inc.	Tunnel of Discovery	061
Public Museum of Grand Rapids	Habitats	031
Roswell Museum and Art Center	P.G.A. Gallery	100
Royal Saskatchewan Museum	Lower Gallery	037
Ruben Fleet Science Center	Symmetry	066
	Signals	072
San Diego Historical Society	From Bustles to Bikinis: A Century of Changing Beach Fashion	076
San Diego Natural History Museum	Global Warming: Understanding the Forecast (2)	025
San Francisco Museum of Modern Art	Gallery 5	104
Science Museum of Minnesota	Hunters of the Sky (1)	057
Science Museum of Virginia	Harvesting the Sun	063
Science Museum, The (London)	DNA Fingerprinting	049
	Living with Lasers	058
	Passive Smoking	062
St. Louis Science Center	Global Warming: Understanding the Forecast (5)	060
Walker Art Center	Permanent Collection II	099
	Permanent Collection I	092
Worcester Art Museum	Judith Leyster: A Dutch Master and Her World	101

APPENDIX F.

RAW DATA SUMMARY: KEY TO COLUMNS

Column one   is the exhibition code number

Column two   is the exhibition name

Column three   is the institution name

Column four   is the exhibition size in number of square feet

Column five   is the type code for the exhibition:
                  Type numbers with three digits stand for—
                  first digit: topic of exhibition (1 = science, 2 = nonscience)

                  second digit: type of institution (1 = zoo or aquarium, 2 = natural history museum, 3 = cultural history, 4 = science museum or science center, 5 = art museum)

                  third digit: 1 = nondioramalike, 2 = dioramalike

                  Type numbers with four digits beginning with "2" are "old" exhibitions; the following three digits in their code numbers follow the same translation as above.

Column six   is the number of exhibit elements in the exhibition

Column seven   is the average time in minutes spent by a sample of tracked visitors in the exhibition

Column eight   is the median number of stops made by a sample of tracked visitors in the exhibition

Column nine   is the number in the sample of visitors tracked and timed in the exhibition

Column ten   is the Sweep Rate Index (SRI)
                  (See body of report for definition)

Column eleven   is the Percent of Diligent Visitors (% DV)
                  (See body of report for definition)

Names in **boldface** indicate the eleven exhibitions that were "exceptionally thoroughly used" (had SRIs below 300 and % DVs above 50 %).

DATA SUMMARY FOR 110 EXHIBITIONS

(• = missing data; **bold** = exceptionally thoroughly used)

Code #	Exhibition	Institution	Sq. Feet	Type	# Elem.	AvT	Med%S	N =	SRI	%DV
001	OuterBay	MonterB	2014	111	18	6	22	129	336	8
002	O&O	Shedd	1000	111	9	4	23	45	250	41
003	**Frogs**	Shedd	3490	111	25	20	56	58	174	64
004	**SW**	Shedd	2300	111	22	9	59	54	256	58
005	Kopje	BrookZ	2500	111	13	10	39	76	250	30
006	Craft	Shedd	3490	111	14	8	64	61	436	63
007	UVG	Shedd	6200	111	23	18	35	91	344	30
008	Kelp	MonterB	500	111	8	3	38	250	167	29
009	Arctic	Shedd	2300	111	19	9	47	50	256	46
010	Swamp	BrookZ	11251	112	102	14	19	63	804	0
011	SARF	NatAquar	6384	112	26	8	15	70	798	3
012	WGator	Shedd	3490	112	12	6	42	85	582	39
013	Wetland	Bergen	1496	112	21	3	19	101	499	3
014	Habitat	BrookZ	9000	112	13	16	17	100	562	3
015	Mam	Field	6000	121	64	10	28	104	600	11
016	**Amber1**	AmerMNH	7000	121	38	33	76	51	212	86
017	Global3	DenMNH	8000	121	32	27	47	106	296	48
018	HB&E	AmerMNH	7000	121	60	19	38	116	368	32
019	Global6	Oakland	8000	121	31	29	•	99	276	42
020	Landform	Rockies	2450	121	45	16	29	39	153	15
021	Ocean P	NMNH	6000	121	61	11	15	246	545	2
022	**DW1**	Oakland	2000	121	17	13	53	61	154	51
023	Spiders1	NMNH	6000	121	74	15	16	100	400	4
024	WIAA	Field	3500	121	33	11	36	79	318	27
025	Global2	SanDNH	8000	121	33	18	•	65	444	36
026	Global1	AmerMNH	8000	121	33	20	33	80	400	33
027	NewBird	Field	5600	121	44	10	30	97	560	13
028	Spiders2	Field	10500	121	95	45	38	54	233	26
029	Raptors2	DenMNH	8000	121	93	22	25	55	364	0
030	HK2	LouNatC	2000	121	24	41	33	43	49	12
031	Habitats	GrandRap	6500	122	19	20	53	45	325	58
032	PreJourn	DenMNH	14000	122	91	43	44	75	326	37
033	Mead	DenMNH	5000	122	13	8	39	100	625	40
034	NW	Field	5800	122	49	11	22	83	527	11
035	Boett2	DenMNH	7200	122	20	11	25	69	655	17
036	Mess	Field	5600	122	26	9	46	77	622	48
037	Lower	Saskatch	13000	122	83	37	52	32	351	53
038	NAW	Carnegie	8000	122	37	11	30	50	727	16
039	Juras	NewMNH	4668	122	21	8	33	44	584	25
040	**Sand**	Michimac	2000	131	37	14	75	60	143	83
041	SciAmLife	NMAH	12000	131	106	16	8	163	750	0
042	DW2	Anchorag	2250	131	18	11	50	41	205	49
043	Geograp	Nat.Geo	6000	131	81	37	22	97	162	4
044	Monarca	CalAcad	6500	141	54	23	26	135	283	2
045	HBDS	BostonSci	2500	141	58	12	21	154	208	4
046	TUIYH	AdlerP	3000	141	26	9	27	99	333	11
047	Global4	CarnSC	8000	141	33	15	•	155	533	30
048	Inventing	ChgCM	3000	141	9	17	44	62	176	50
049	DNA	SciM(Lon)	500	141	11	3	18	60	167	7

DATA SUMMARY FOR 110 EXHIBITIONS

(• = missing data; **bold** = exceptionally thoroughly used)

Code #	Exhibition	Institution	Sq. Feet	Type	# Elem.	AvT	Med%S	N =	SRI	%DV
050	Jurass	CalAcad	1950	141	47	5	9	113	390	1
051	**Whodun1**	FtWorthSH	4500	141	25	25	60	75	180	57
052	**Prenatal**	MSI	1000	141	42	6	62	49	167	59
053	Amber2	CalAcad	6797	141	40	21	38	52	324	37
054	Numbers2	NYHOS	6000	141	34	36	41	37	167	35
055	Slices	MSI	400	141	14	4	40	77	100	41
056	Numbers1	MrlndSC	6000	141	45	9	17	64	667	0
057	Raptors1	Sci Minn	5000	141	99	29	24	46	172	9
058	Lasers	SciM(Lon)	500	141	15	3	21	60	167	20
059	Whodun2	MSI	6000	141	40	18	23	81	333	16
060	Global5	StLouSC	8000	141	32	14	•	132	571	34
061	Tunnel	OrlanSC	2800	141	23	10	30	32	280	16
062	Smoke	SciM(Lon)	500	141	13	3	15	58	167	3
063	Sun	VirgSC	2500	141	25	7	20	42	357	5
064	Rites	CopChris	2000	141	55	10	20	33	200	3
065	**Molecule**	CalMSI	2000	141	11	10	55	80	200	61
066	Symmet	RubFleSC	3000	141	26	16	31	84	188	14
067	Turbland	Explora	3000	141	34	11	32	60	273	15
068	LTT	CalAcad	4000	141	56	15	30	47	267	30
069	Seams	Dis.Place	5500	141	39	8	18	83	688	2
070	HK1	CalMSI	2000	141	25	11	36	54	182	15
071	Size	Explora	1000	141	19	4	16	22	250	0
072	Signals	RubFleSC	3000	141	31	23	42	47	130	28
073	Feather	CalAcad	2100	141	52	4	9	102	525	2
074	HandsOn	CalAcad	2300	141	43	9	9	114	256	0
075	Wild CA	CalAcad	9175	142	22	8	23	55	1147	16
076	**Bikini**	SanDHS	3500	231	32	17	74	47	206	77
077	OSMH	OldSouth	6500	231	28	26	50	104	250	45
078	Confront	Civil Rts	384	231	8	1	50	56	384	29
079	NextStop	HudsRM	3000	231	33	19	24	55	158	23
080	TrailHis	Kalama	4500	231	42	18	20	56	250	9
081	Encount	NMAH	3800	231	55	8	15	82	475	4
082	BTN	NatPost	3400	231	34	10	26	45	340	18
083	Ground	MinnHS	4000	231	56	19	•	129	211	9
084	C&C	NatPost	3200	231	39	14	36	42	229	24
085	MOT	BrklnCM	2200	231	24	8	42	45	275	32
086	HistBox	NatPost(Can)	2000	231	10	7	50	40	286	38
087	Motor	DetHS	8000	231	64	27	31	40	296	28
088	ABCs	Mystic	3000	231	23	14	44	54	214	43
089	Families	MinnHS	2100	231	179	17	9	123	124	0
090	Pants	MinnHS	1450	231	4	3	75	47	483	53
091	Tribute	MilwPub	6500	232	25	6	20	458	1083	3
092	perm.galI	Walker	10700	251	61	13	21	85	823	19
093	Activist	Smithso	2000	251	77	15	38	43	133	35
094	Cyclad	GettyM	700	251	11	3	27	101	233	30
095	Deceit	NelsonAt	4200	251	18	19	43	42	221	49
096	**Dia de los**	MexFA	3500	251	39	20	68	38	175	66
097	Gal 218	CleveAM	890	251	29	3	24	25	297	20
098	Tomb	GettyM	2800	251	24	15	42	40	187	33

DATA SUMMARY FOR 110 EXHIBITIONS

(• = missing data; **bold** = exceptionally thoroughly used)

Code #	Exhibition	Institution	Sq. Feet	Type	# Elem.	AvT	Med%S	N =	SRI	%DV
099	perm.galII	Walker	10700	251	83	15	25	83	713	18
100	P.G.A.	Roswell	1345	251	11	3	36	40	448	26
101	**Leyster**	Worcest	3200	251	48	32	73	49	100	79
102	ArtWorks	AIC	2000	251	22	7	•	23	286	4
103	Calaver	MexFA	3500	251	39	18	46	44	194	48
104	SF MOMA	SanFMOMA	1040	251	21	3	29	76	347	21
105	Bird old	Field	7000	2121	65	9	21	24	778	17
106	Mam old	AmerMNH	12000	2122	32	7	34	123	1714	35
107	Asian old	Field	7000	2122	21	4	29	42	1750	26
108	Boett old	DenMNH	7200	2122	8	2	25	131	3600	18
109	Astro old	AdlerP	2500	2141	17	2	12	100	1250	11
110	Afr. old	CalAcad	9475	2142	24	5	21	47	1895	17

APPENDIX G.

HISTOGRAMS FOR TIME, HISTOGRAMS FOR STOPS, AND SCATTERGRAMS FOR TIME AND STOPS FOR 102 EXHIBITIONS

Each page contains three graphs that apply to one exhibition. The top two are bar graphs of the frequency distributions of time or stops on the horizontal axis. Each bar represents the number of visitors ("Count" on the vertical axis) who spent the corresponding total time or number of stops on the graph's horizontal axis.

The bottom graph is a scattergram. Each dot represents one visitor, and the dots correspond to each visitor's total time spent (vertical axis) and the percentage of stops they made out of the total number of exhibit elements in the exhibition (horizontal axis). Some dots may overlap exactly, which results in showing fewer dots than visitors listed for the sample.

Pages are labeled with the same code numbers (001-110) as used in the previous appendixes, the abbreviated name of the exhibition, the institution's name and the number of visitors in the tracking and timing sample for that exhibition. (Eight pages of data are missing for numbers 019, 025, 032, 047, 056, 060, 092, and 099.)

An alphabetical list of the abbreviated exhibition names and the full titles is on the next page.

LIST ALPHABETIZED BY ABBREVIATED EXHIBITION NAMES

Abbreviation	Full Name	Abbreviation	Full Name
ABCs	ABCs of Sailor Language	Kopje	Kopje
Activist	Art as Activist	Landform	Landforms/Lifeforms
Afr. old	African Hall	Lasers	Living with Lasers
Amber1	Amber: Window to the Past (1)	Leyster	Judith Leyster: A Dutch Master and Her World
Amber2	Amber: Window to the Past (2)	Lower	Lower Gallery
Arctic	On Arctic Ice	LTT	Life Through Time
ArtWorks	Art That Works	Mam	Mammals of the World
Asian old	Asian Mammals	Mam old	North American Mammals Hall
Astro old	Astronomical Instruments	Mead	Explore Colorado
Bikini	From Bustles to Bikinis: A Century of Changing Beach Fashion	Mess	Messages from the Wilderness
		Molecule	Molecules in Motion
Bird old	Hall of Birds	Monarca	Monarca
Boett old	Boettcher Hall	MOT	Mystery of Things
Boett2	Edge of the Wild	Motor	Motor City
BTN	Binding the Nation	NAW	North American Wildlife Hall
C&C	Customers & Communities	NewBird	Birds of the World
Calaver	Calaveras Pa Todos	NextStop	Next Stop Westchester!
Confront	Confrontation Gallery	Numbers1	Beyond Numbers (1)
Craft	Classic Craft	Numbers2	Beyond Numbers (2)
Cyclad	Cycladic Art	NW	Nature Walk
Deceit	Discovery and Deceit	O&O	Otters & Oil
Dia de los	Dia de los Muertos: Where Past and Present Meet	Ocean P	Ocean Planet
DNA	DNA Fingerprinting	OSMH	Old South Meeting House
DW1	Darkened Waters: Profile of an Oil Spill (1)	OuterBay	Exploring the Outer Bay
DW2	Darkened Waters: Profile of an Oil Spill (2)	P.G.A.	P.G.A. Gallery
Encount	American Encounters	Pants	History by the Seat of Your Pants
Families	Families	perm.gal1	Permanent Collection I
Feather	Birds of a Feather	perm.gal2	Permanent Collection II
Frogs	Frogs!	PreJourn	Prehistoric Journey
Gal 218	Gallery 218	Prenatal	Prenatal Development
Geograp	Geographica	Raptors1	Hunters of the Sky (1)
Global1	Global Warming: Understanding the Forecast (1)	Raptors2	Hunters of the Sky (2)
Global2	Global Warming: Understanding the Forecast (2)	Rites	Rites of Passage: Celebration of Life
Global3	Global Warming: Understanding the Forecast (3)	Sand	Treasures from the Sand
Global4	Global Warming: Understanding the Forecast (4)	SARF	South American Tropical Rainforest
Global5	Global Warming: Understanding the Forecast (5)	SciAmLife	Science in American Life
Global6	Global Warming: Understanding the Forecast (6)	Seams	Behind the Seams
Ground	A Common Ground	SF MOMA	Gallery 5
Habitat	Habitat Africa!	Signals	Signals
Habitats	Habitats	Size	A Question of Size
HandsOn	Hands-On Science	Slices	Anatomical Sections
HB&E	Hall of Human Biology & Evolution	Smoke	Passive Smoking
HBDS	Human Body Discovery Zone	Spiders1	Spiders! (1)
HistBox	History in a Box	Spiders2	Spiders! (2)
HK1	Hidden Kingdoms: The World of Microbes (1)	Sun	Harvesting the Sun
HK2	Hidden Kingdoms: The World of Microbes (2)	SW	Silent Witness
Inventing	Inventing Lab	Swamp	The Swamp: Wonders of Our Wetlands
Juras	Jurassic Hall	Symmet	Symmetry
Jurass	Jurassic!	Tomb	In the Tomb of Nefertari
Kelp	Kelp Lab	TrailHis	On the Trail of History

LIST ALPHABETIZED BY ABBREVIATED OF EXHIBITION NAMES

Abbreviation	Full Name
Tribute	A Tribute to Survival
TUIYH	The Universe in Your Hands
Tunnel	Tunnel of Discovery
Turbland	Turbulent Landscapes
UVG	Underwater Viewing Gallery
Wetland	Wetland Aviary
WGator	White Alligator: Secret of the Swamp
Whodun1	Whodunit? The Science of Solving Crime (1)
Whodun2	Whodunit? The Science of Solving Crime (2)
WIAA	What is an Animal?
Wild CA	Wild California

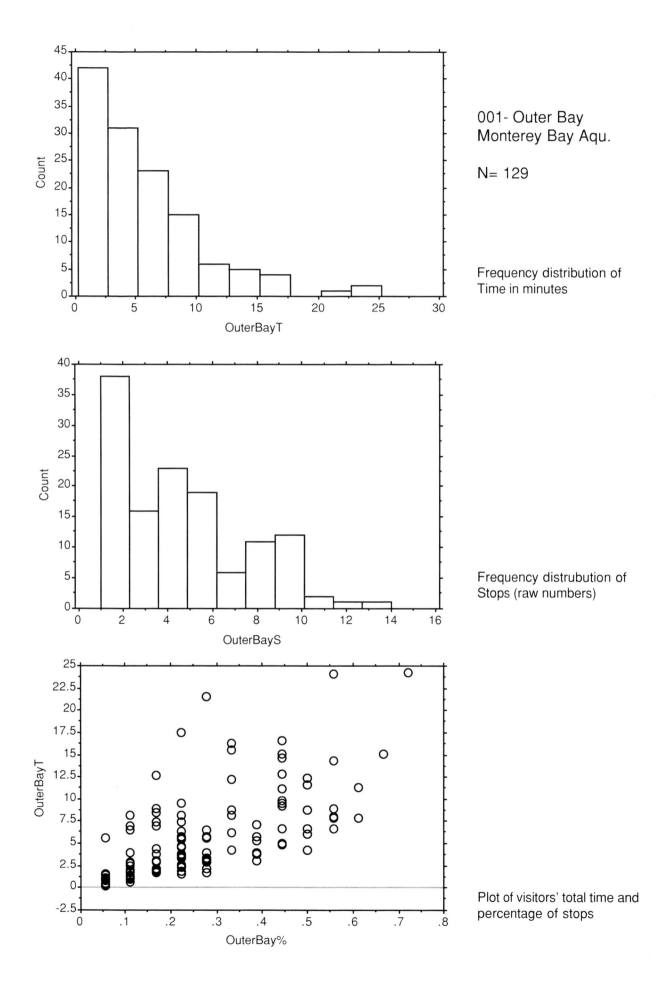

001- Outer Bay
Monterey Bay Aqu.

N= 129

Frequency distribution of
Time in minutes

Frequency distrubution of
Stops (raw numbers)

Plot of visitors' total time and
percentage of stops

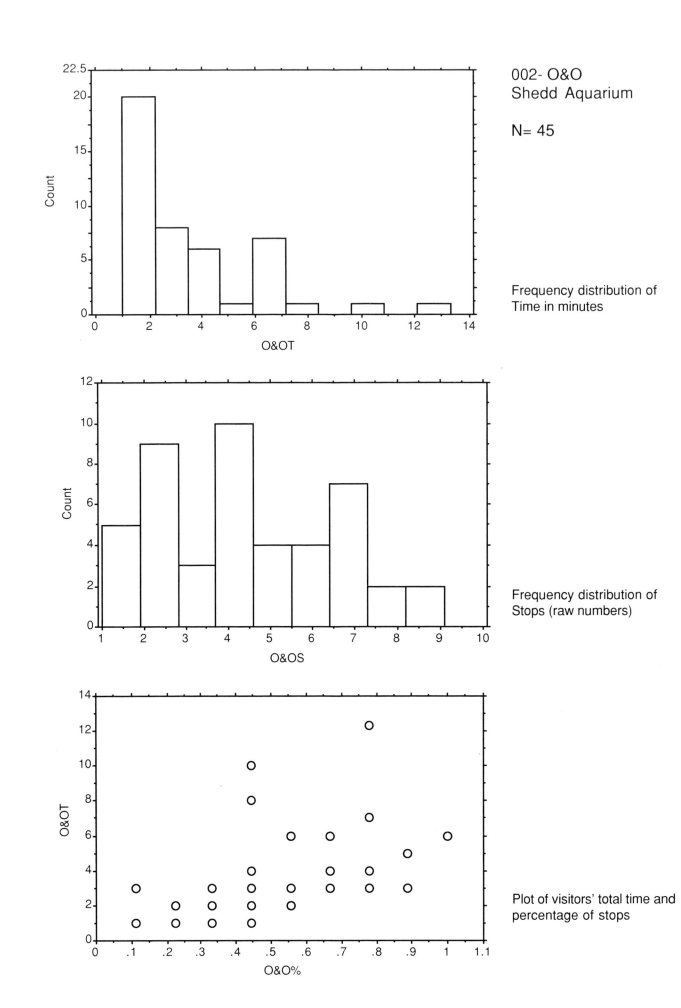

002- O&O
Shedd Aquarium

N= 45

Frequency distribution of
Time in minutes

Frequency distribution of
Stops (raw numbers)

Plot of visitors' total time and
percentage of stops

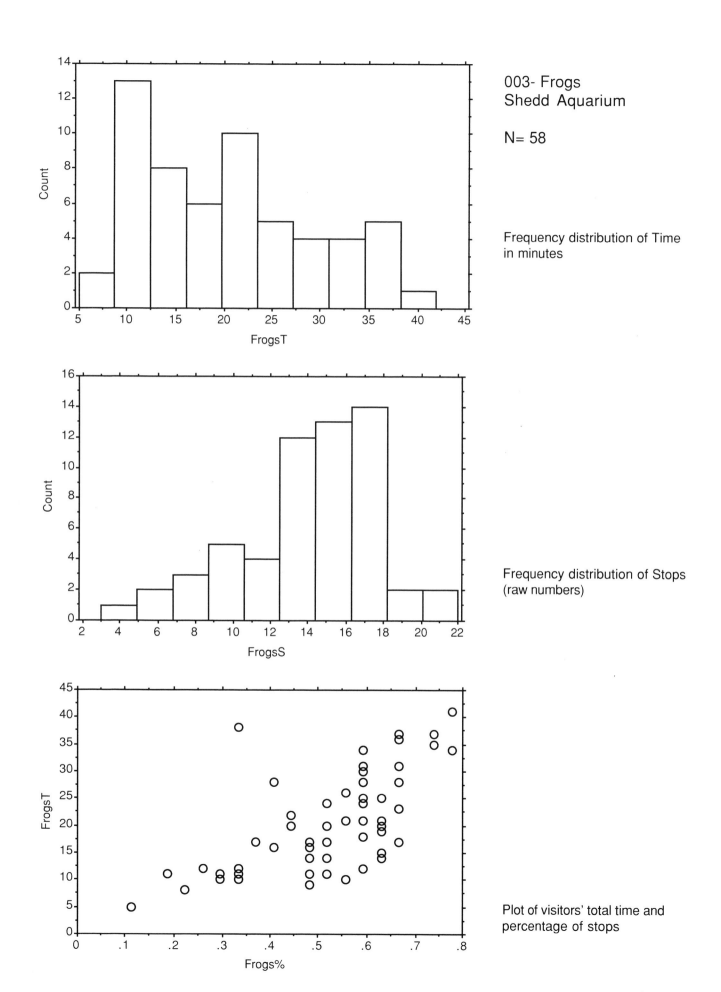

003- Frogs
Shedd Aquarium

N= 58

Frequency distribution of Time
in minutes

Frequency distribution of Stops
(raw numbers)

Plot of visitors' total time and
percentage of stops

Ten prototype interactive stations about wildlife forensic science in *Silent Witness* were tested with adult visitors. Elements were revised until approximately 80 % of the visitors could successfully complete each activity in less than a minute. Final versions of the stations were used thoroughly by children and families alike.

Photo by author

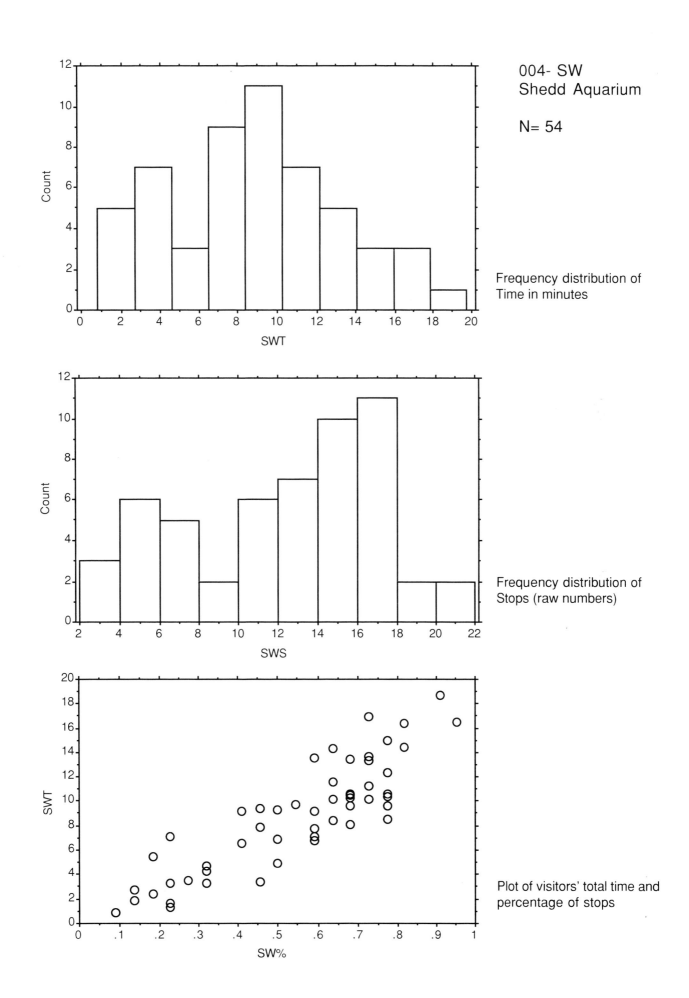

004- SW
Shedd Aquarium

N= 54

Frequency distribution of
Time in minutes

Frequency distribution of
Stops (raw numbers)

Plot of visitors' total time and
percentage of stops

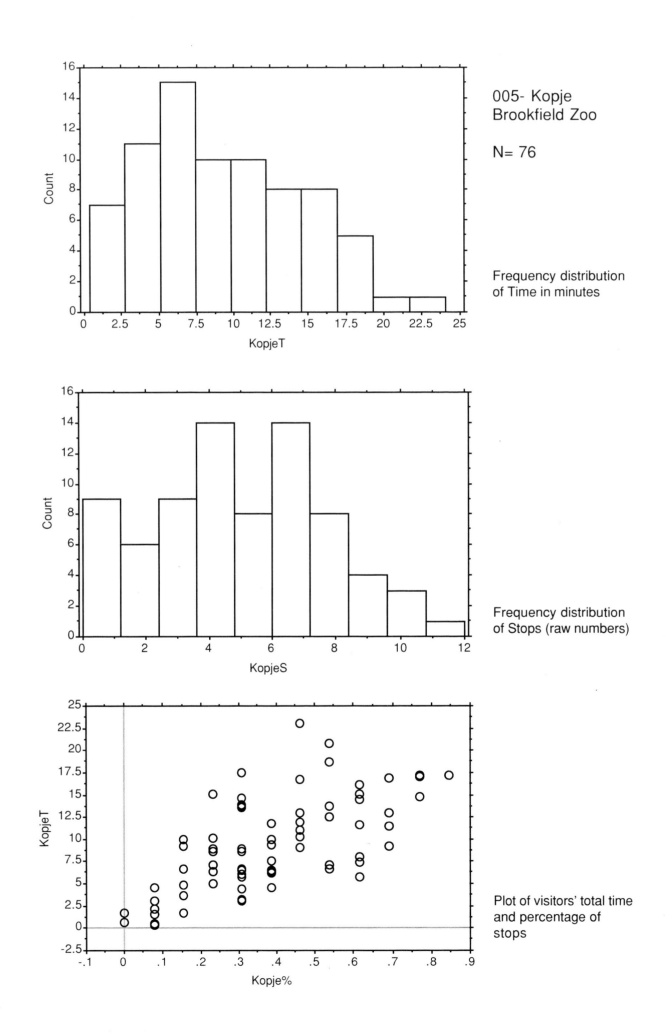

005- Kopje
Brookfield Zoo

N= 76

Frequency distribution
of Time in minutes

Frequency distribution
of Stops (raw numbers)

Plot of visitors' total time
and percentage of
stops

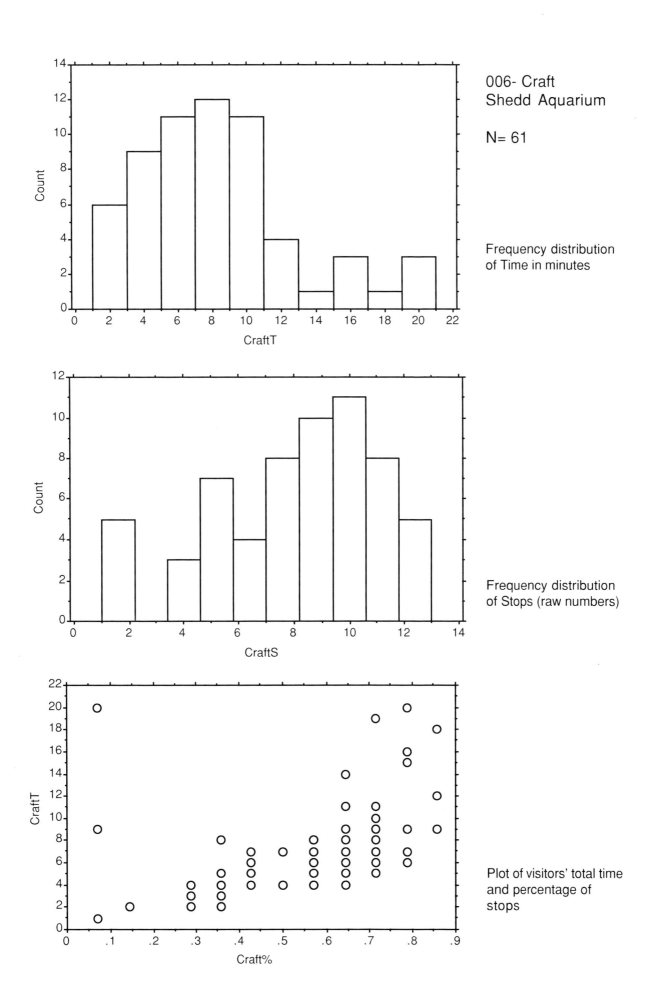

006- Craft
Shedd Aquarium

N= 61

Frequency distribution
of Time in minutes

Frequency distribution
of Stops (raw numbers)

Plot of visitors' total time
and percentage of
stops

In Shedd Aquarium's Underwater Viewing Gallery, graphics and low-tech interactives that compare humans and whales were among the most popular and memorable parts of the exhibition. Tracking showed that the majority of visitors stopped at those elements, and exit questionnaires revealed that visitors found the information memorable.

Photo by author

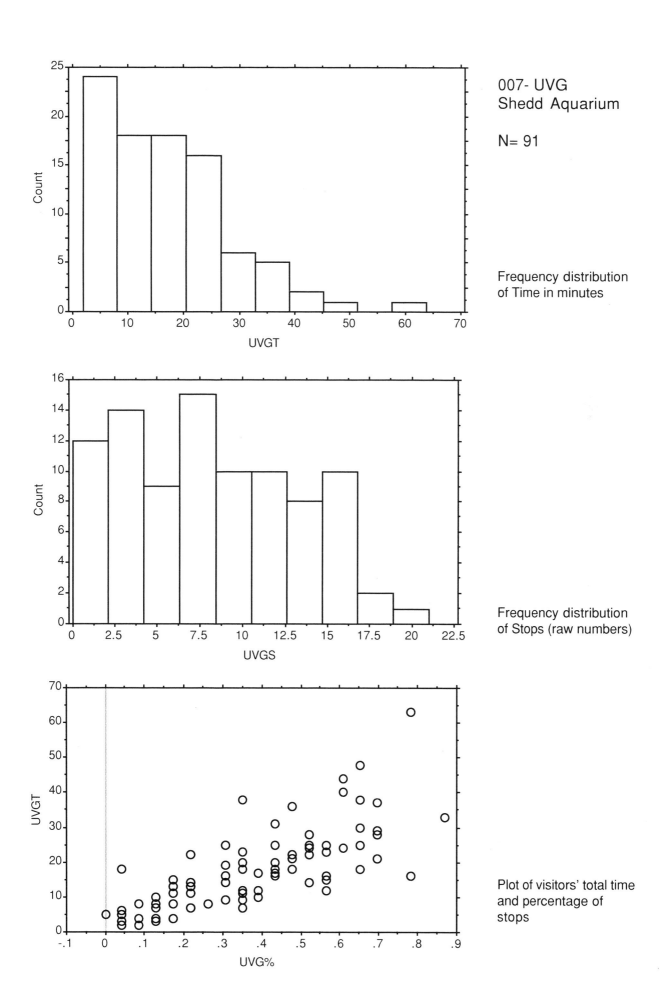

007- UVG
Shedd Aquarium

N= 91

Frequency distribution
of Time in minutes

Frequency distribution
of Stops (raw numbers)

Plot of visitors' total time
and percentage of
stops

Live animals, especially ones that visitors can touch (here in "Kelp Lab"), are popular with adults and children in almost any exhibition in any museum. But there is a high cost for staffing and maintaining such exhibits, especially when they are part of a traveling exhibition.

Photo courtesy of Monterey Bay Aquarium

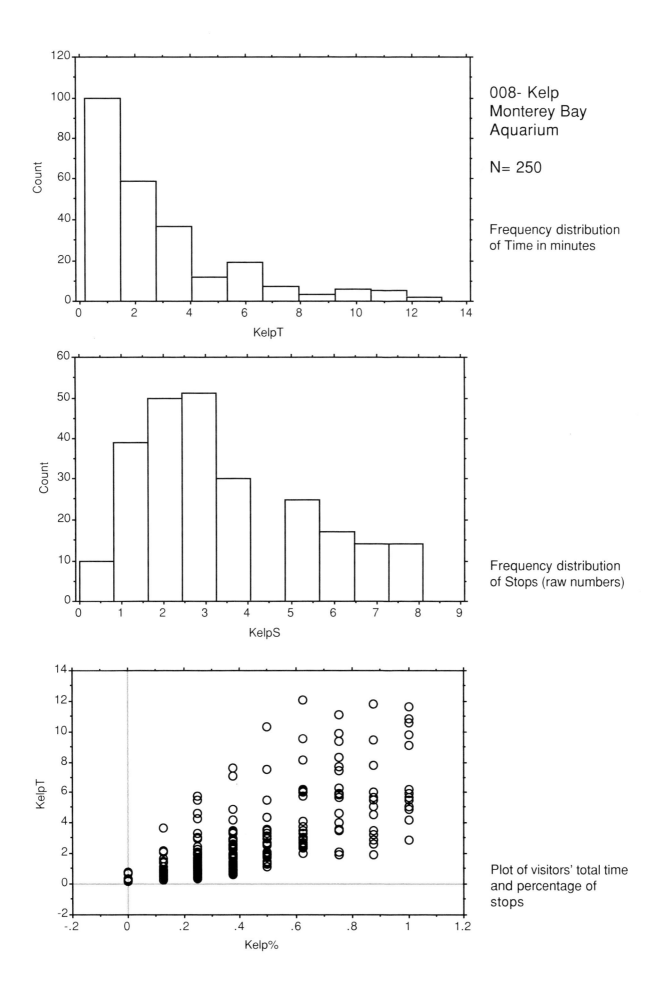

008- Kelp
Monterey Bay
Aquarium

N= 250

Frequency distribution
of Time in minutes

Frequency distribution
of Stops (raw numbers)

Plot of visitors' total time
and percentage of
stops

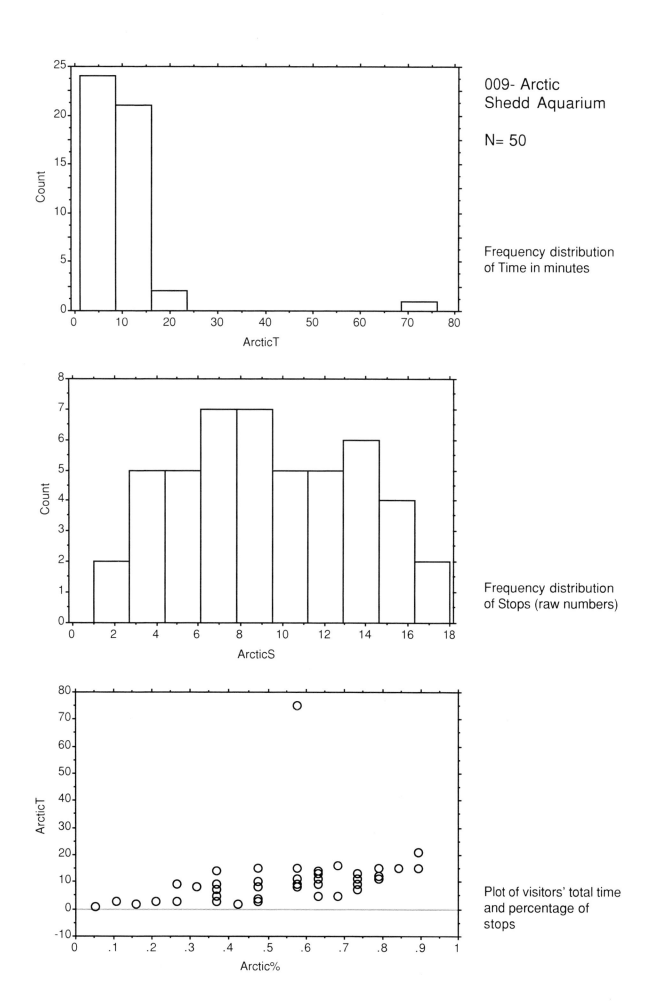

009- Arctic
Shedd Aquarium

N= 50

Frequency distribution
of Time in minutes

Frequency distribution
of Stops (raw numbers)

Plot of visitors' total time
and percentage of
stops

Paying attention to interpretive devices may not be what most zoo visitors expect to do. In "The Swamp," far more visitors stopped at the live-animal exhibits than at the graphics and interactives (such as this one about bird migration). If enough of the devices are engaging, could visitors' expectations change?

Photo courtesy of Brookfield Zoo (Chicago Zoological Society)

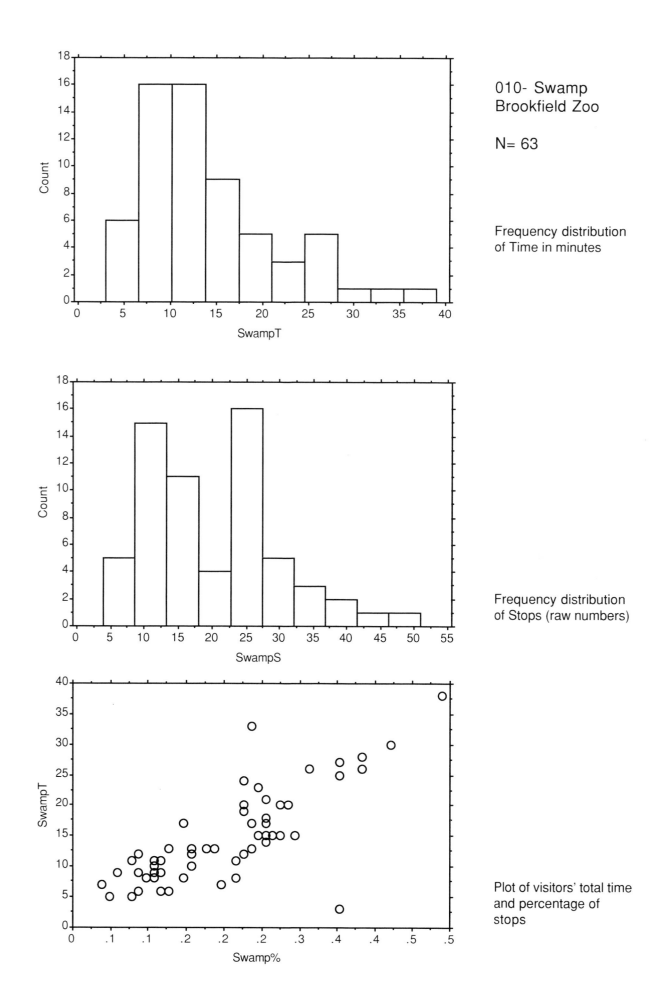

010- Swamp
Brookfield Zoo

N= 63

Frequency distribution
of Time in minutes

Frequency distribution
of Stops (raw numbers)

Plot of visitors' total time
and percentage of
stops

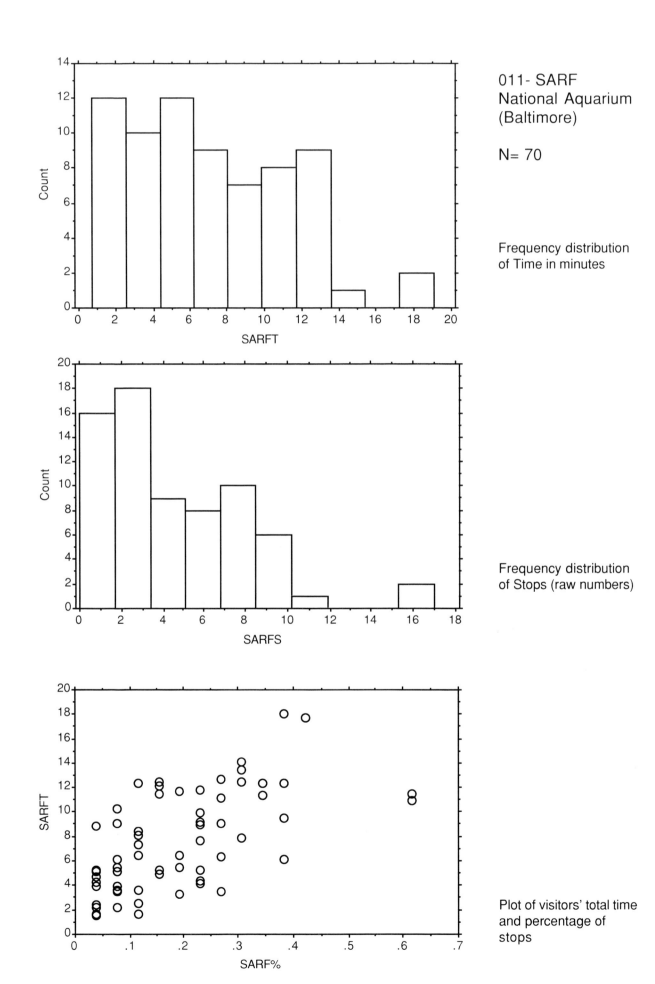

011- SARF
National Aquarium
(Baltimore)

N= 70

Frequency distribution
of Time in minutes

Frequency distribution
of Stops (raw numbers)

Plot of visitors' total time
and percentage of
stops

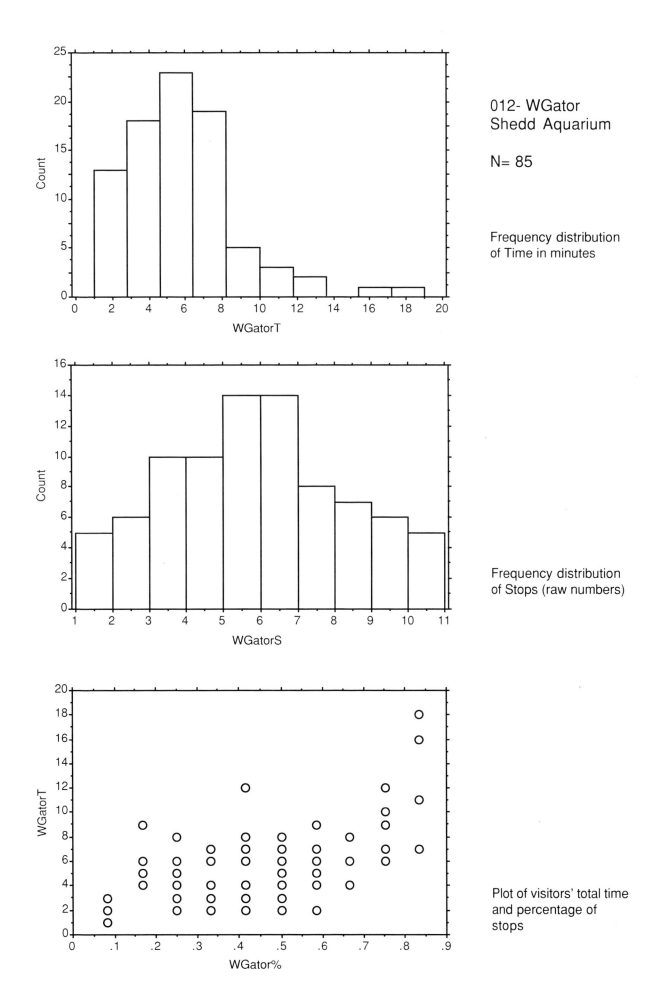

012- WGator
Shedd Aquarium

N= 85

Frequency distribution
of Time in minutes

Frequency distribution
of Stops (raw numbers)

Plot of visitors' total time
and percentage of
stops

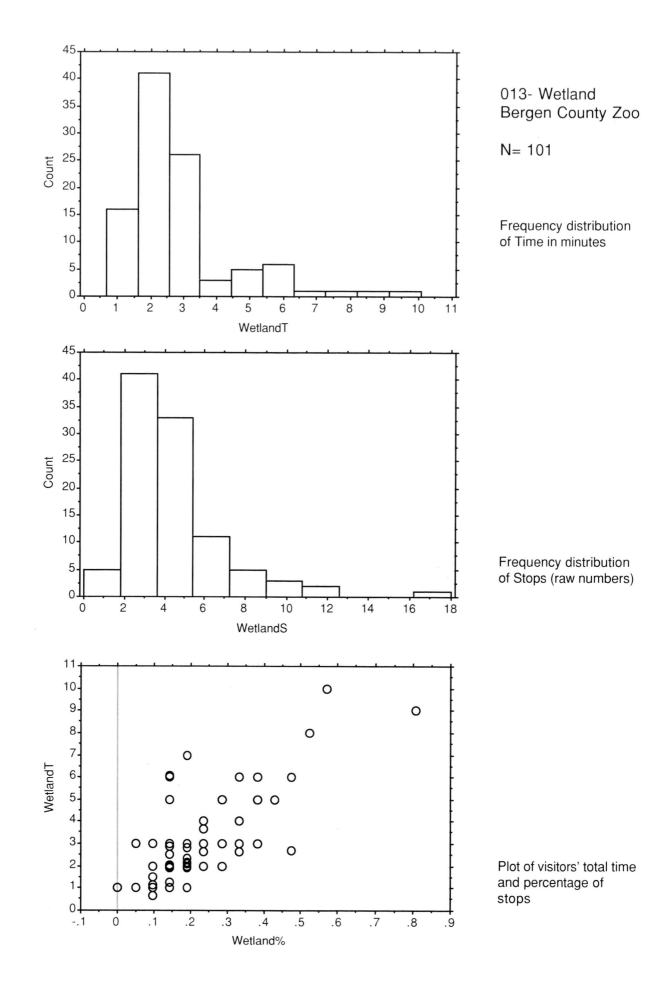

013- Wetland
Bergen County Zoo

N= 101

Frequency distribution
of Time in minutes

Frequency distribution
of Stops (raw numbers)

Plot of visitors' total time
and percentage of
stops

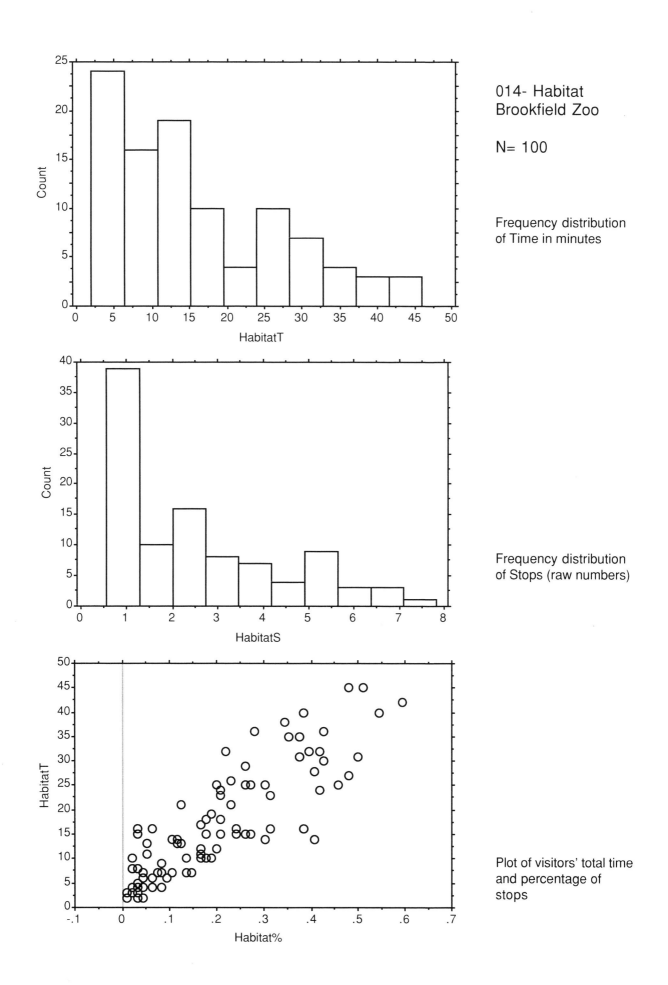

014- Habitat
Brookfield Zoo

N= 100

Frequency distribution
of Time in minutes

Frequency distribution
of Stops (raw numbers)

Plot of visitors' total time
and percentage of
stops

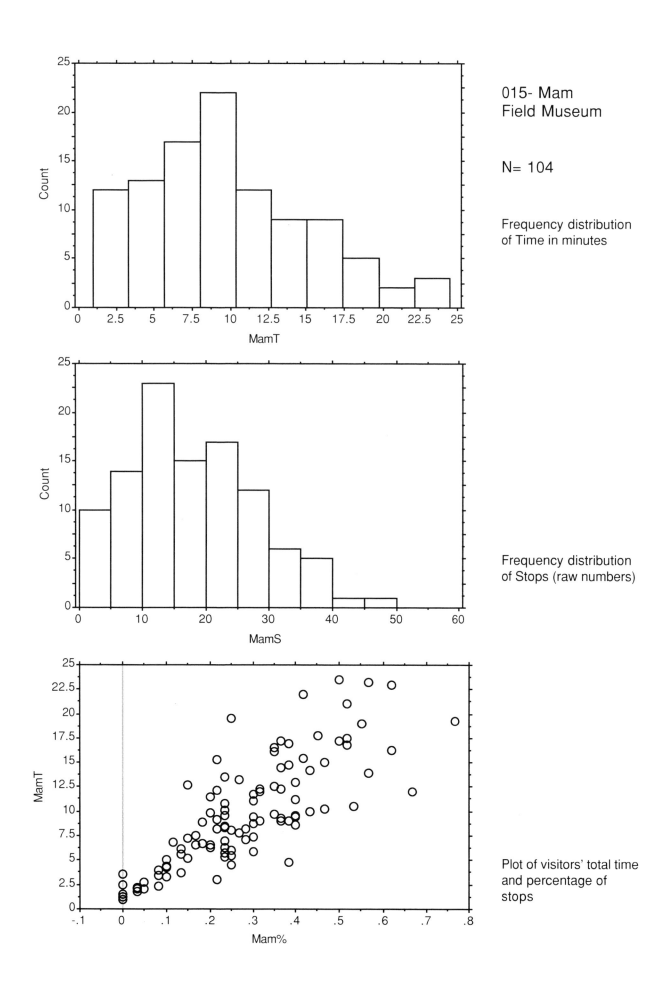

015- Mam
Field Museum

N= 104

Frequency distribution
of Time in minutes

Frequency distribution
of Stops (raw numbers)

Plot of visitors' total time
and percentage of
stops

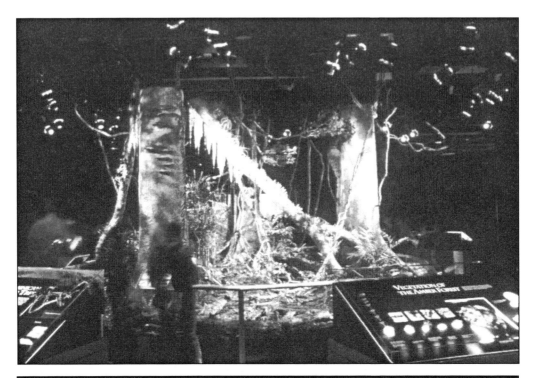

"Amber: Window to the Past" combined aspects of science (top photo), and art (bottom photo) in displays that encourage careful looking and reading. Visitors to the American Museum of Natural History used this exhibition more thoroughly than any other in the Paying Attention study (SRI = 212, % DV = 86 %). When it traveled to other sites, the average time visitors spent in the exhibition was also relatively high.

Detail from photograph, courtesy Department of Library Services,
Photo courtesy of American Museum of Natural History

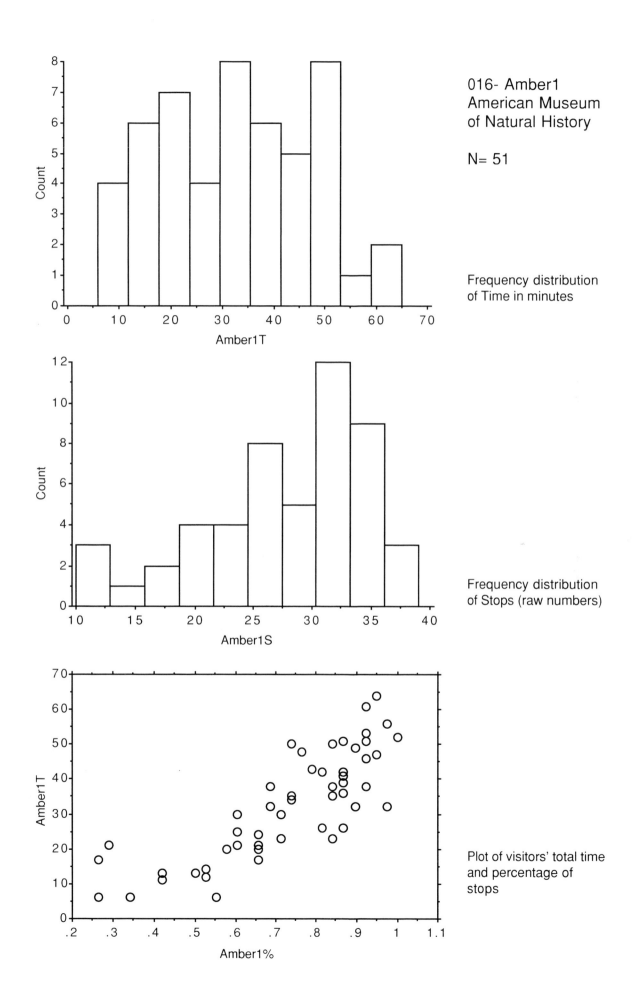

016- Amber1
American Museum
of Natural History

N= 51

Frequency distribution
of Time in minutes

Frequency distribution
of Stops (raw numbers)

Plot of visitors' total time
and percentage of
stops

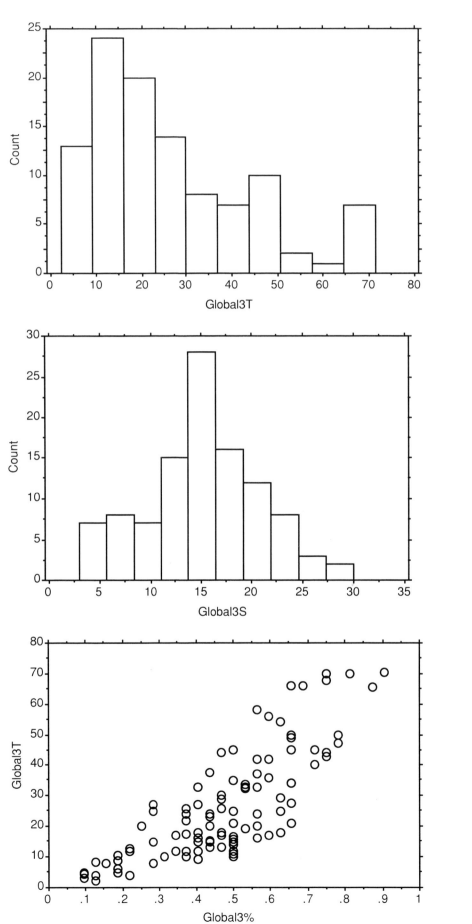

017- Global3
Denver Museum of
Natural History

N= 106

Frequency distribution
of Time in minutes

Frequency distribution
of Stops (raw numbers)

Plot of visitors' total time
and percentage of
stops

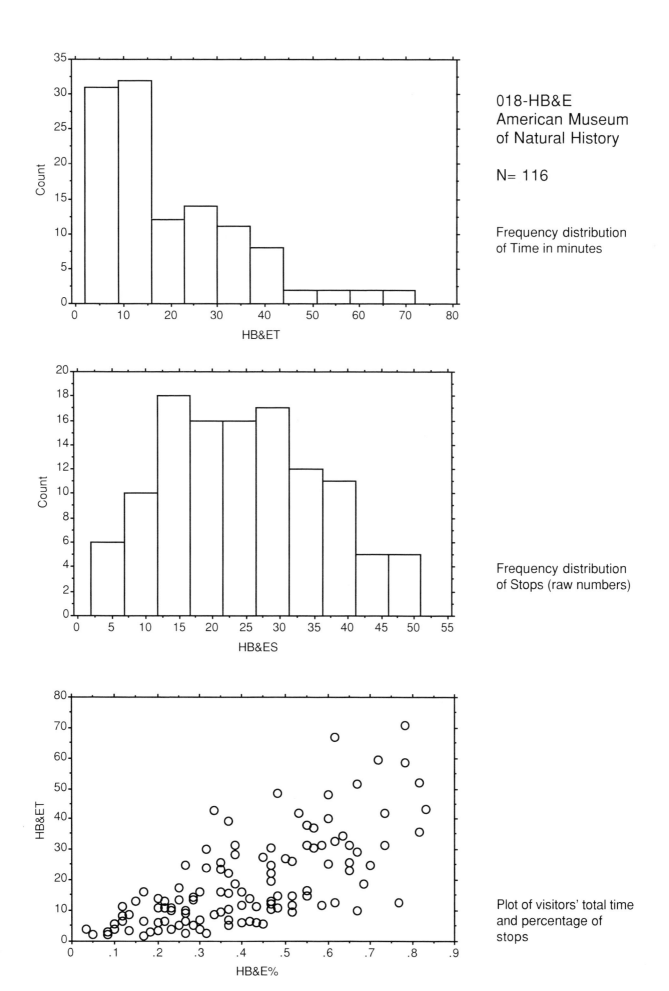

018-HB&E
American Museum
of Natural History

N= 116

Frequency distribution
of Time in minutes

Frequency distribution
of Stops (raw numbers)

Plot of visitors' total time
and percentage of
stops

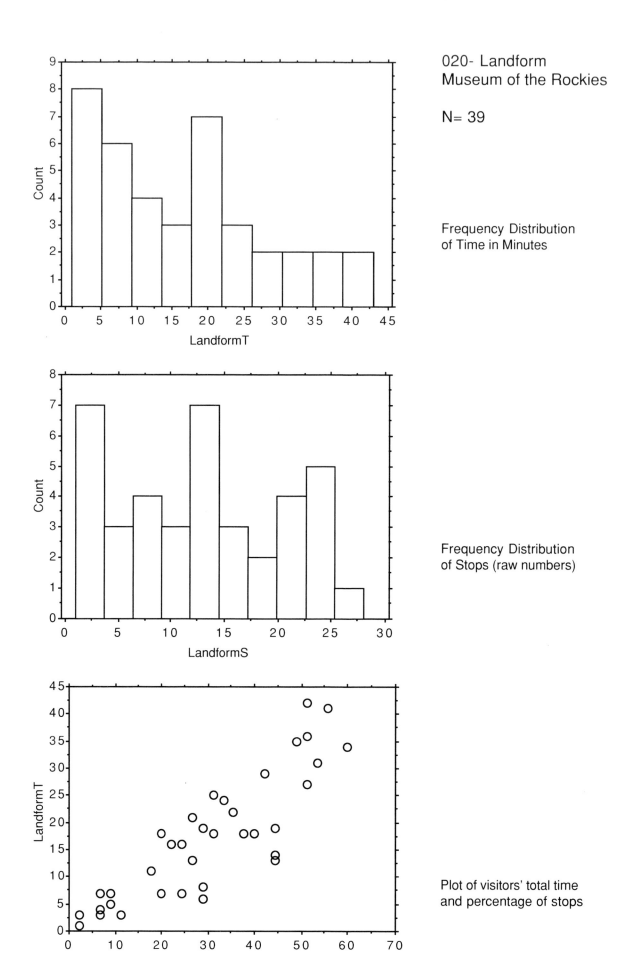

020- Landform
Museum of the Rockies

N= 39

Frequency Distribution
of Time in Minutes

Frequency Distribution
of Stops (raw numbers)

Plot of visitors' total time
and percentage of stops

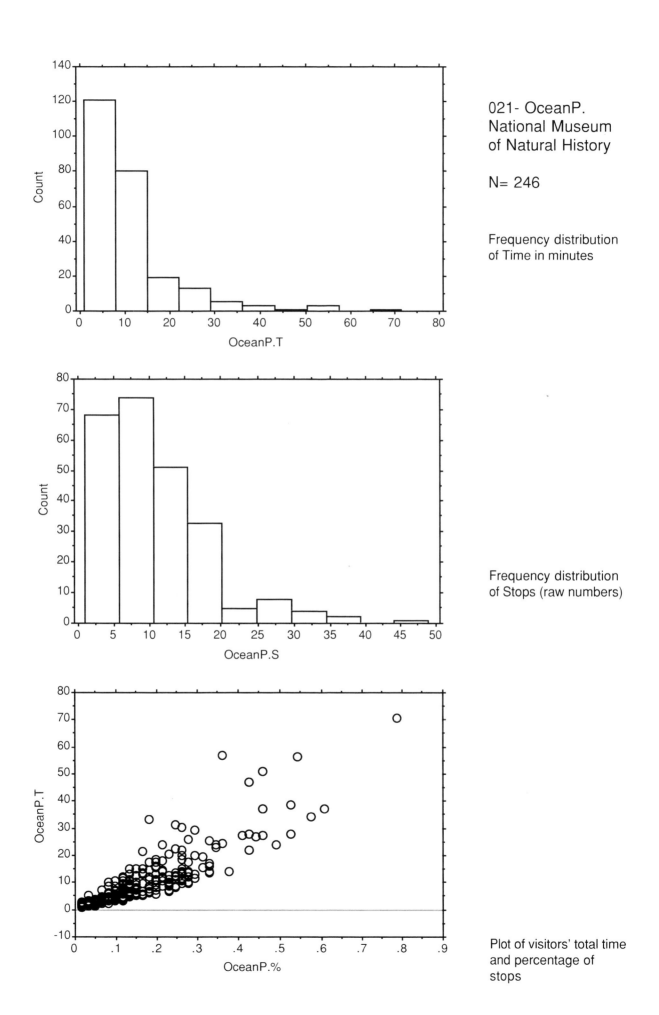

021- OceanP.
National Museum
of Natural History

N= 246

Frequency distribution
of Time in minutes

Frequency distribution
of Stops (raw numbers)

Plot of visitors' total time
and percentage of
stops

Words, images, and specimens worked together closely to communicate a coherent, clear story in the traveling exhibition, "Darkened Waters: Profile of an Oil Spill." Tracking studies at two sites showed exceptionally thorough use by visitors in this 2,000-square-foot exhibition.

Photo by author

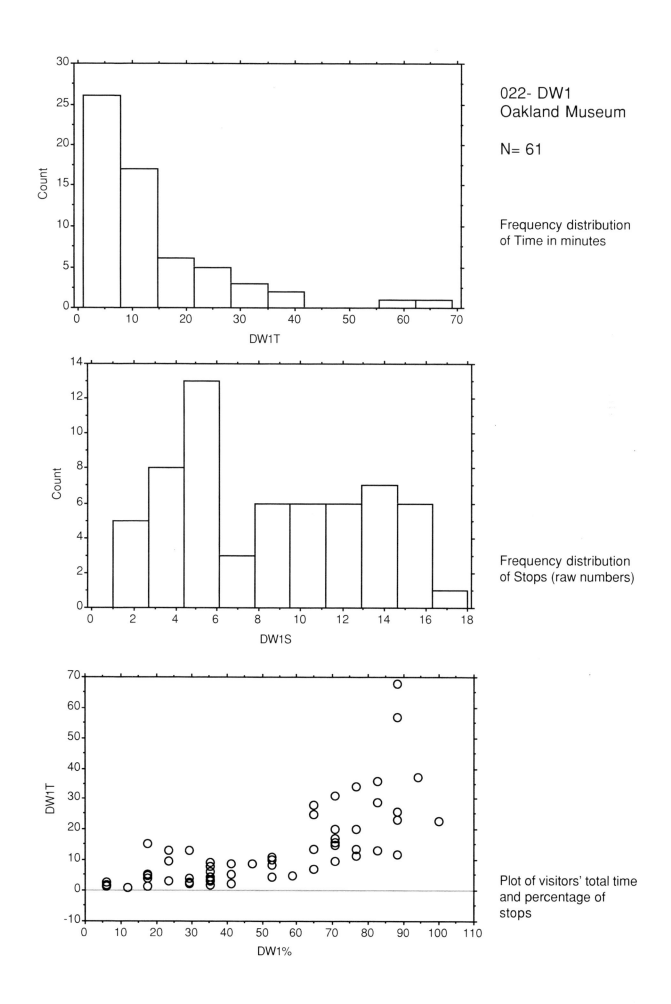

022- DW1
Oakland Museum

N= 61

Frequency distribution
of Time in minutes

Frequency distribution
of Stops (raw numbers)

Plot of visitors' total time
and percentage of
stops

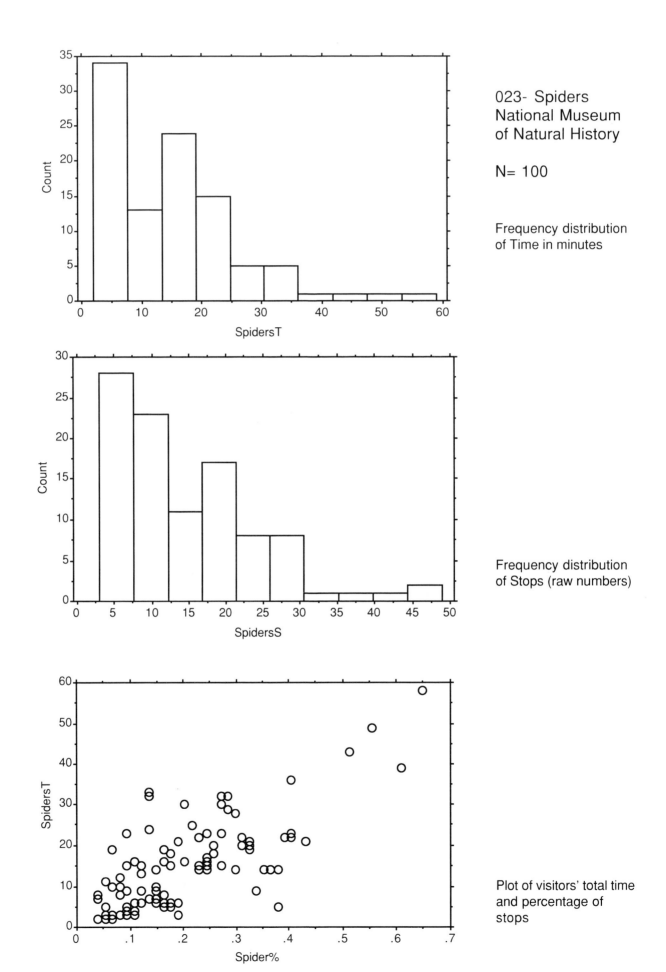

023- Spiders
National Museum
of Natural History

N= 100

Frequency distribution
of Time in minutes

Frequency distribution
of Stops (raw numbers)

Plot of visitors' total time
and percentage of
stops

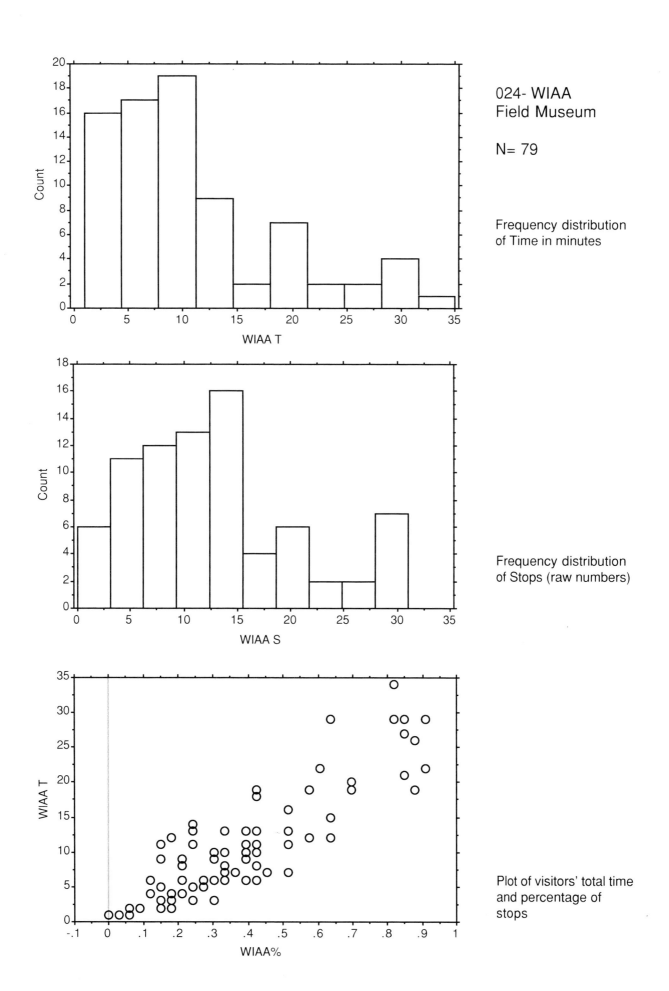

024- WIAA
Field Museum

N= 79

Frequency distribution
of Time in minutes

Frequency distribution
of Stops (raw numbers)

Plot of visitors' total time
and percentage of
stops

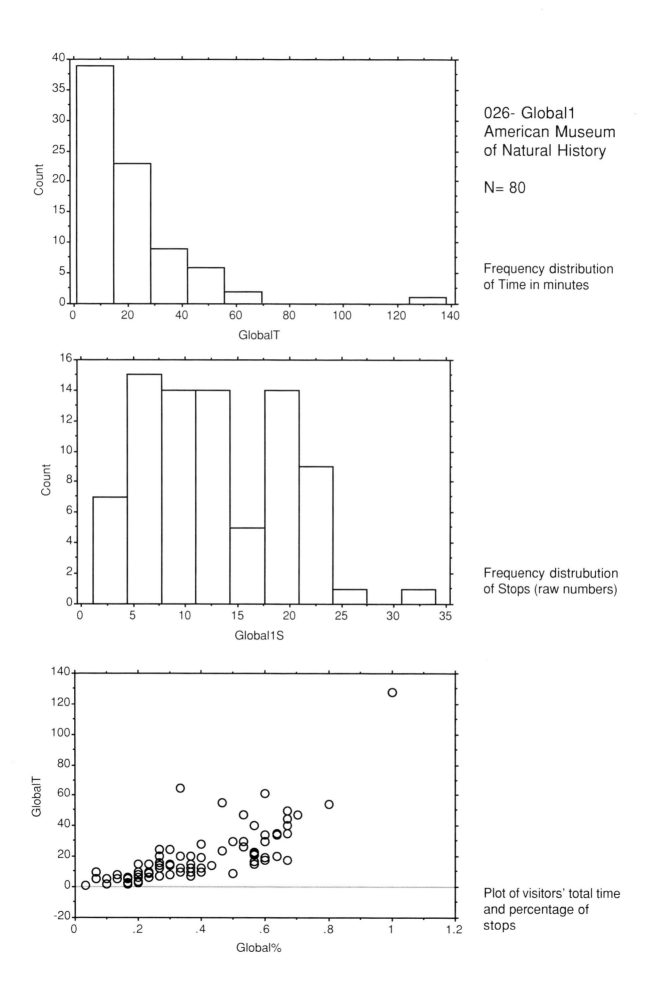

026- Global1
American Museum
of Natural History

N= 80

Frequency distribution
of Time in minutes

Frequency distrubution
of Stops (raw numbers)

Plot of visitors' total time
and percentage of
stops

In the new bird hall, "Birds of the World," at Field Museum, summed up by one visitor as "gleaming talons and sparkling beaks," interactive devices along a low rail helped engage visitors through different modalities. Tracking studies showed that visitors spent more time here than in the old bird hall (#105).

Photo by author

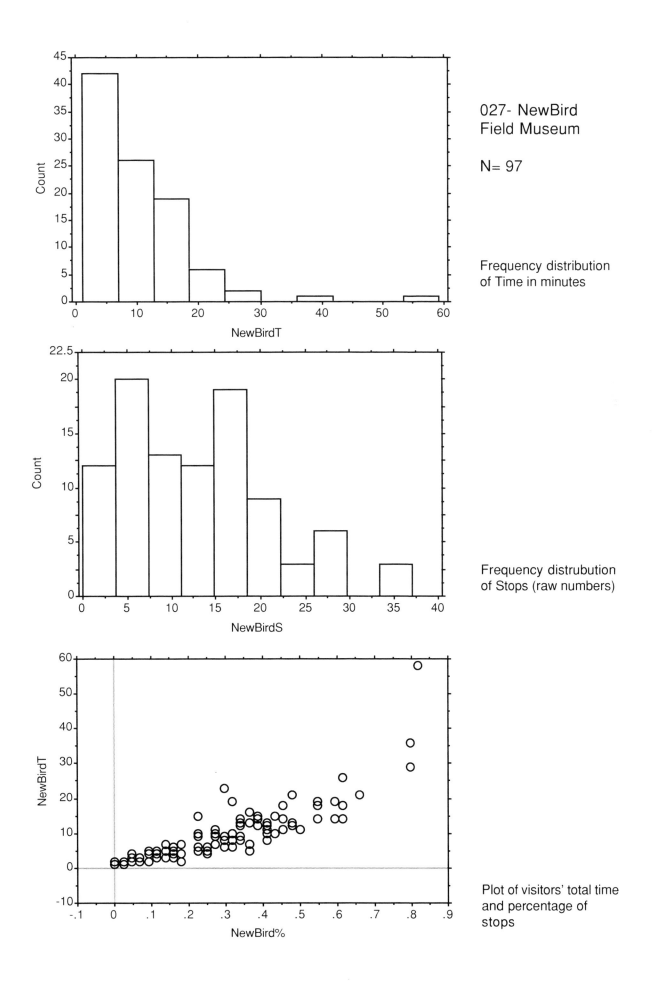

027- NewBird
Field Museum

N= 97

Frequency distribution
of Time in minutes

Frequency distrubution
of Stops (raw numbers)

Plot of visitors' total time
and percentage of
stops

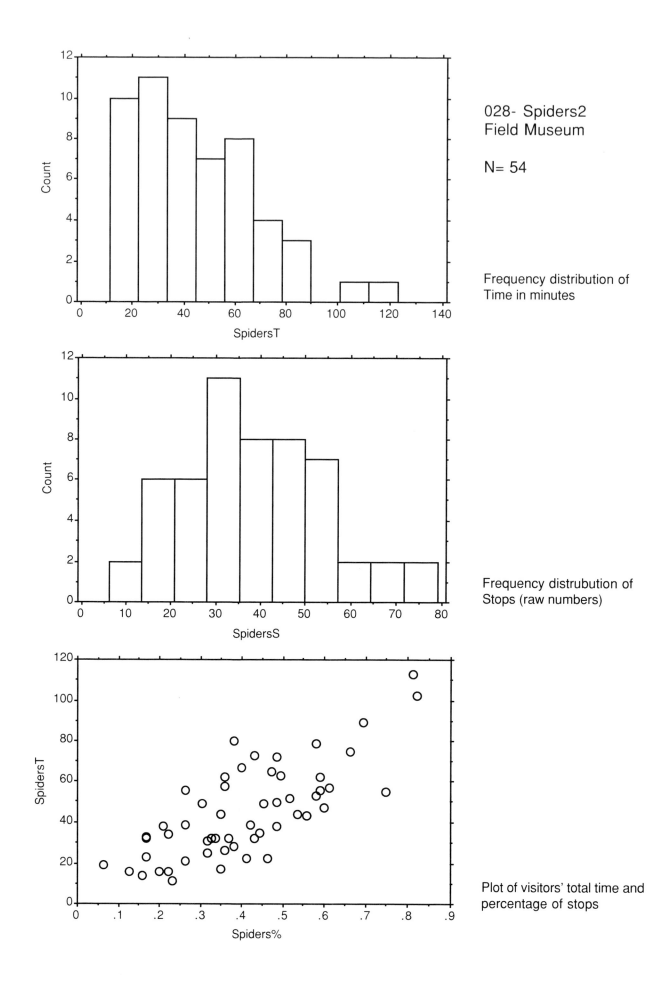

028- Spiders2
Field Museum

N= 54

Frequency distribution of
Time in minutes

Frequency distrubution of
Stops (raw numbers)

Plot of visitors' total time and
percentage of stops

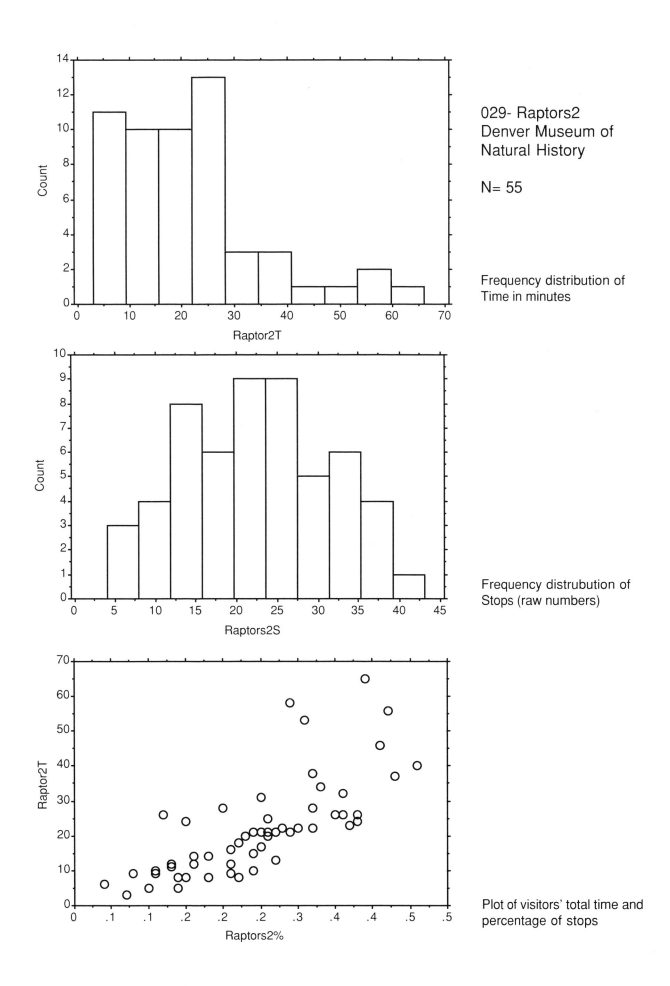

029- Raptors2
Denver Museum of
Natural History

N= 55

Frequency distribution of
Time in minutes

Frequency distrubution of
Stops (raw numbers)

Plot of visitors' total time and
percentage of stops

"There's something moving in here!" Microscopes with views of living microbes were clearly the most popular elements in the traveling show, "Hidden Kingdoms: The World of Microbes." This was true no matter where the exhibit traveled. (Photo taken at New York Hall of Science.)

Photo courtesy of the New York Hall of Science

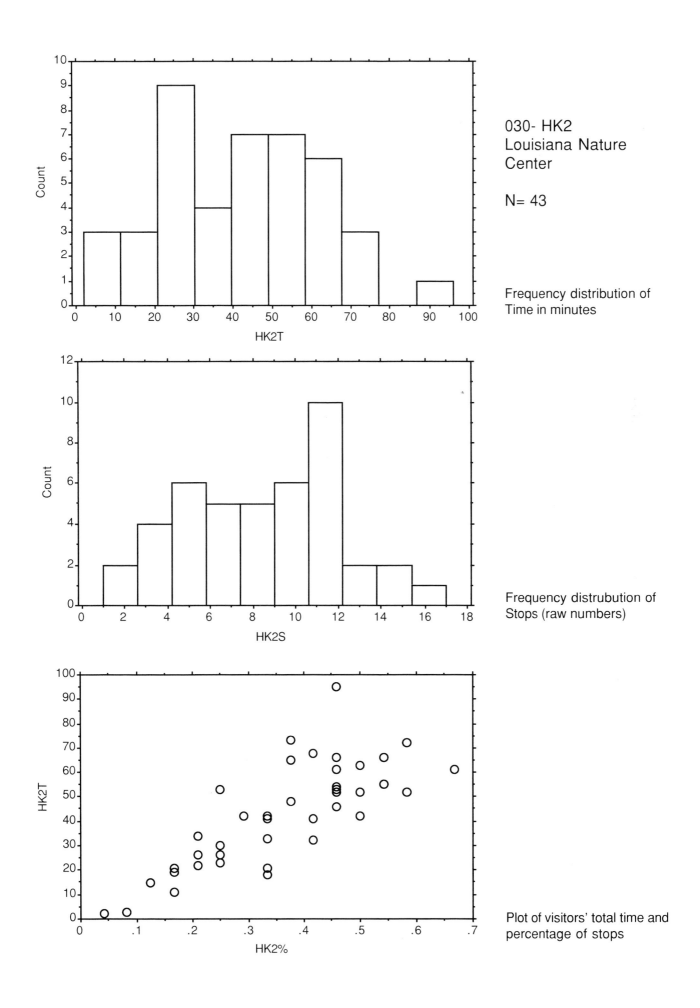

030- HK2
Louisiana Nature
Center

N= 43

Frequency distribution of
Time in minutes

Frequency distrubution of
Stops (raw numbers)

Plot of visitors' total time and
percentage of stops

"Habitats" has several large, open, naturalistic environments with engaging interactives. Subtle signs of human habitation inside the dioramas provide an element of surprise. "Habitats" held visitors' attention longer than any other diorama-based exhibition tested in the study.

Photo courtesy of Grand Rapids Public Museum

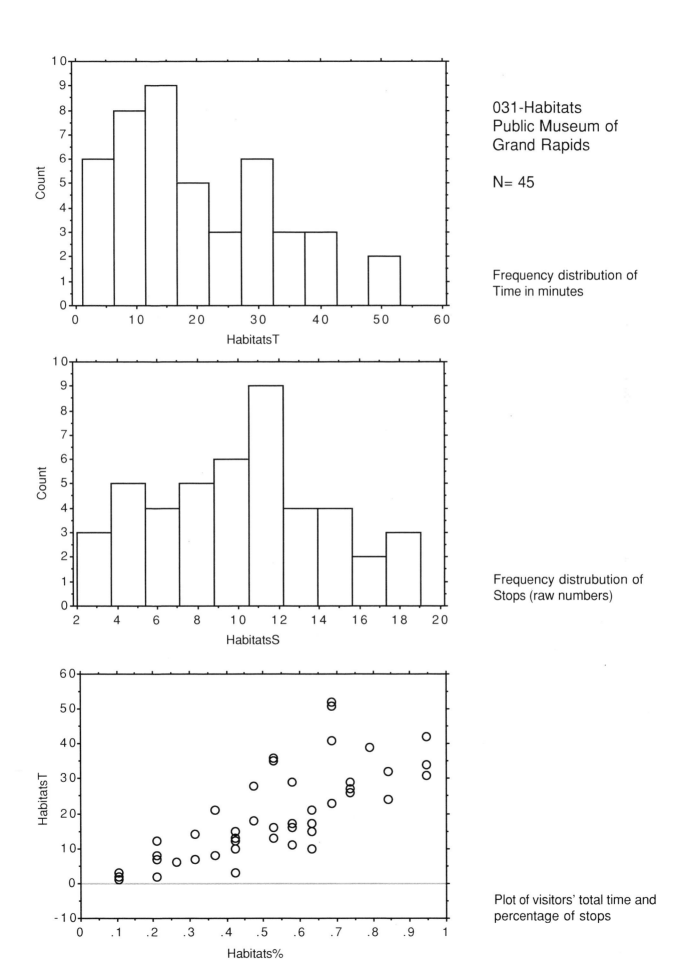

031-Habitats
Public Museum of
Grand Rapids

N= 45

Frequency distribution of
Time in minutes

Frequency distrubution of
Stops (raw numbers)

Plot of visitors' total time and
percentage of stops

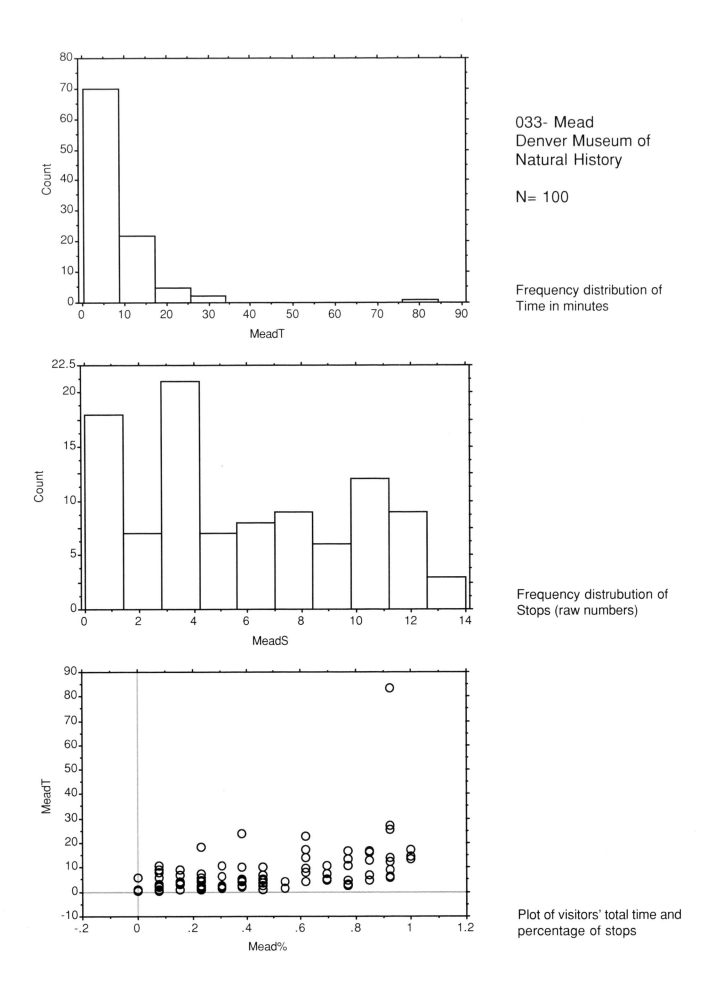

033- Mead
Denver Museum of
Natural History

N= 100

Frequency distribution of
Time in minutes

Frequency distrubution of
Stops (raw numbers)

Plot of visitors' total time and
percentage of stops

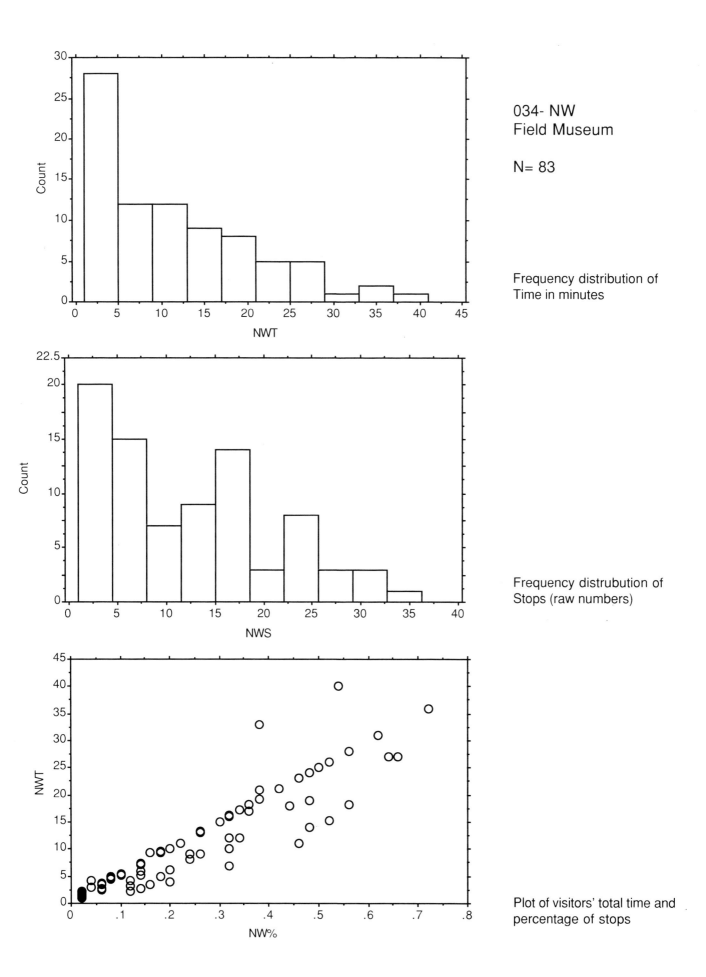

034- NW
Field Museum

N= 83

Frequency distribution of
Time in minutes

Frequency distrubution of
Stops (raw numbers)

Plot of visitors' total time and
percentage of stops

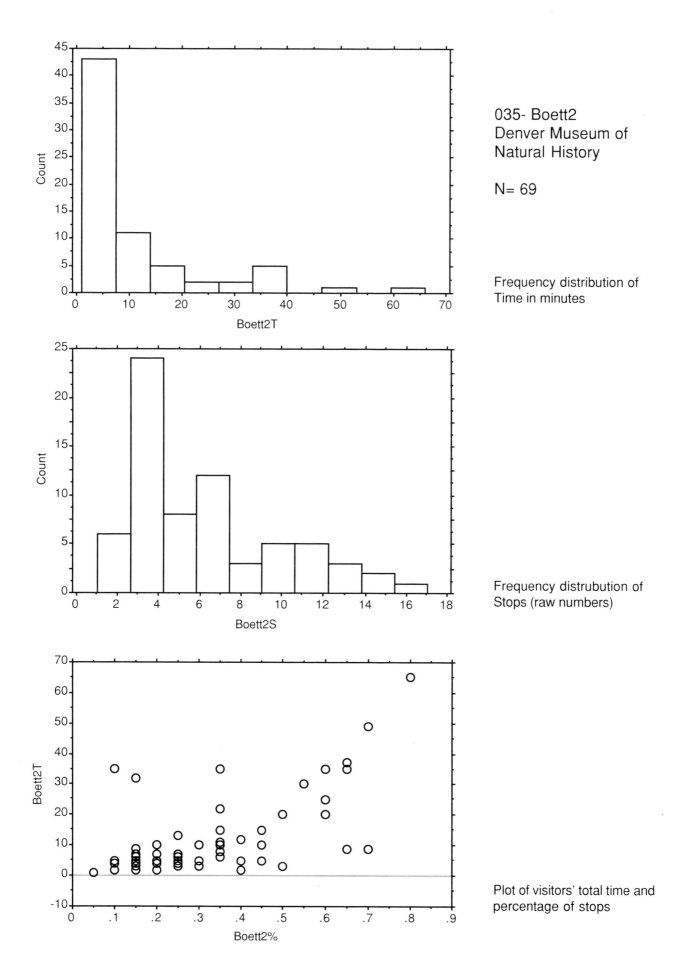

035- Boett2
Denver Museum of
Natural History

N= 69

Frequency distribution of
Time in minutes

Frequency distrubution of
Stops (raw numbers)

Plot of visitors' total time and
percentage of stops

Moose diorama in "Messages from the Wilderness" at Field Museum in Chicago.

Photo by author

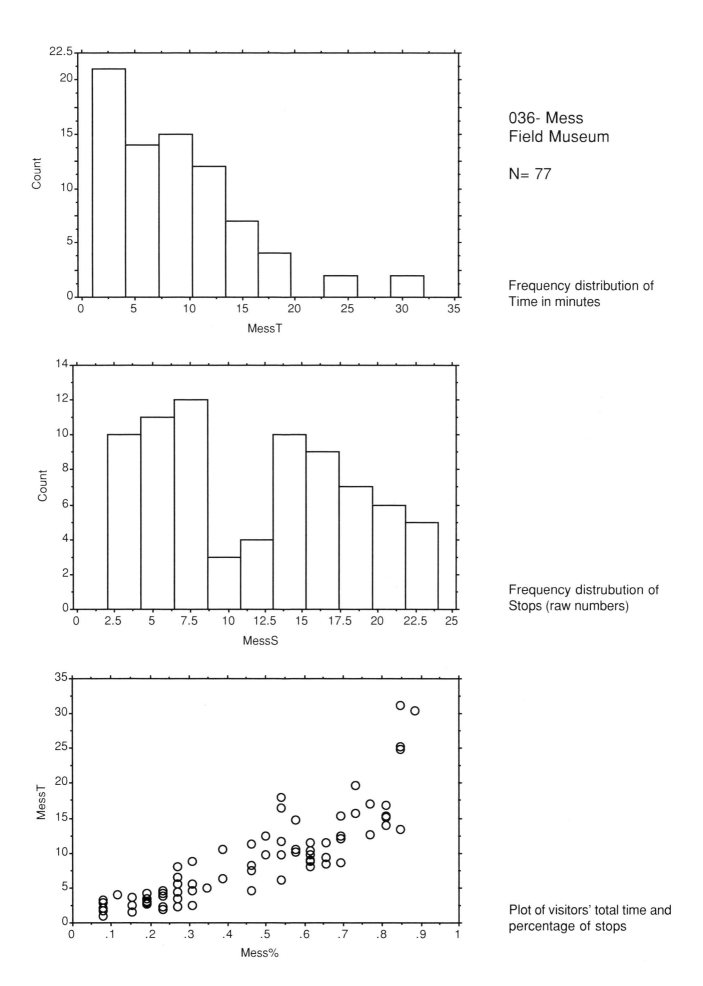

036- Mess
Field Museum

N= 77

Frequency distribution of
Time in minutes

Frequency distrubution of
Stops (raw numbers)

Plot of visitors' total time and
percentage of stops

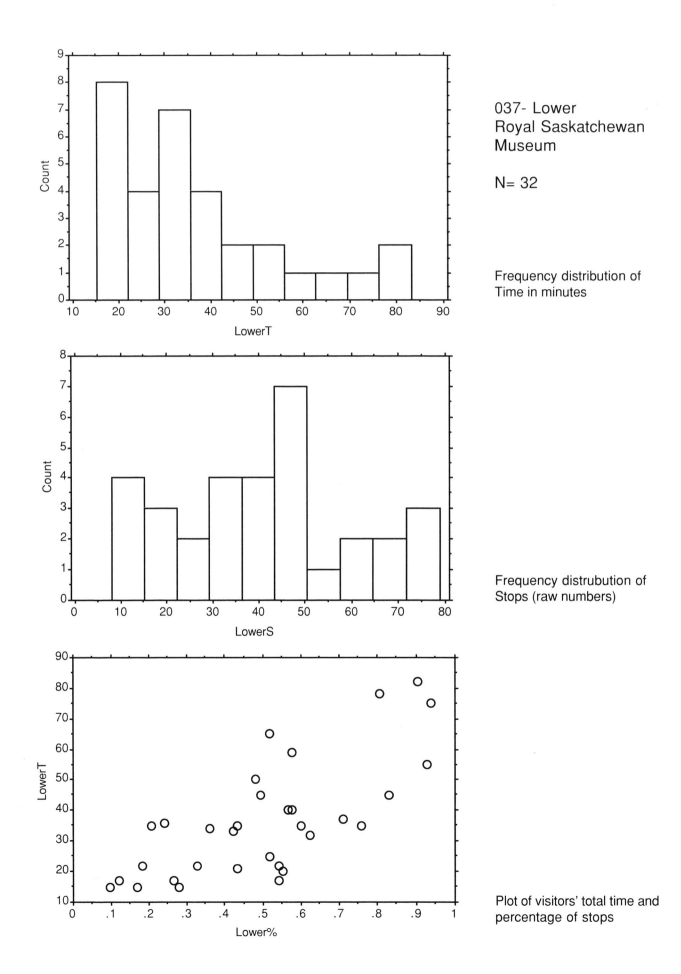

037- Lower
Royal Saskatchewan
Museum

N= 32

Frequency distribution of
Time in minutes

Frequency distrubution of
Stops (raw numbers)

Plot of visitors' total time and
percentage of stops

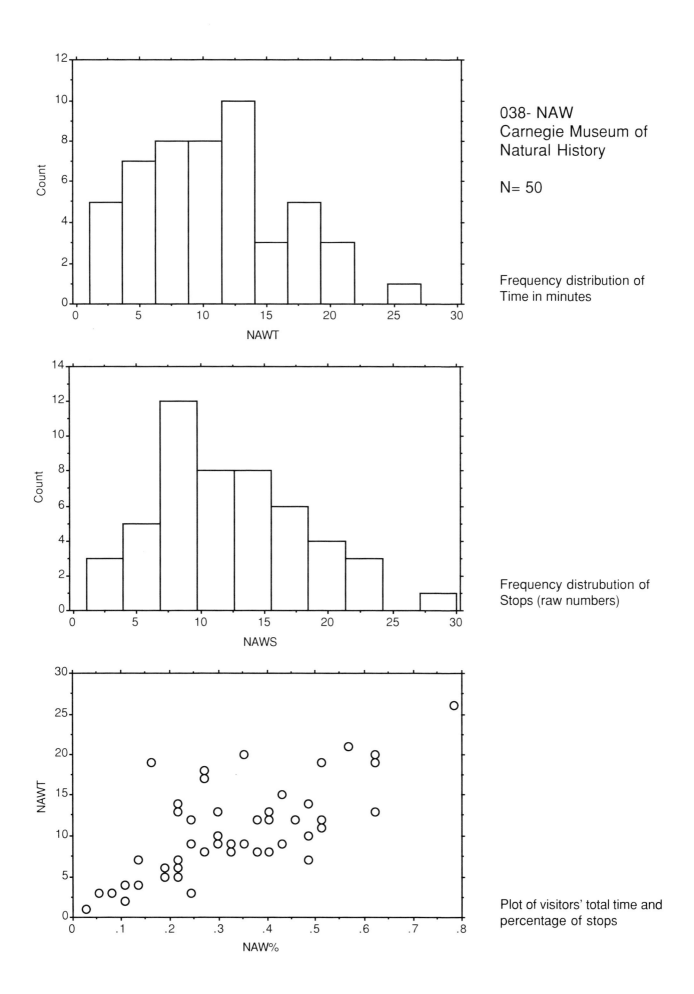

038- NAW
Carnegie Museum of
Natural History

N= 50

Frequency distribution of
Time in minutes

Frequency distrubution of
Stops (raw numbers)

Plot of visitors' total time and
percentage of stops

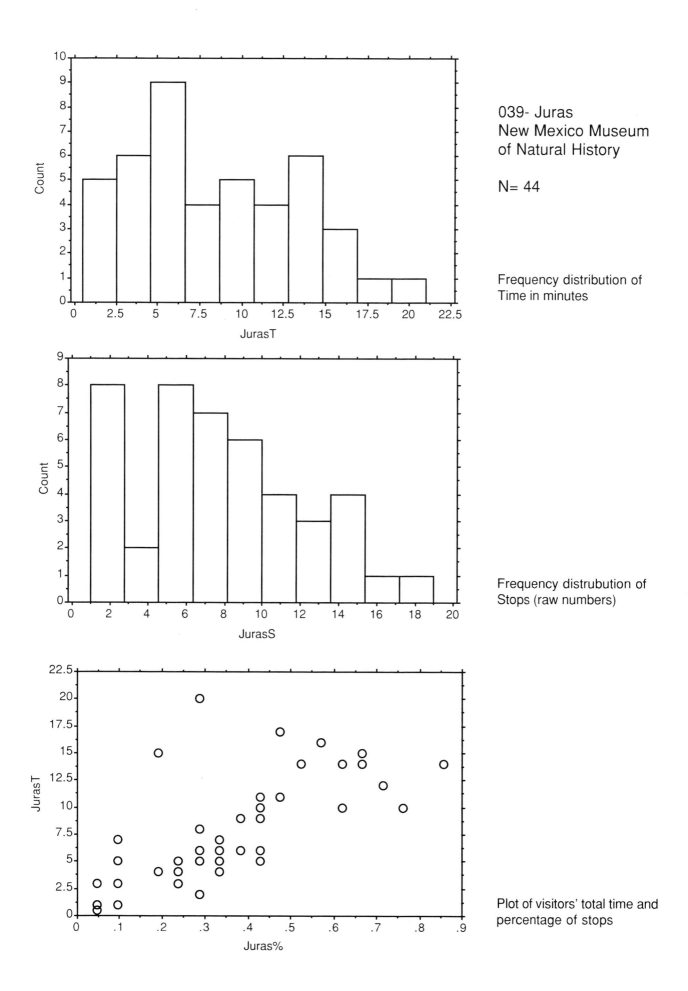

039- Juras
New Mexico Museum
of Natural History

N= 44

Frequency distribution of
Time in minutes

Frequency distrubution of
Stops (raw numbers)

Plot of visitors' total time and
percentage of stops

In the original installation of "Treasures from the Sand" (top photo), many visitors did not stop at the introductory panel. Instead, they were drawn immediately inside, lured by photos and artifacts. Exhibit developers added a larger title and subtitle to the panel as well as an artifact that helped hide the view inside (bottom photo). After these changes, evaluations showed that more visitors read the introduction and grasped the main idea of the exhibition—testimony to the power of good orientation.

Photo courtesy of Mackinac State Historic Parks, Michigan

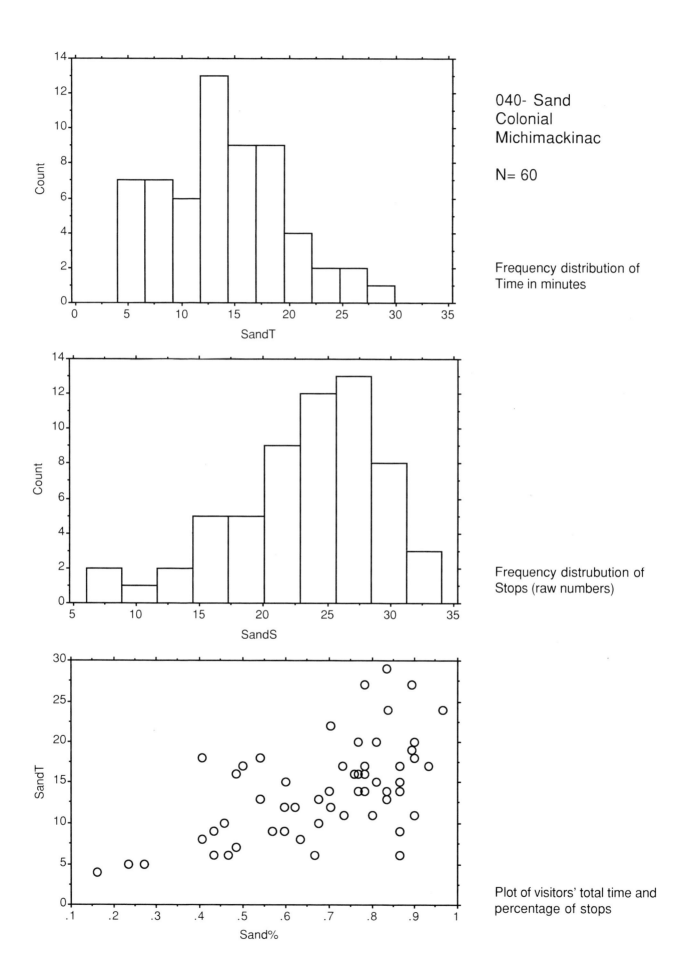

040- Sand
Colonial
Michimackinac

N= 60

Frequency distribution of
Time in minutes

Frequency distrubution of
Stops (raw numbers)

Plot of visitors' total time and
percentage of stops

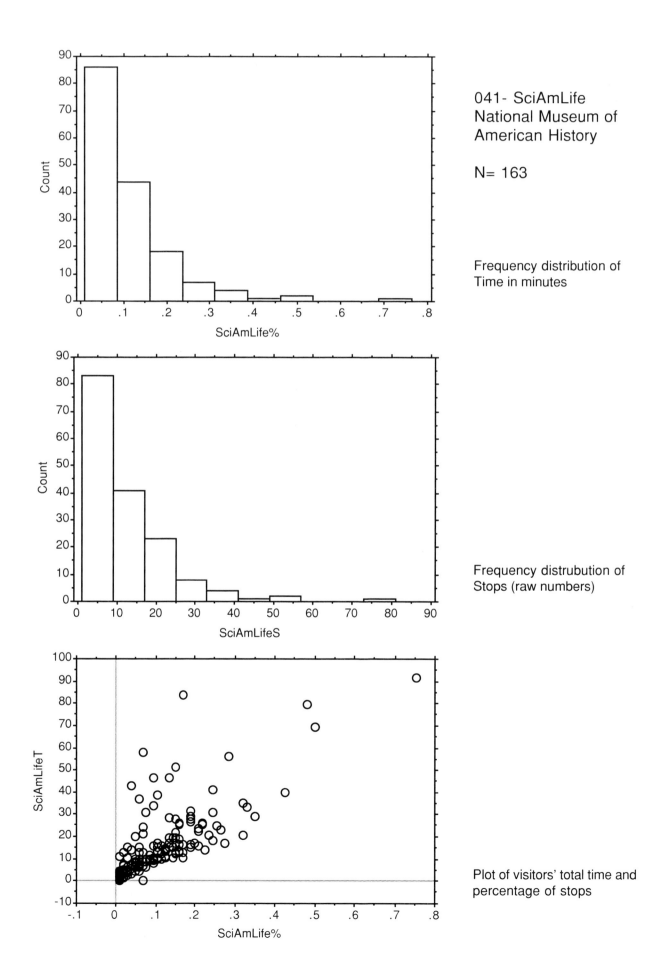

041- SciAmLife
National Museum of
American History

N= 163

Frequency distribution of
Time in minutes

Frequency distrubution of
Stops (raw numbers)

Plot of visitors' total time and
percentage of stops

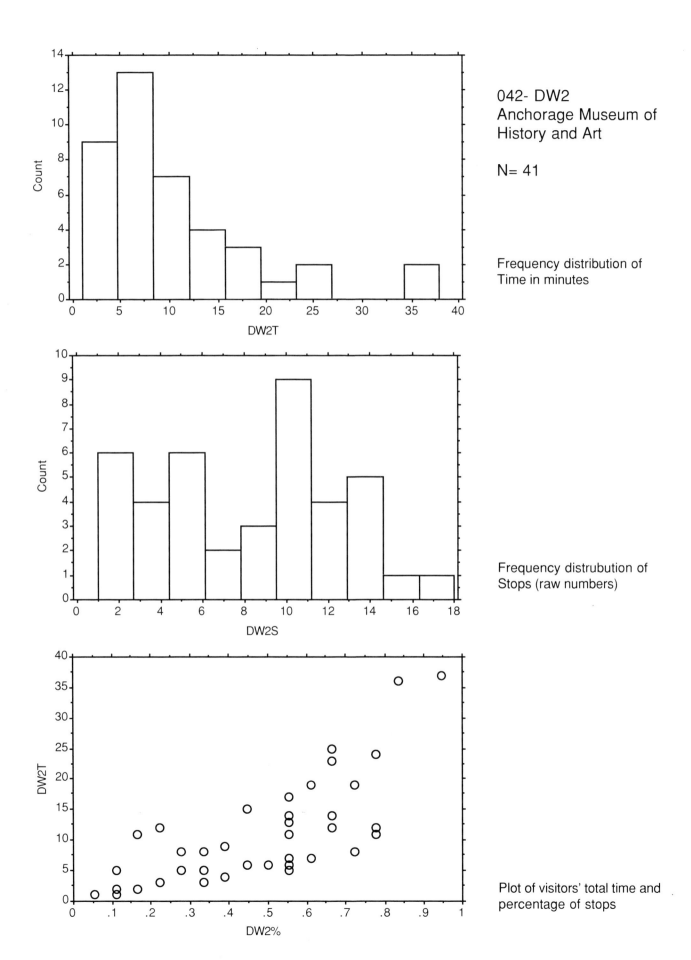

042- DW2
Anchorage Museum of
History and Art

N= 41

Frequency distribution of
Time in minutes

Frequency distrubution of
Stops (raw numbers)

Plot of visitors' total time and
percentage of stops

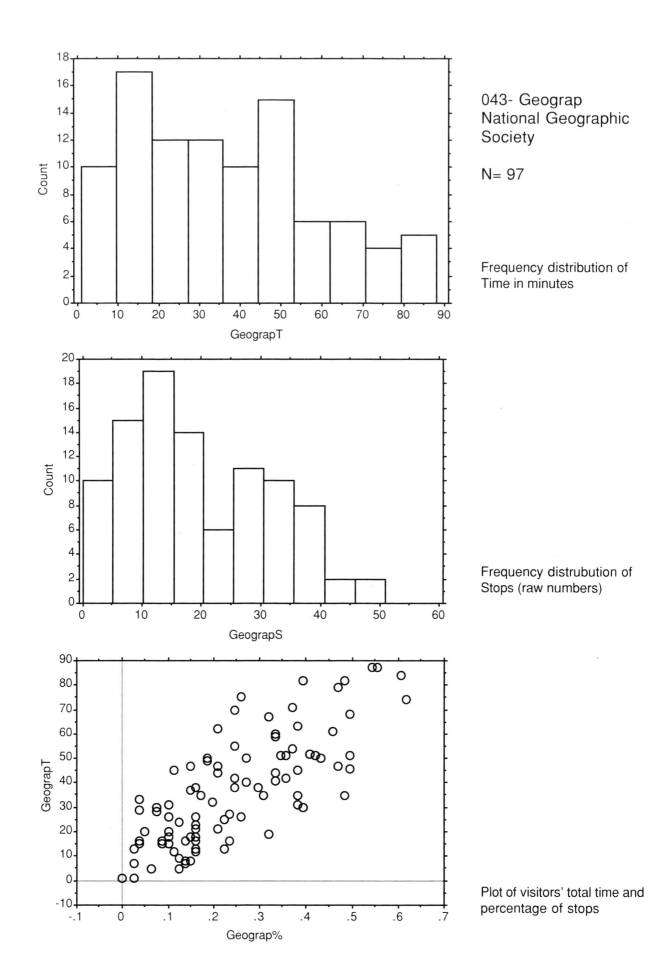

043- Geograp
National Geographic
Society

N= 97

Frequency distribution of
Time in minutes

Frequency distrubution of
Stops (raw numbers)

Plot of visitors' total time and
percentage of stops

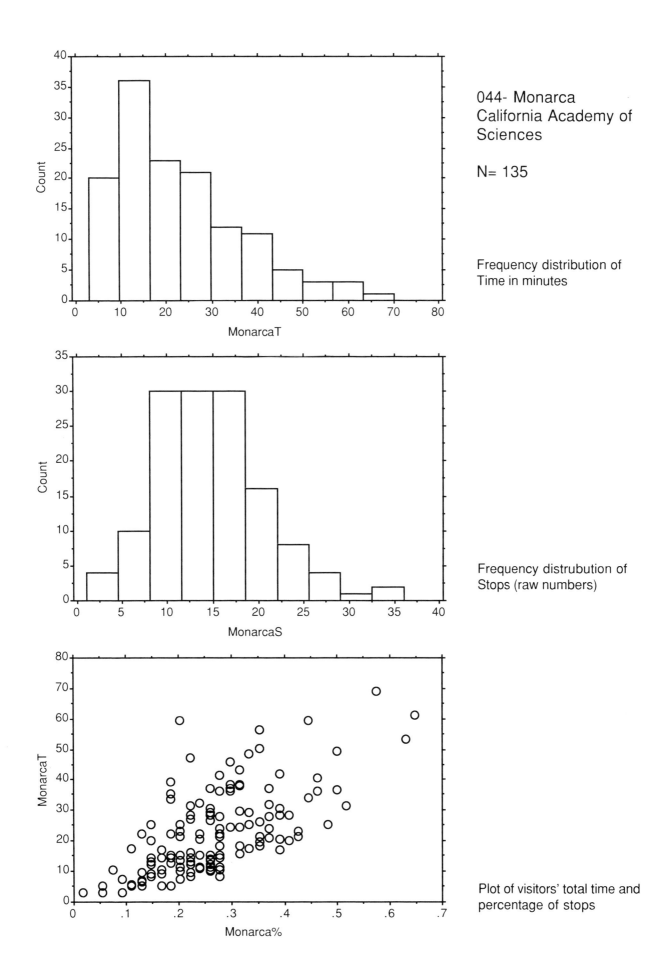

044- Monarca
California Academy of
Sciences

N= 135

Frequency distribution of
Time in minutes

Frequency distrubution of
Stops (raw numbers)

Plot of visitors' total time and
percentage of stops

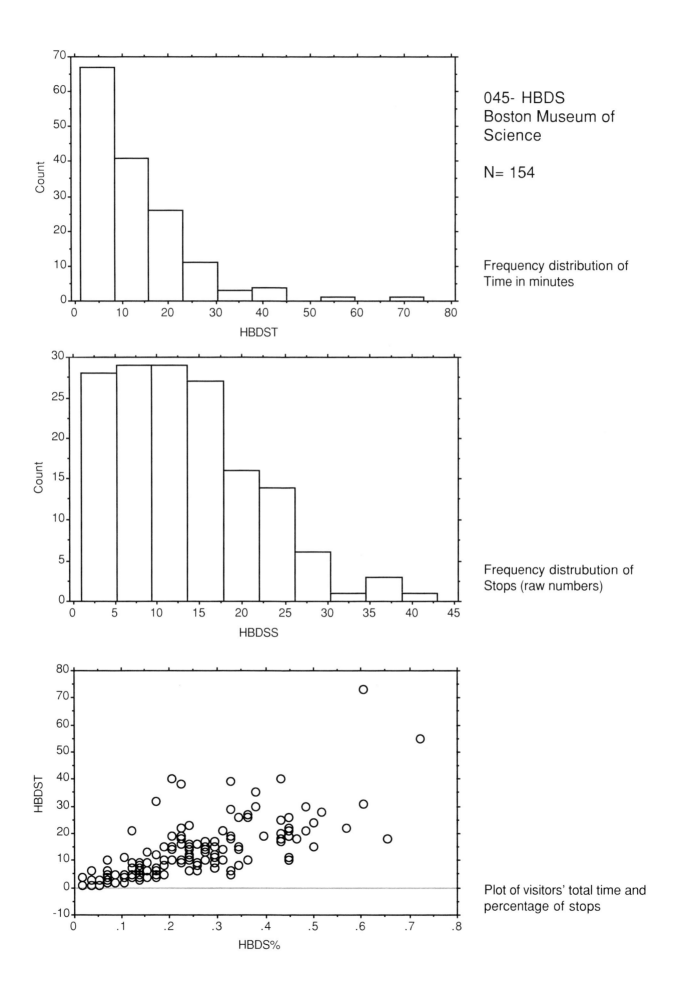

045- HBDS
Boston Museum of
Science

N= 154

Frequency distribution of
Time in minutes

Frequency distrubution of
Stops (raw numbers)

Plot of visitors' total time and
percentage of stops

At the popular Mystery Objects case, part of "The Universe In Your Hands: Early Tools of Astronomy," visitors interacted with the "slider" labels and looked closely and carefully at the instruments. Although tracking showed that most visitors did not use the exhibition thoroughly, other evaluations revealed that visitors clearly understood the main messages.

Photo courtesy of Adler Planetarium & Astronomy Museum

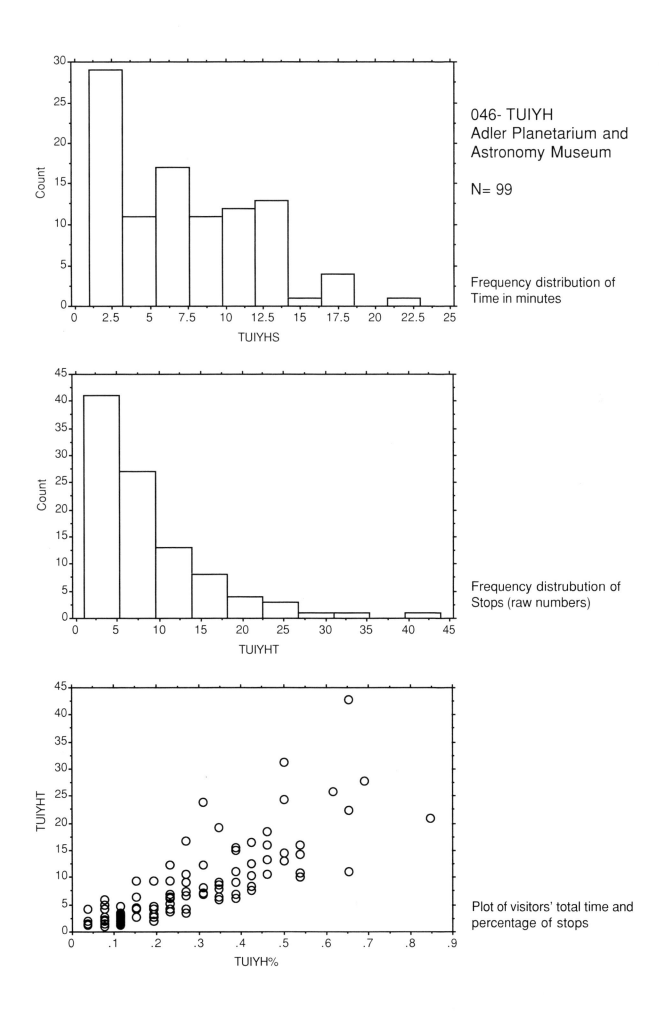

046- TUIYH
Adler Planetarium and
Astronomy Museum

N= 99

Frequency distribution of
Time in minutes

Frequency distrubution of
Stops (raw numbers)

Plot of visitors' total time and
percentage of stops

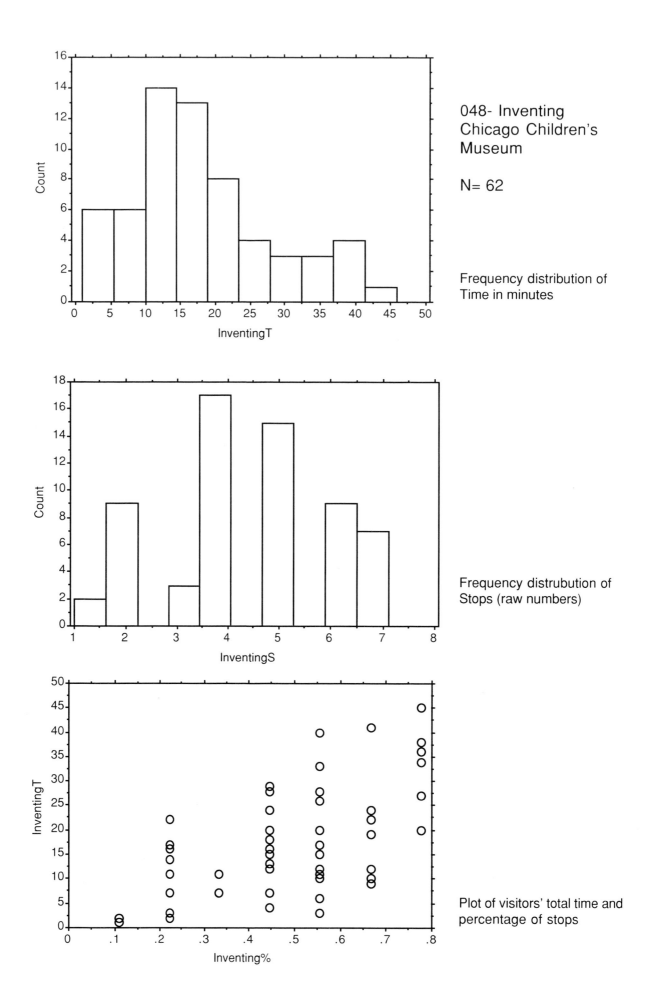

048- Inventing
Chicago Children's
Museum

N= 62

Frequency distribution of
Time in minutes

Frequency distrubution of
Stops (raw numbers)

Plot of visitors' total time and
percentage of stops

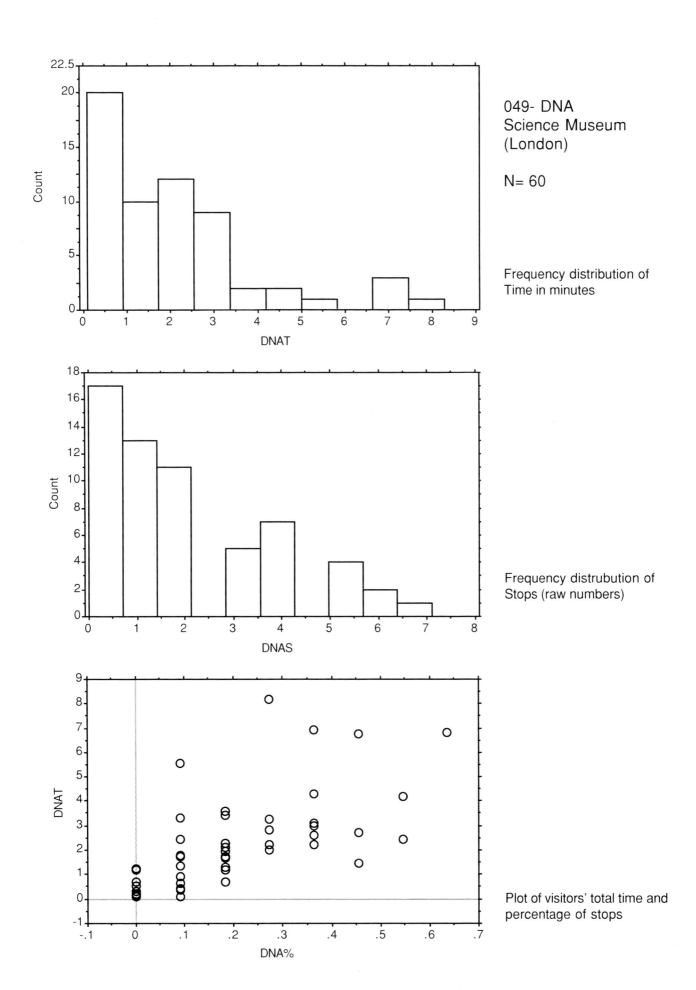

049- DNA
Science Museum
(London)

N= 60

Frequency distribution of
Time in minutes

Frequency distrubution of
Stops (raw numbers)

Plot of visitors' total time and
percentage of stops

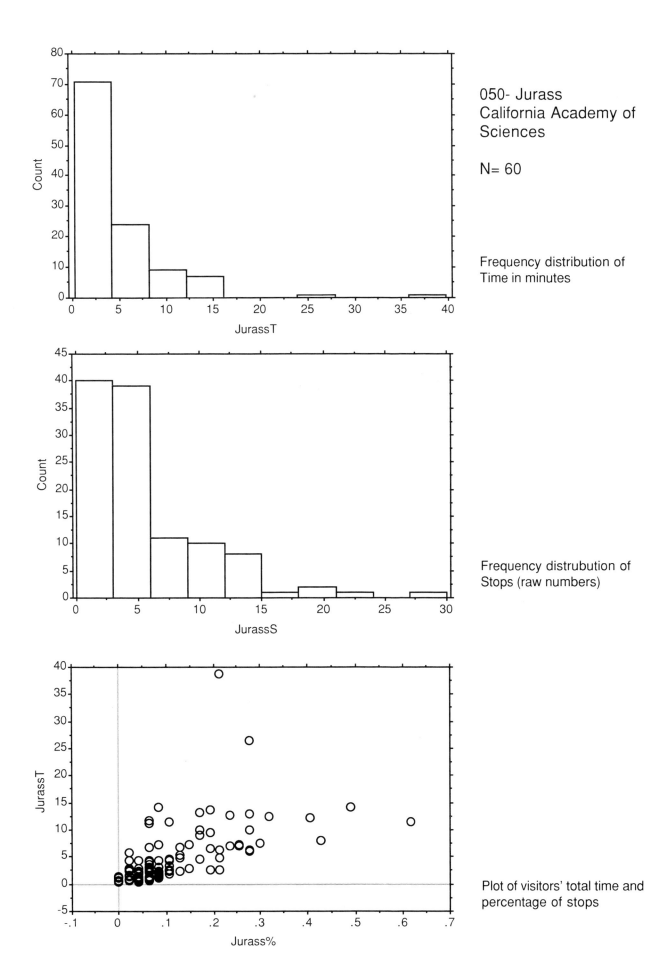

050- Jurass
California Academy of
Sciences

N= 60

Frequency distribution of
Time in minutes

Frequency distrubution of
Stops (raw numbers)

Plot of visitors' total time and
percentage of stops

A realistic cafe, alley crime scene and video autopsy contributed to the success of "Whodunit: The Science of Solving Crime." When it was pared down to fewer square feet and fewer elements (in Fort Worth, compared to Chicago), visitors used this traveling exhibit more thoroughly.

Photo courtesy of Fort Worth Museum of History and Science

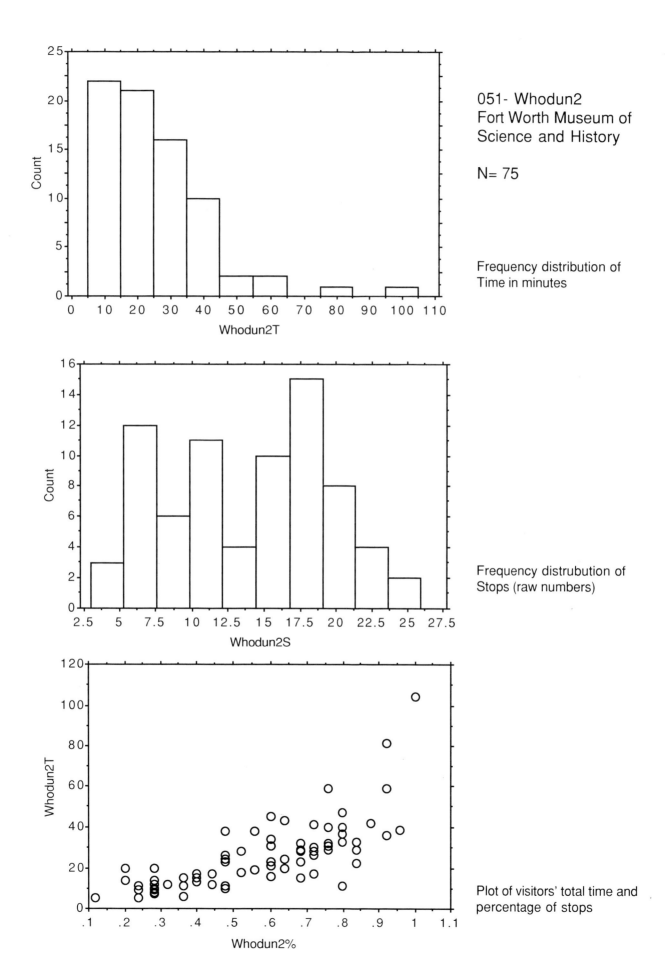

051- Whodun2
Fort Worth Museum of
Science and History

N= 75

Frequency distribution of
Time in minutes

Frequency distrubution of
Stops (raw numbers)

Plot of visitors' total time and
percentage of stops

One of the oldest exhibits at the Museum of Science and Industry in Chicago, "Prenatal Development" is a linear display of 40 embryos and fetuses. Many visitors moved slowly, spent a relatively long time, and stopped at a high percentage of the exhibit elements. Others left quickly.

Photo by the author

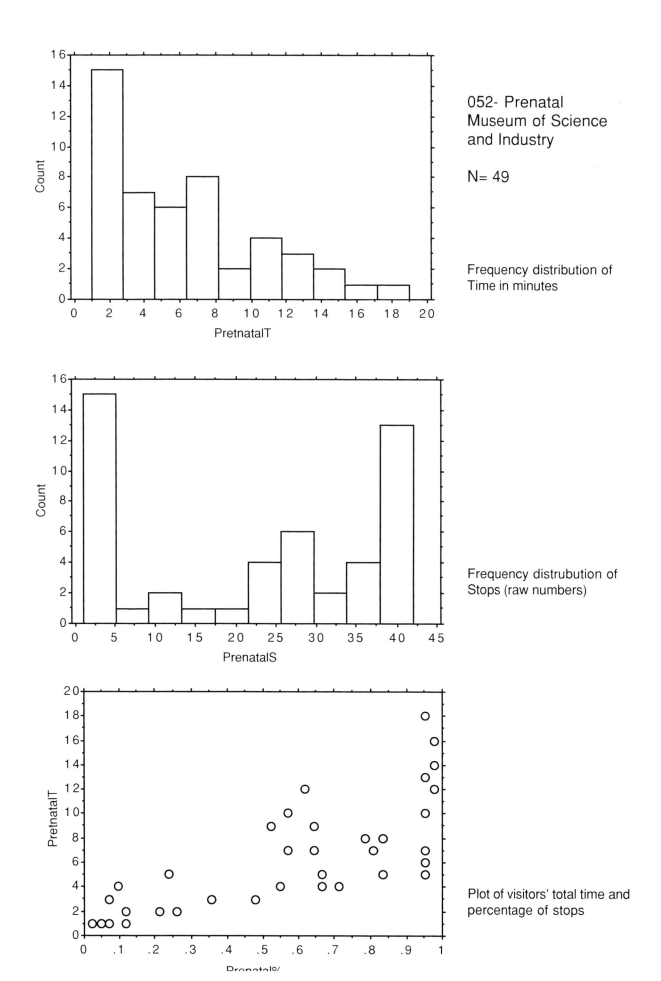

052- Prenatal
Museum of Science
and Industry

N= 49

Frequency distribution of
Time in minutes

Frequency distrubution of
Stops (raw numbers)

Plot of visitors' total time and
percentage of stops

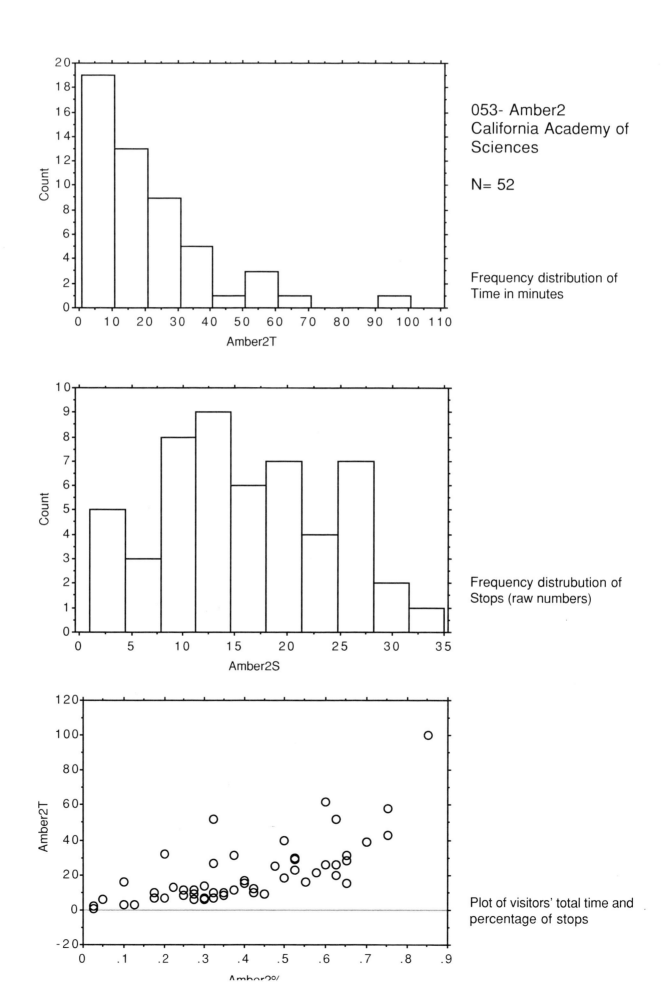

053- Amber2
California Academy of Sciences

N= 52

Frequency distribution of Time in minutes

Frequency distrubution of Stops (raw numbers)

Plot of visitors' total time and percentage of stops

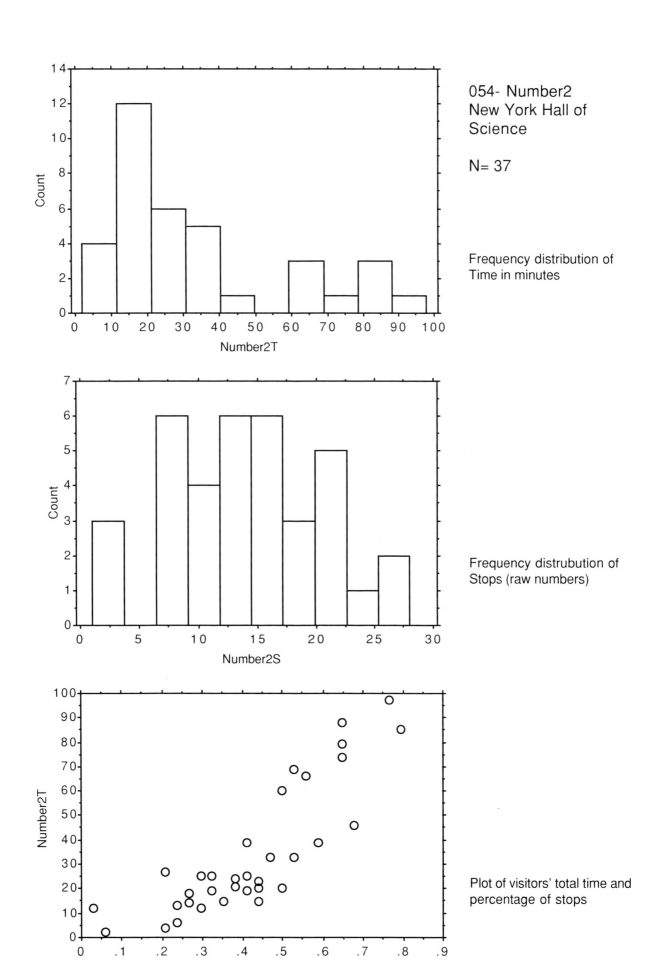

054- Number2
New York Hall of
Science

N= 37

Frequency distribution of
Time in minutes

Frequency distrubution of
Stops (raw numbers)

Plot of visitors' total time and
percentage of stops

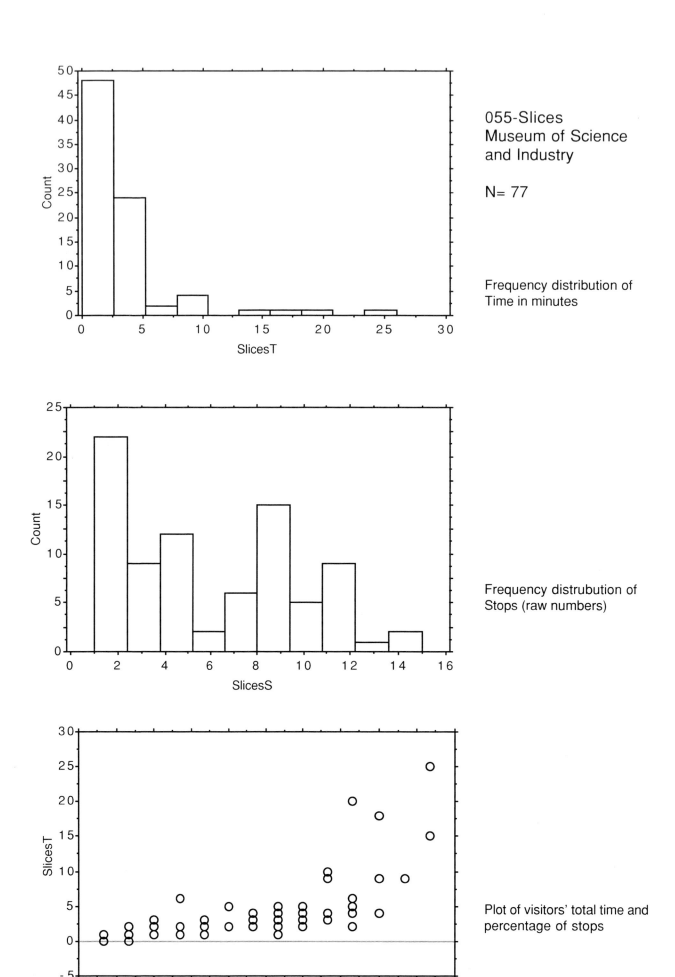

055-Slices
Museum of Science
and Industry

N= 77

Frequency distribution of
Time in minutes

Frequency distrubution of
Stops (raw numbers)

Plot of visitors' total time and
percentage of stops

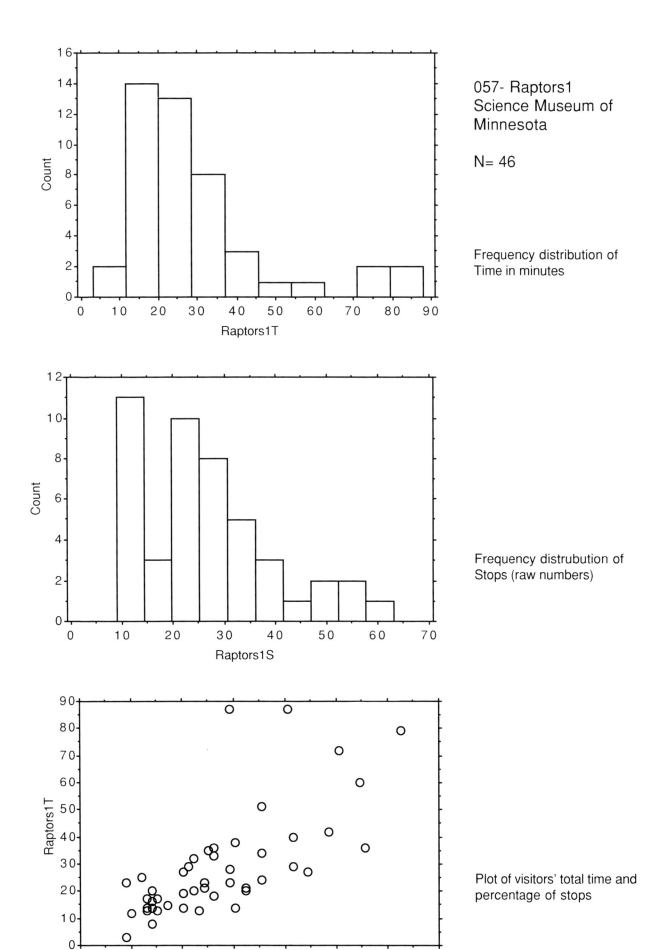

057- Raptors1
Science Museum of
Minnesota

N= 46

Frequency distribution of
Time in minutes

Frequency distrubution of
Stops (raw numbers)

Plot of visitors' total time and
percentage of stops

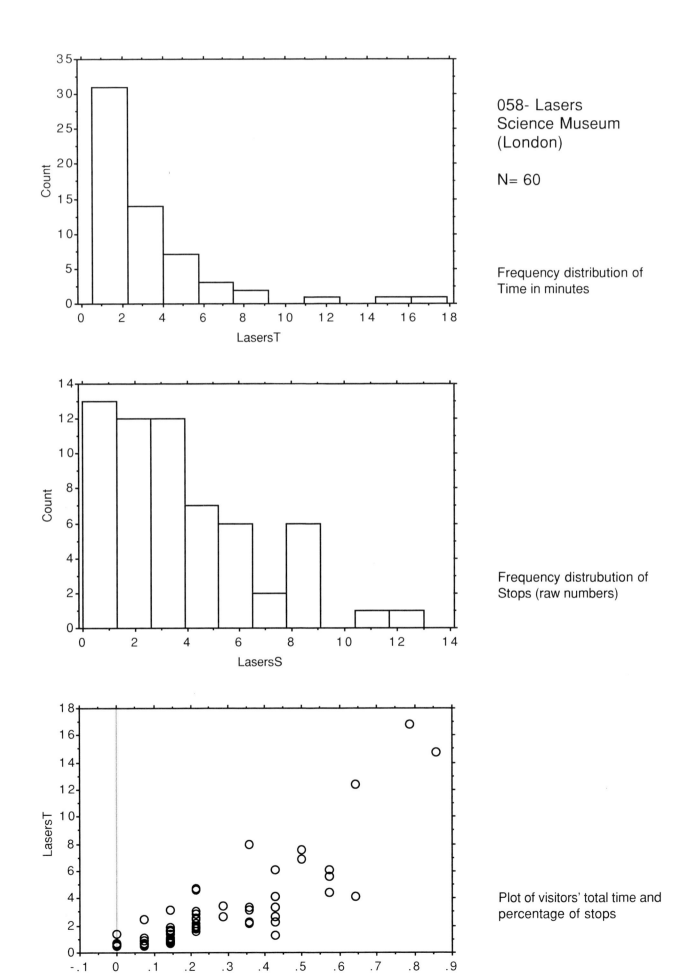

058- Lasers
Science Museum
(London)

N= 60

Frequency distribution of
Time in minutes

Frequency distrubution of
Stops (raw numbers)

Plot of visitors' total time and
percentage of stops

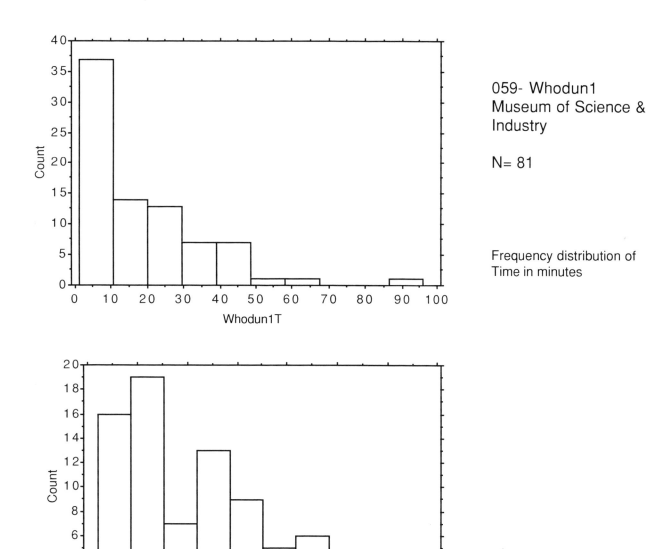

059- Whodun1
Museum of Science &
Industry

N= 81

Frequency distribution of
Time in minutes

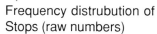

Frequency distrubution of
Stops (raw numbers)

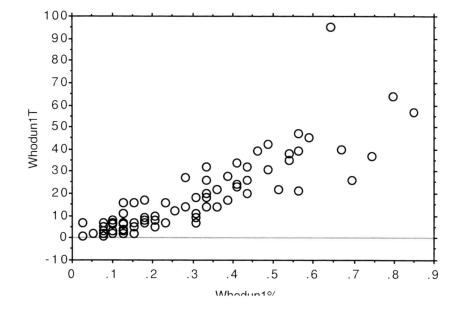

Plot of visitors' total time and
percentage of stops

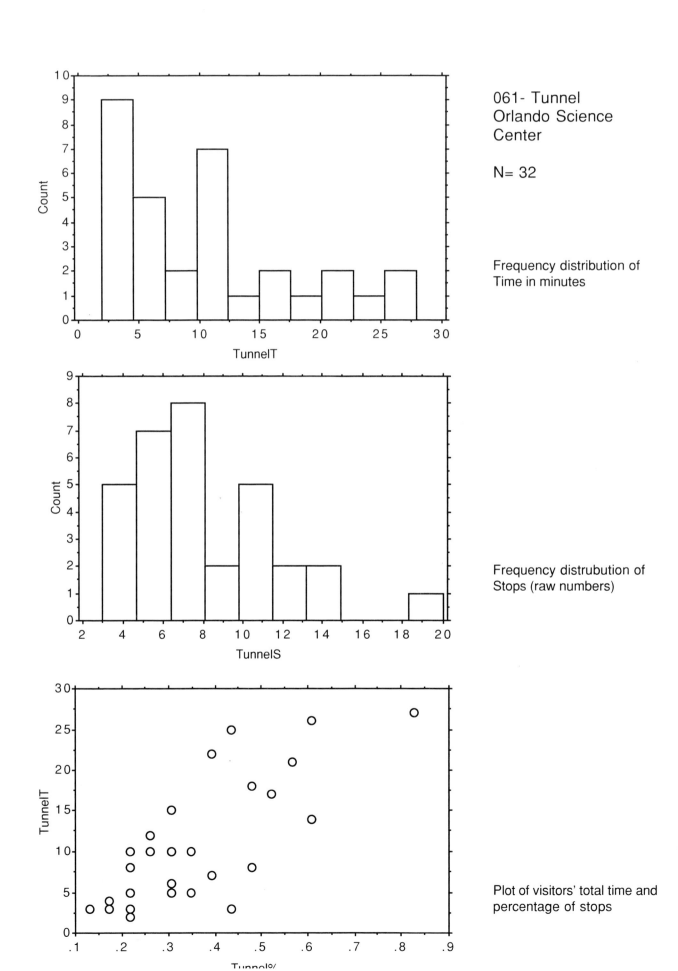

061- Tunnel
Orlando Science
Center

N= 32

Frequency distribution of
Time in minutes

Frequency distrubution of
Stops (raw numbers)

Plot of visitors' total time and
percentage of stops

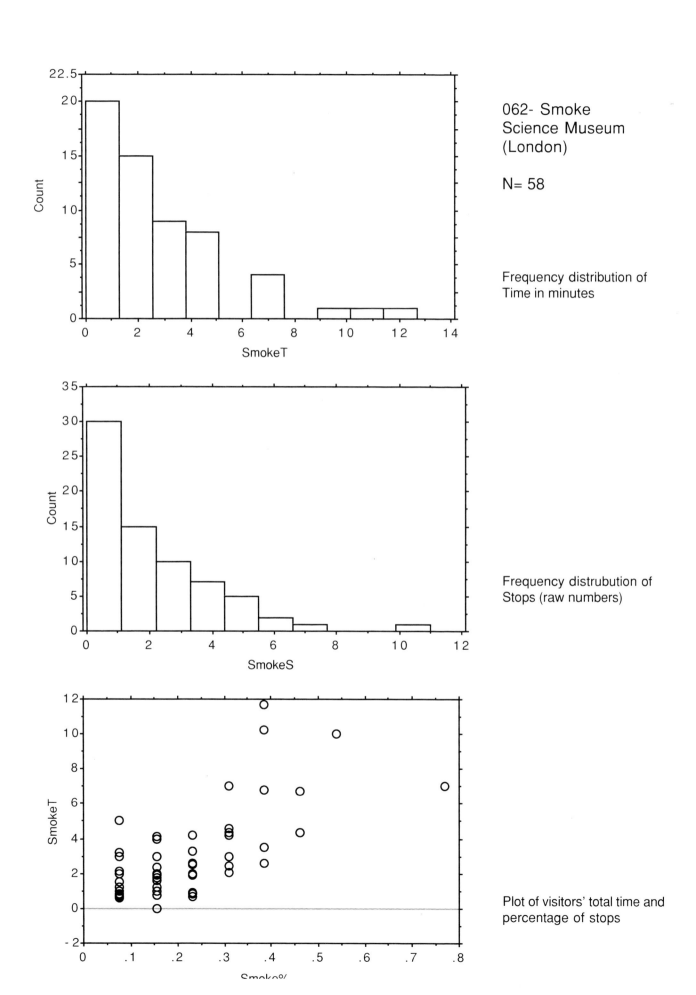

062- Smoke
Science Museum
(London)

N= 58

Frequency distribution of
Time in minutes

Frequency distrubution of
Stops (raw numbers)

Plot of visitors' total time and
percentage of stops

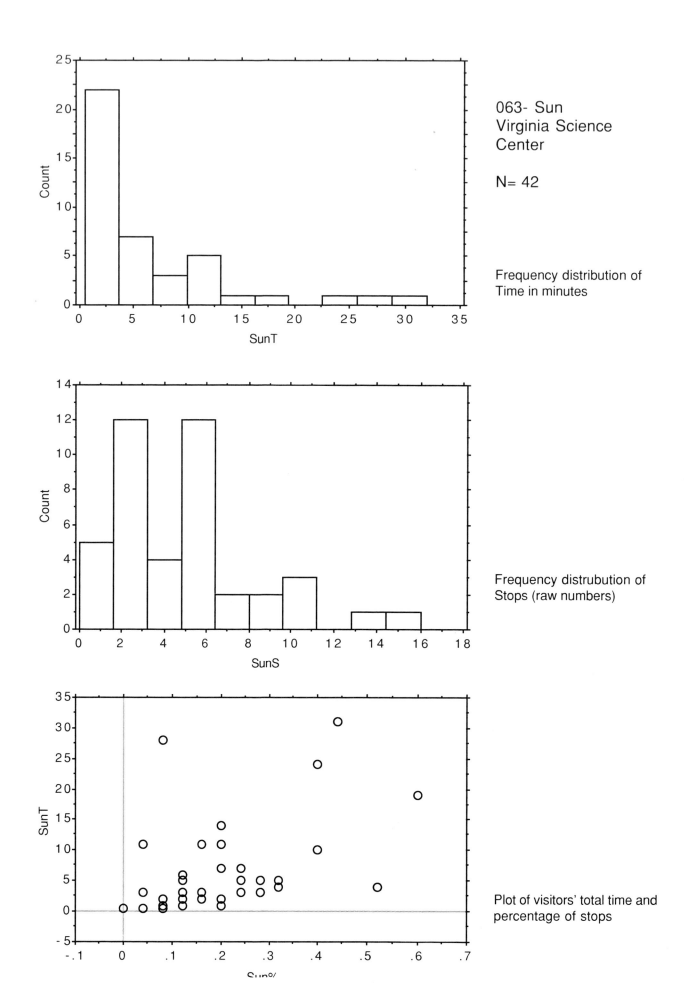

063- Sun
Virginia Science
Center

N= 42

Frequency distribution of
Time in minutes

Frequency distrubution of
Stops (raw numbers)

Plot of visitors' total time and
percentage of stops

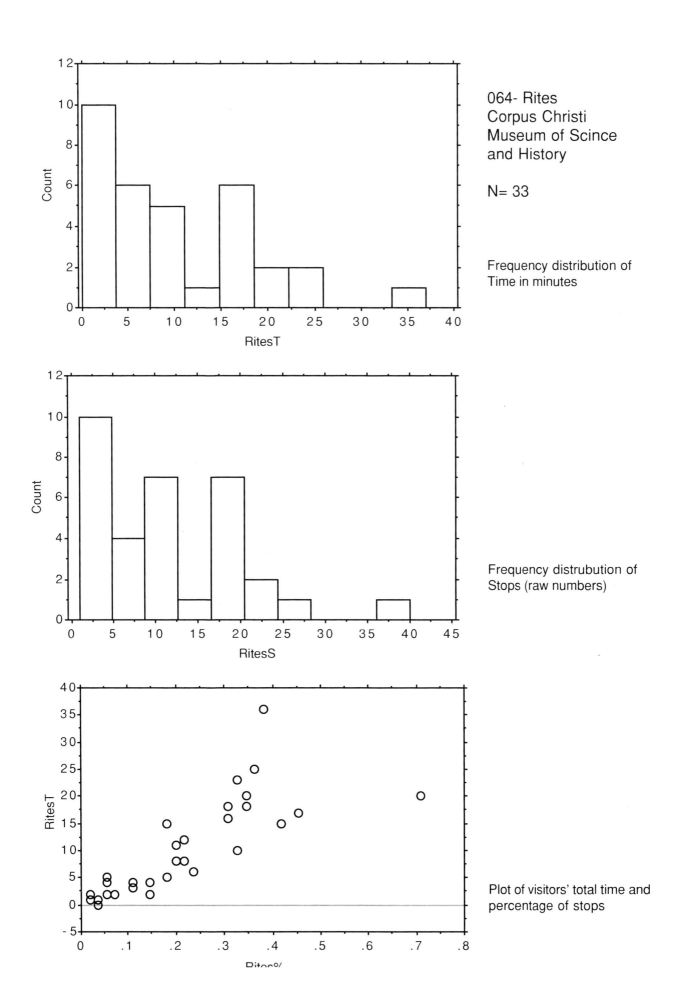

064- Rites
Corpus Christi
Museum of Scince
and History

N= 33

Frequency distribution of
Time in minutes

Frequency distrubution of
Stops (raw numbers)

Plot of visitors' total time and
percentage of stops

Interaction, clarity of content, and an element of surprise held visitors' attention and communicated effectively at this exhibit in "Molecules in Motion" at the California Museum of Science and Industry. Most of the exhibit elements were used by a majority of visitors, but not all of the components successfully communicated their messages about chemistry.

Photo by the author

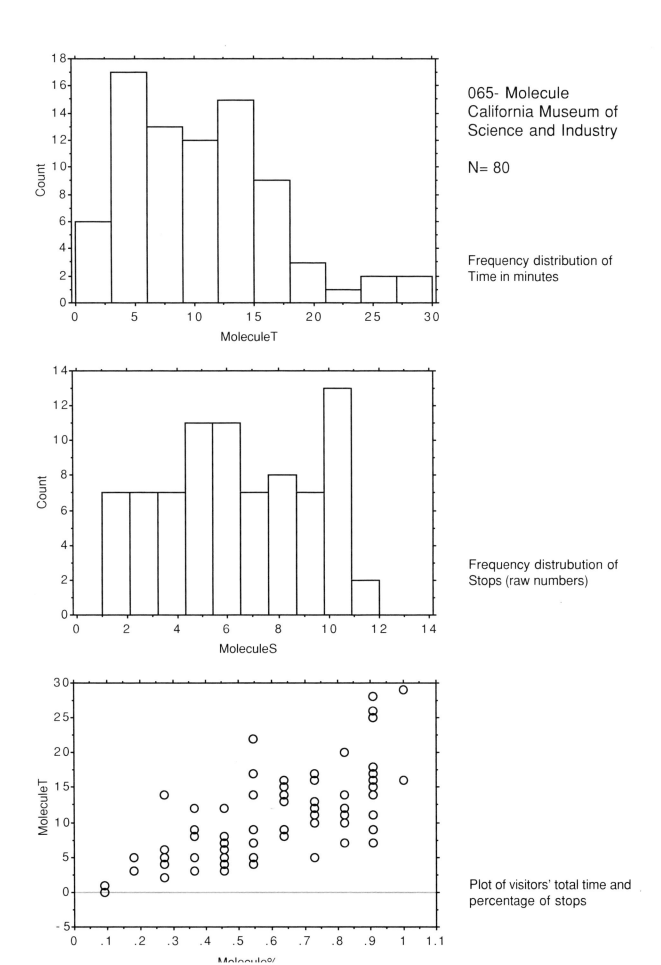

065- Molecule
California Museum of
Science and Industry

N= 80

Frequency distribution of
Time in minutes

Frequency distrubution of
Stops (raw numbers)

Plot of visitors' total time and
percentage of stops

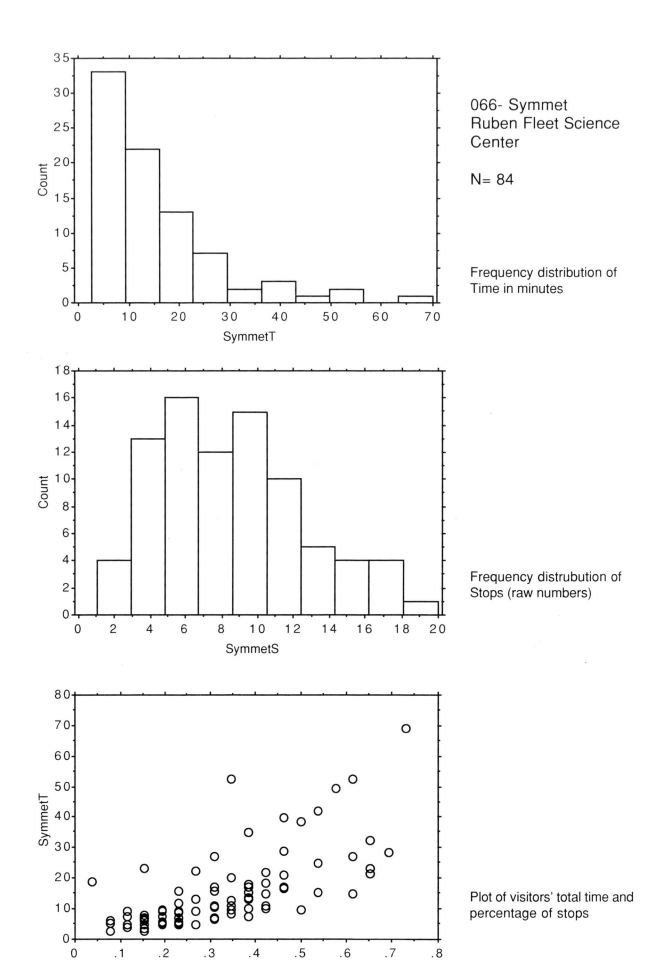

066- Symmet
Ruben Fleet Science
Center

N= 84

Frequency distribution of
Time in minutes

Frequency distrubution of
Stops (raw numbers)

Plot of visitors' total time and
percentage of stops

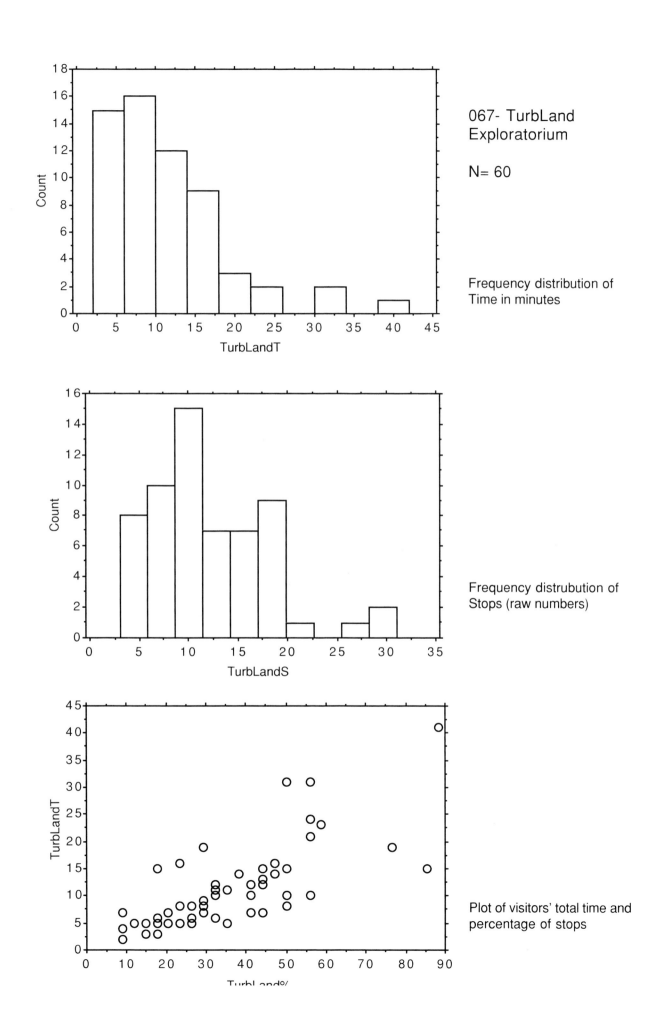

067- TurbLand Exploratorium

N= 60

Frequency distribution of Time in minutes

Frequency distrubution of Stops (raw numbers)

Plot of visitors' total time and percentage of stops

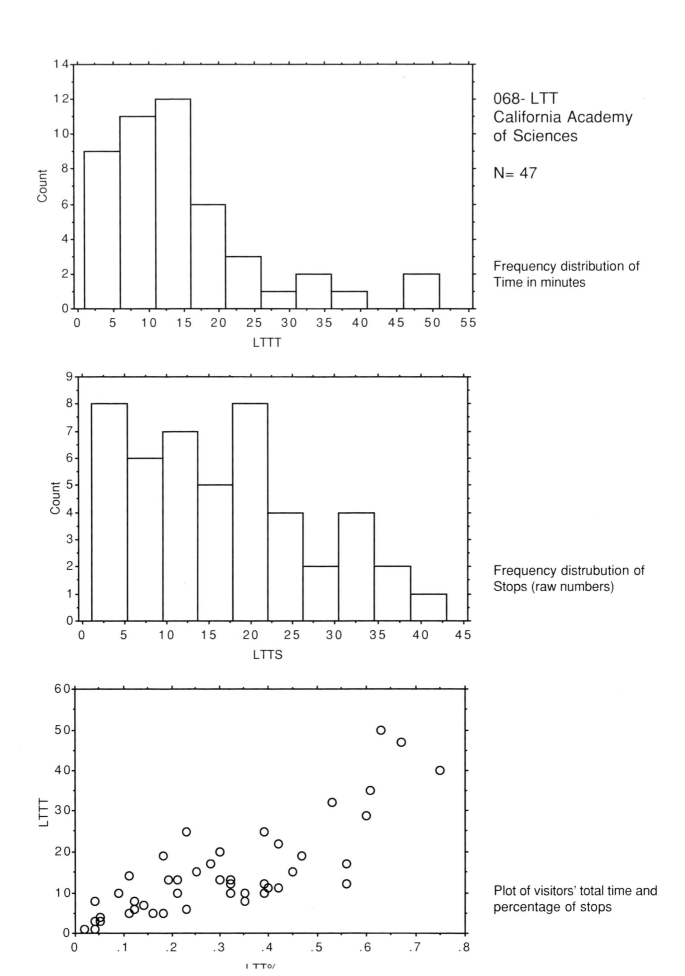

068- LTT
California Academy
of Sciences

N= 47

Frequency distribution of
Time in minutes

Frequency distrubution of
Stops (raw numbers)

Plot of visitors' total time and
percentage of stops

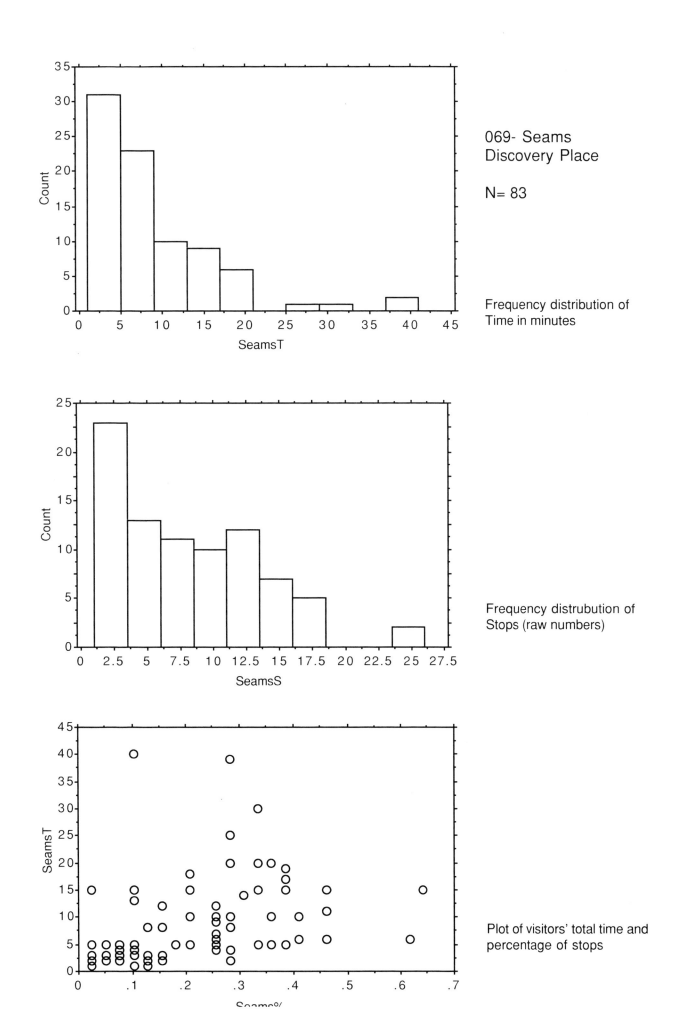

069- Seams
Discovery Place

N= 83

Frequency distribution of
Time in minutes

Frequency distrubution of
Stops (raw numbers)

Plot of visitors' total time and
percentage of stops

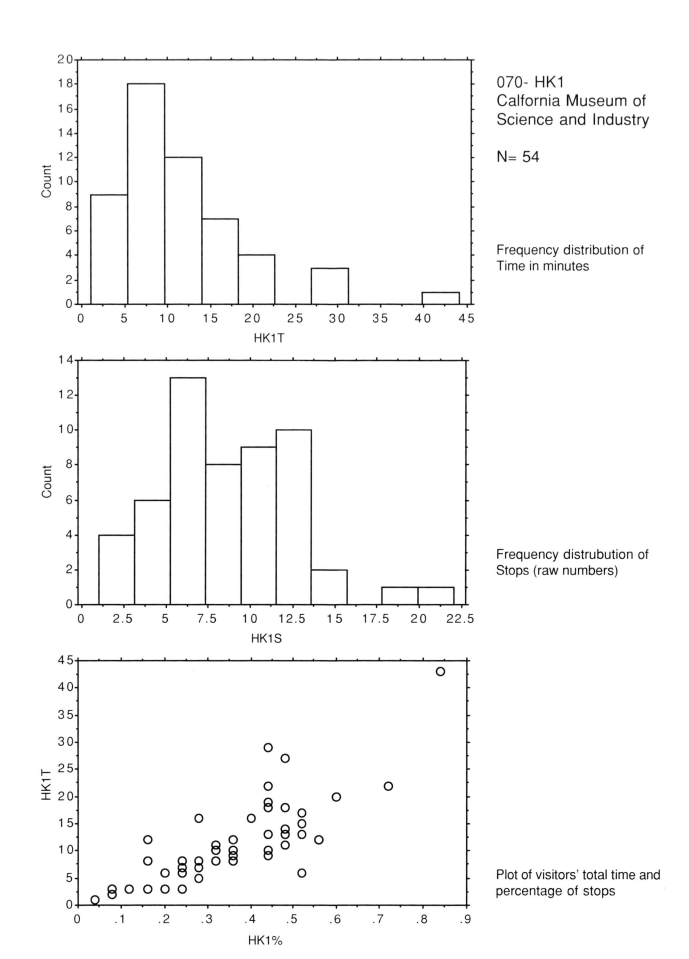

070- HK1
Calfornia Museum of
Science and Industry

N= 54

Frequency distribution of
Time in minutes

Frequency distrubution of
Stops (raw numbers)

Plot of visitors' total time and
percentage of stops

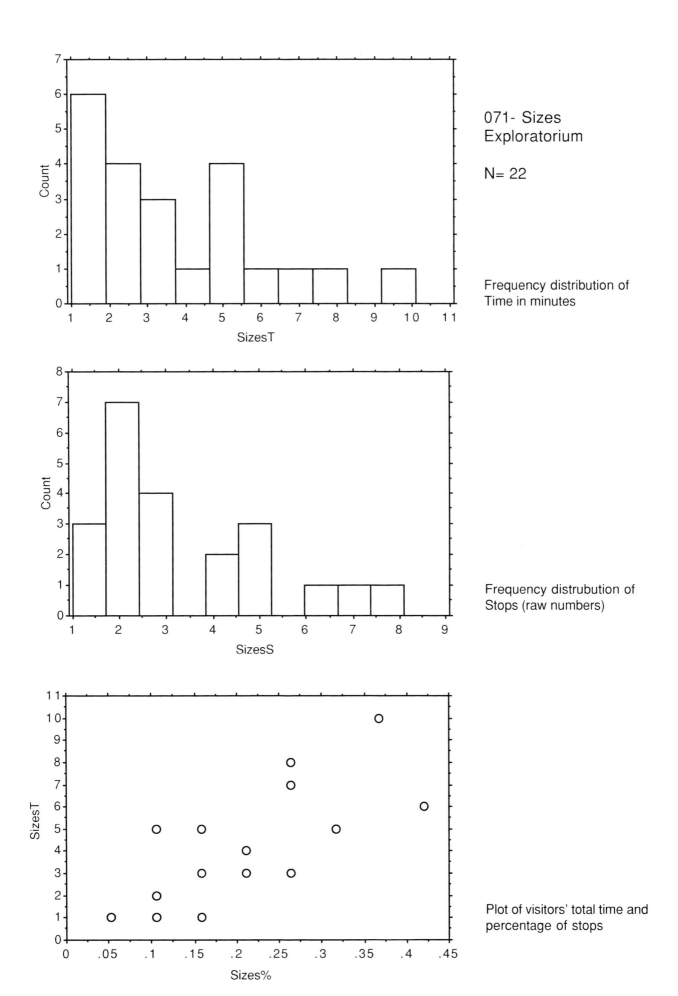

071- Sizes
Exploratorium

N= 22

Frequency distribution of
Time in minutes

Frequency distrubution of
Stops (raw numbers)

Plot of visitors' total time and
percentage of stops

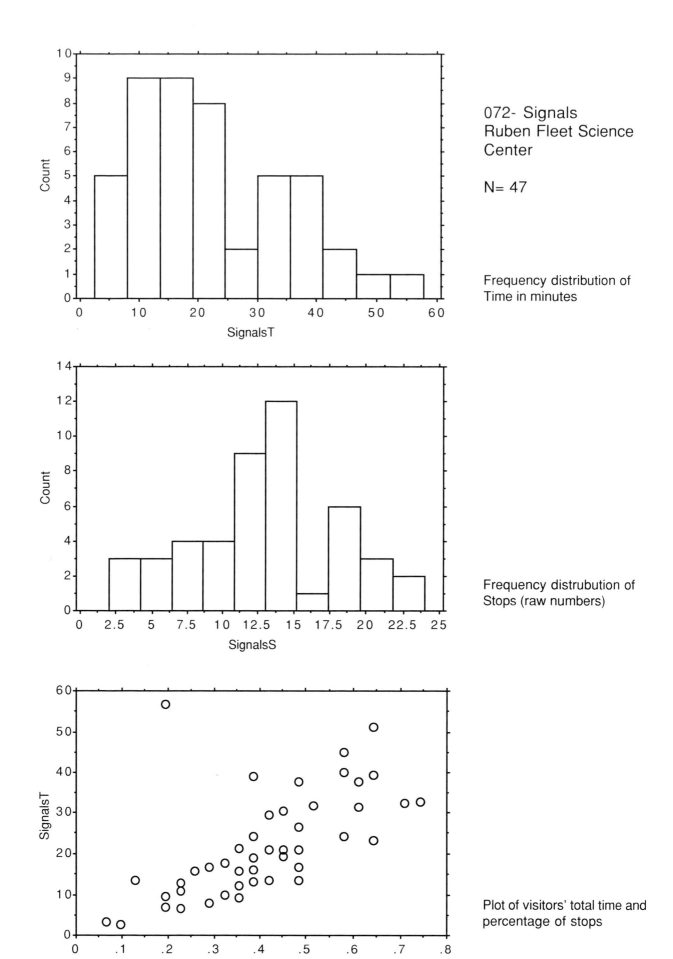

072- Signals
Ruben Fleet Science
Center

N= 47

Frequency distribution of
Time in minutes

Frequency distrubution of
Stops (raw numbers)

Plot of visitors' total time and
percentage of stops

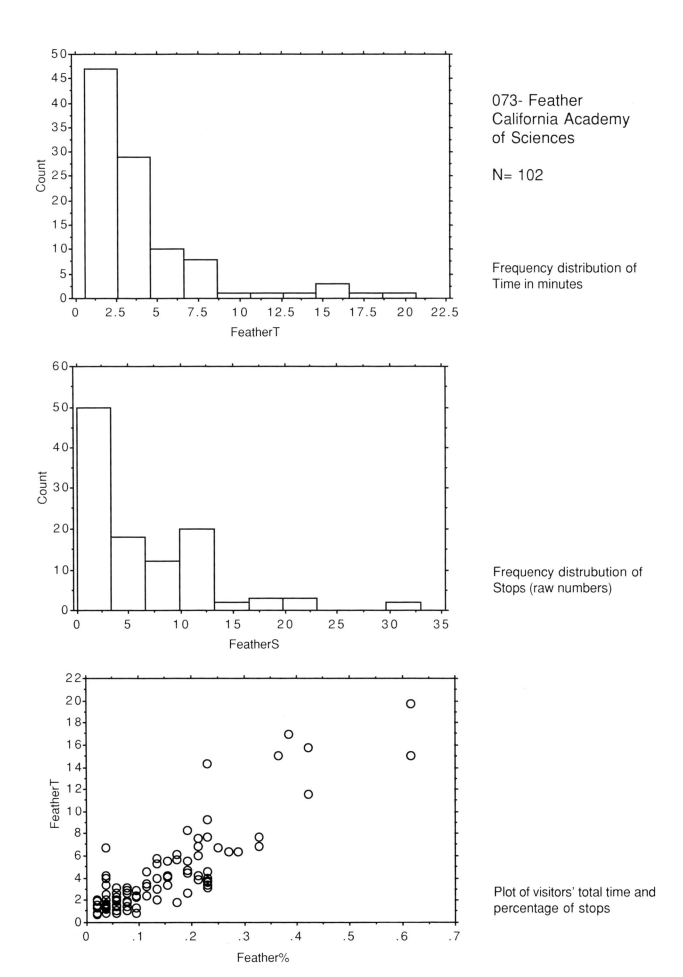

073- Feather
California Academy
of Sciences

N= 102

Frequency distribution of
Time in minutes

Frequency distrubution of
Stops (raw numbers)

Plot of visitors' total time and
percentage of stops

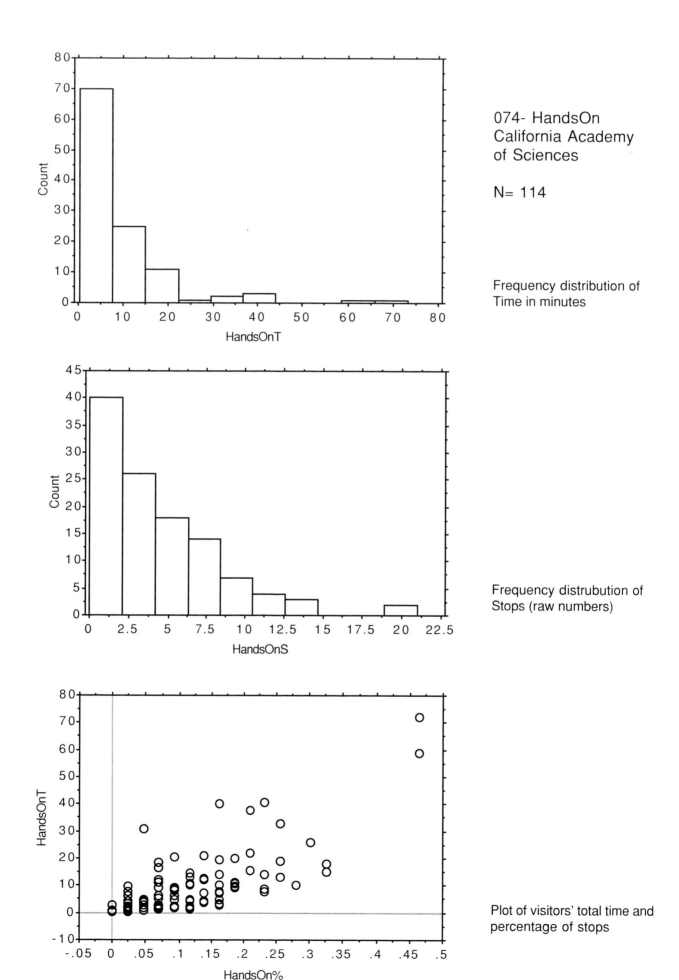

074- HandsOn
California Academy
of Sciences

N= 114

Frequency distribution of
Time in minutes

Frequency distrubution of
Stops (raw numbers)

Plot of visitors' total time and
percentage of stops

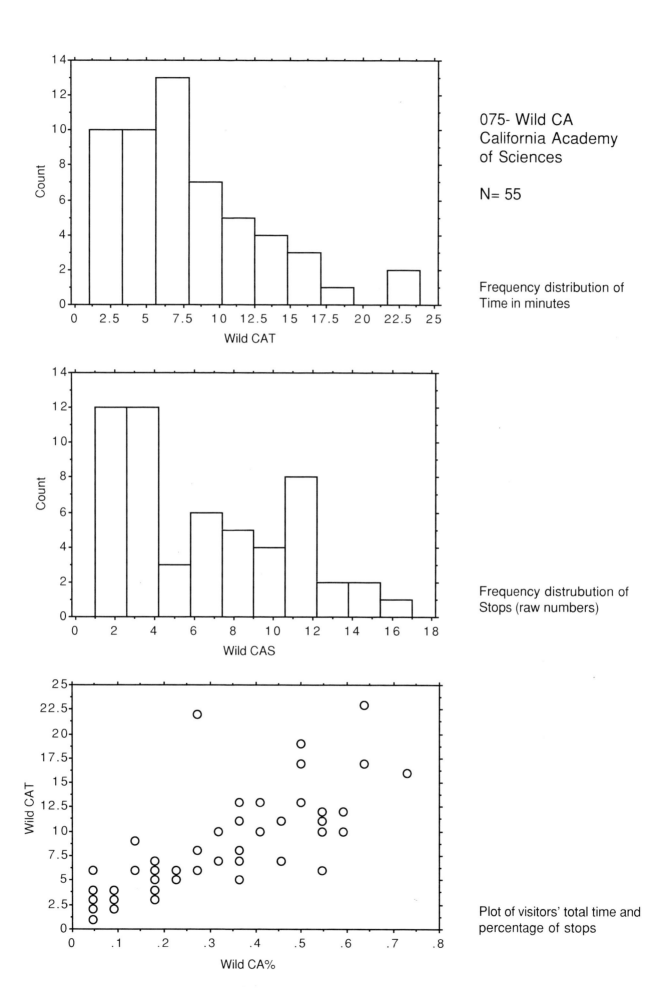

075- Wild CA
California Academy
of Sciences

N= 55

Frequency distribution of
Time in minutes

Frequency distrubution of
Stops (raw numbers)

Plot of visitors' total time and
percentage of stops

Typically, a majority of visitors do not stop at introductory exhibits, but in "From Bustles to Bikinis," far more visitors than usual did stop. Visitors also stopped at a high percentage of elements throughout the exhibition, making it one of the most thoroughly used in the Paying Attention study.

Photo courtesy of San Diego Historical Society/Carina Woolrich Photography

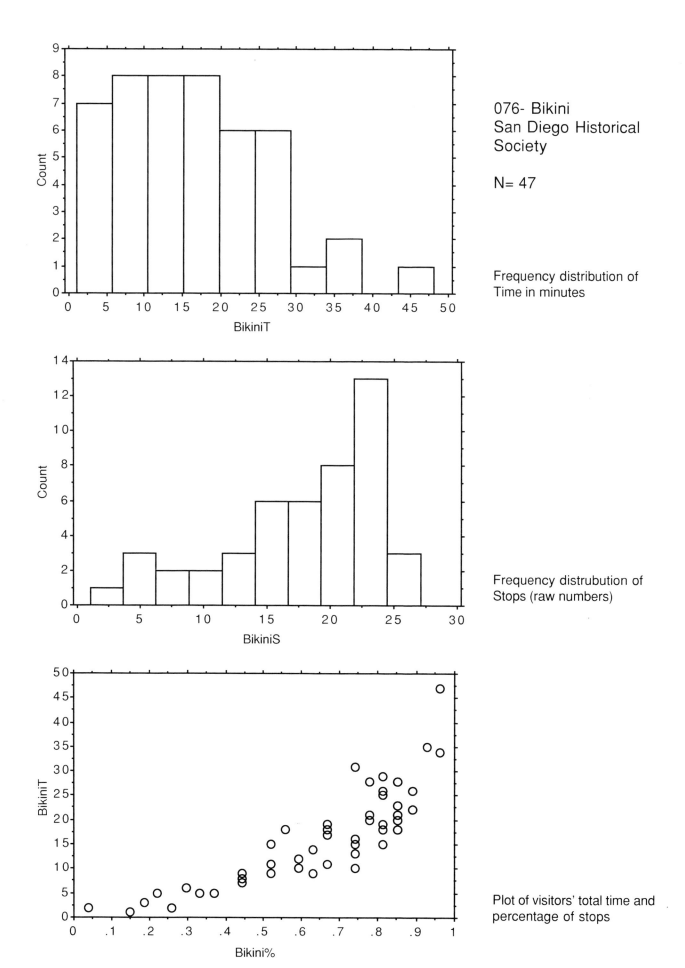

076- Bikini
San Diego Historical
Society

N= 47

Frequency distribution of
Time in minutes

Frequency distrubution of
Stops (raw numbers)

Plot of visitors' total time and
percentage of stops

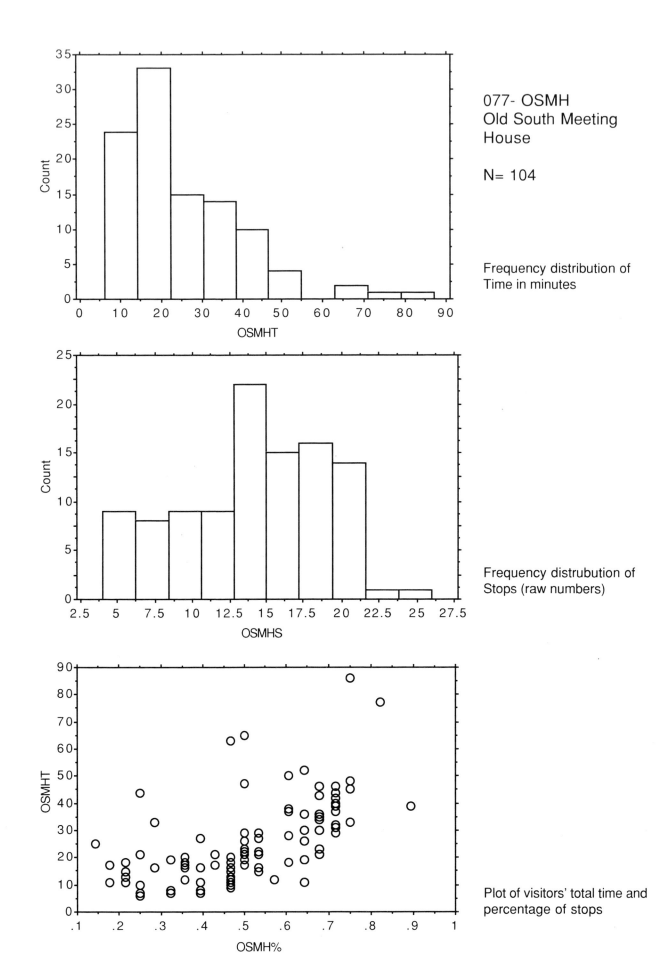

077- OSMH
Old South Meeting
House

N= 104

Frequency distribution of
Time in minutes

Frequency distrubution of
Stops (raw numbers)

Plot of visitors' total time and
percentage of stops

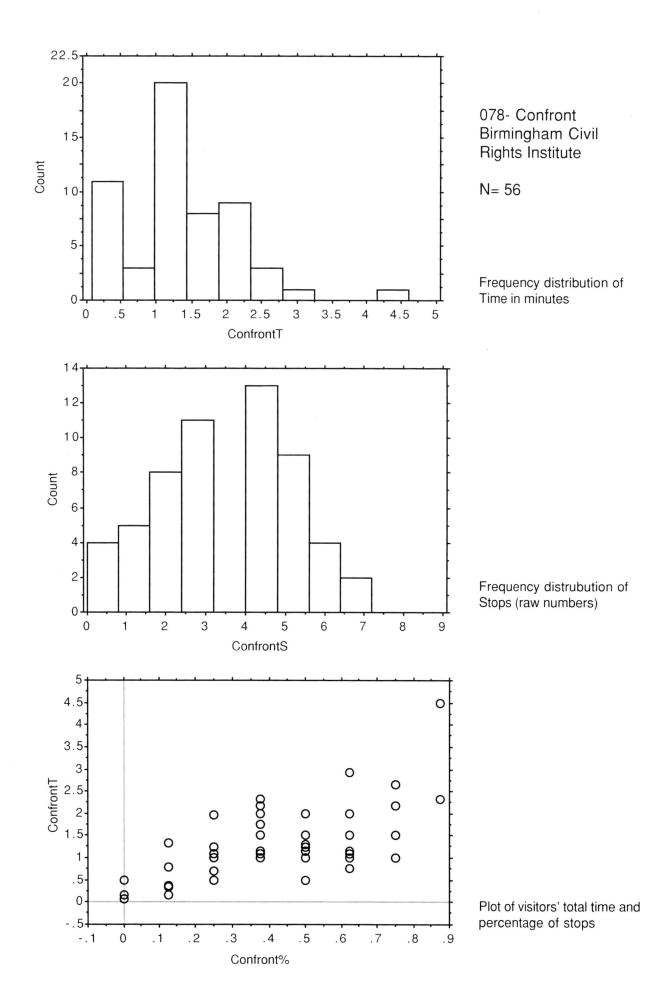

078- Confront
Birmingham Civil
Rights Institute

N= 56

Frequency distribution of
Time in minutes

Frequency distrubution of
Stops (raw numbers)

Plot of visitors' total time and
percentage of stops

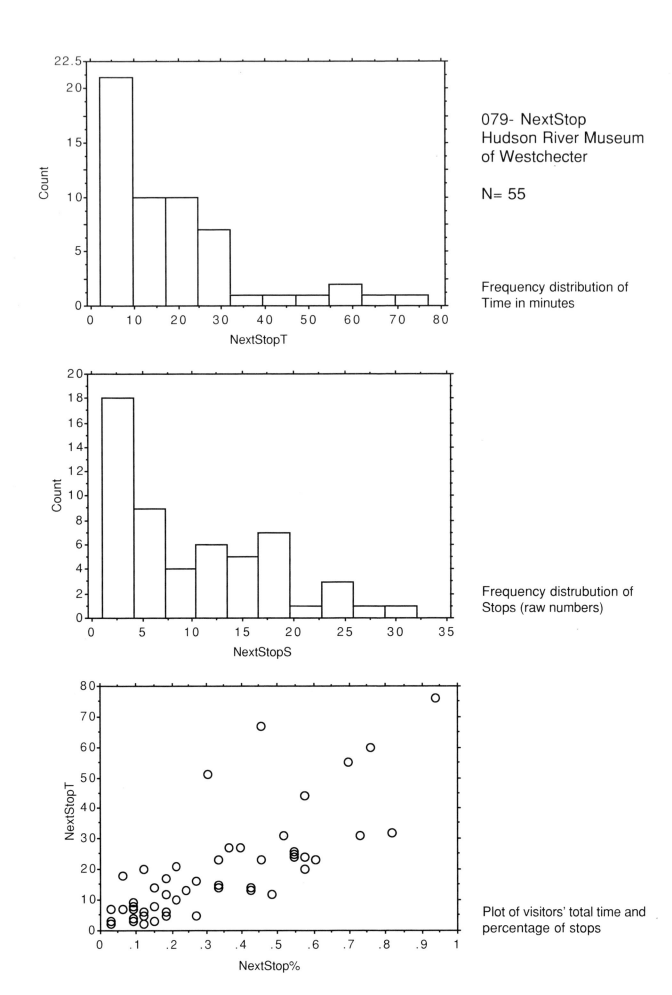

079- NextStop
Hudson River Museum
of Westchecter

N= 55

Frequency distribution of
Time in minutes

Frequency distrubution of
Stops (raw numbers)

Plot of visitors' total time and
percentage of stops

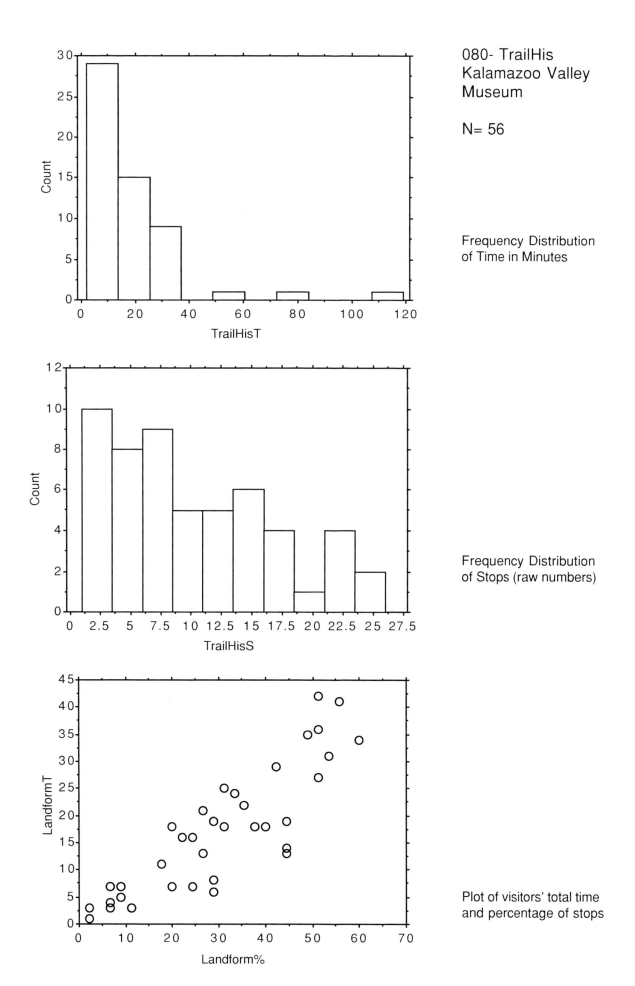

080- TrailHis
Kalamazoo Valley
Museum

N= 56

Frequency Distribution
of Time in Minutes

Frequency Distribution
of Stops (raw numbers)

Plot of visitors' total time
and percentage of stops

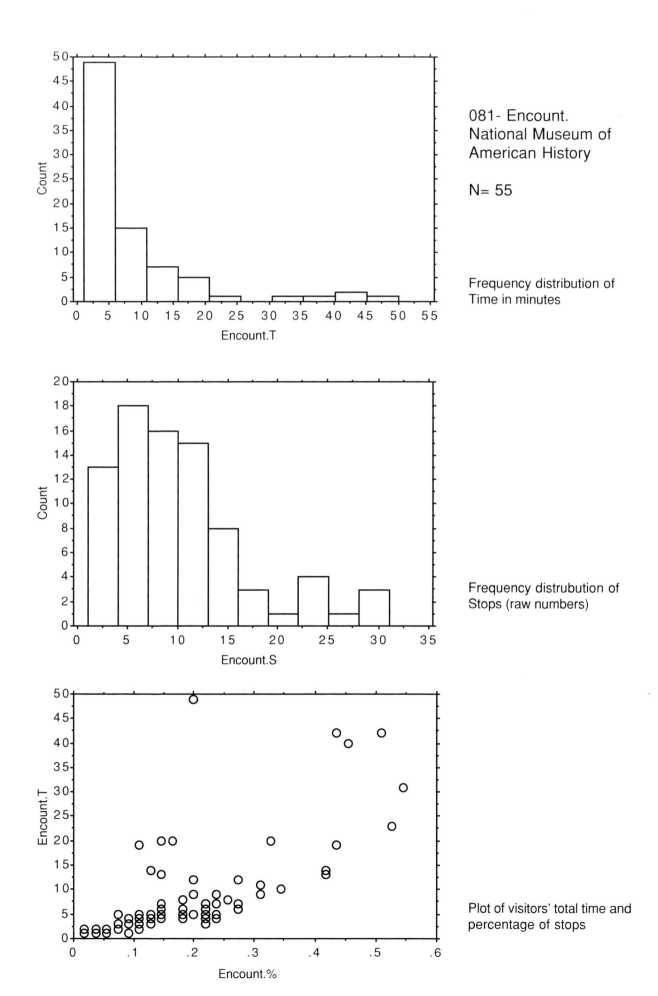

081- Encount.
National Museum of
American History

N= 55

Frequency distribution of
Time in minutes

Frequency distrubution of
Stops (raw numbers)

Plot of visitors' total time and
percentage of stops

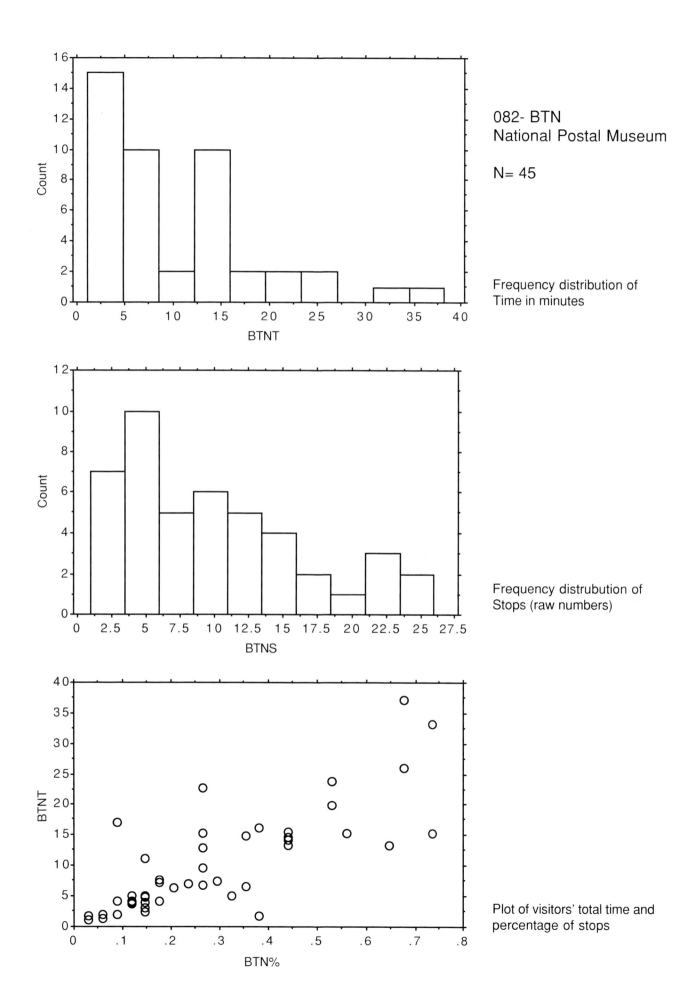

082- BTN
National Postal Museum

N= 45

Frequency distribution of
Time in minutes

Frequency distrubution of
Stops (raw numbers)

Plot of visitors' total time and
percentage of stops

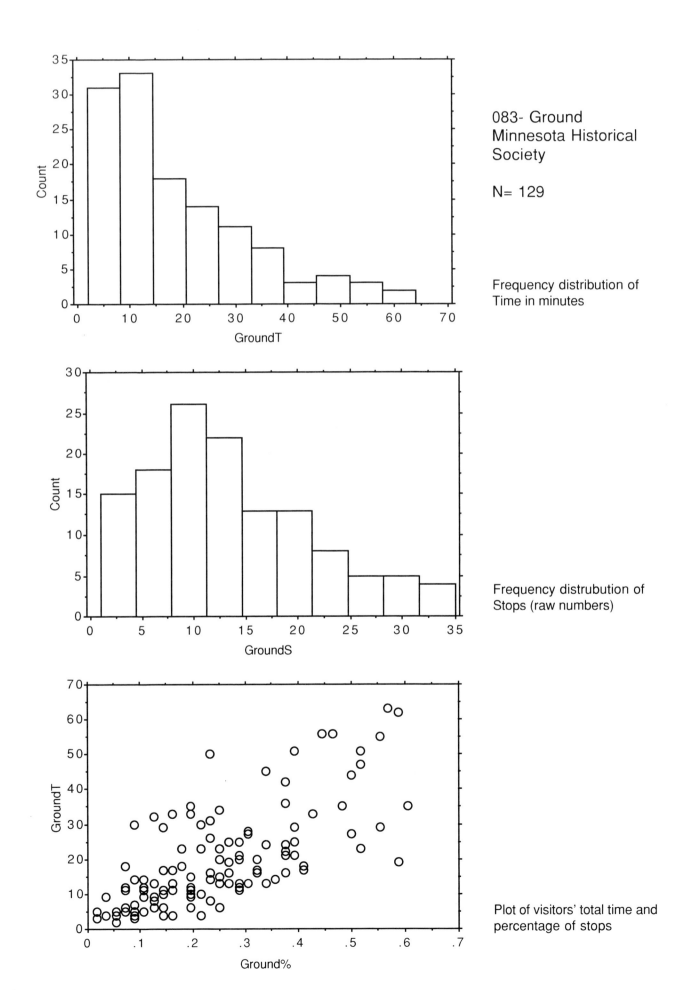

083- Ground
Minnesota Historical
Society

N= 129

Frequency distribution of
Time in minutes

Frequency distrubution of
Stops (raw numbers)

Plot of visitors' total time and
percentage of stops

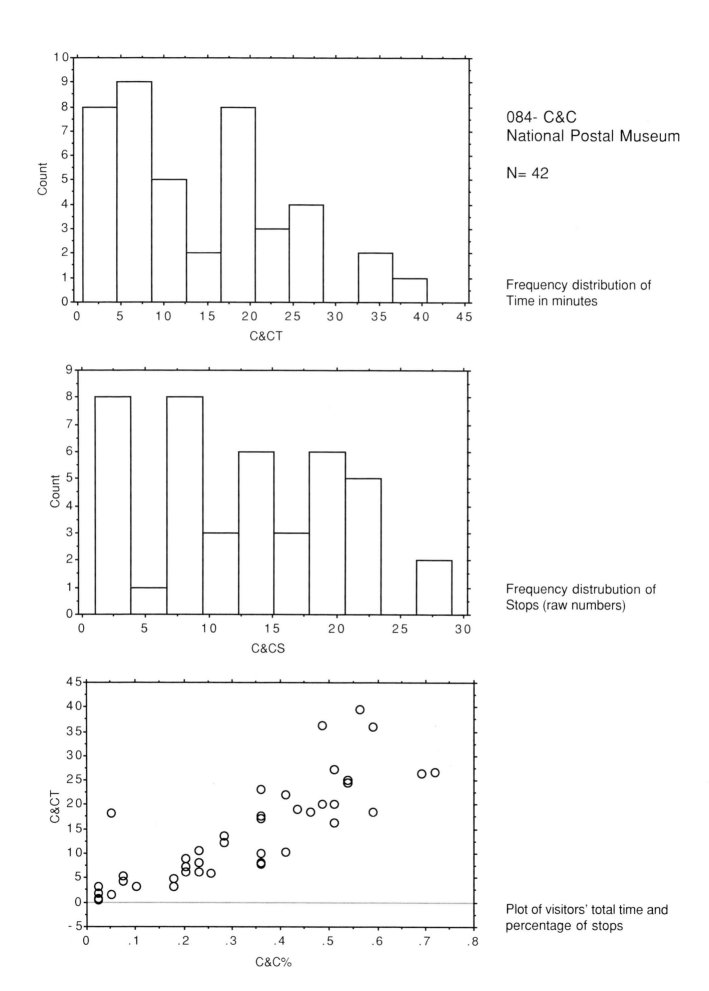

084- C&C
National Postal Museum

N= 42

Frequency distribution of
Time in minutes

Frequency distrubution of
Stops (raw numbers)

Plot of visitors' total time and
percentage of stops

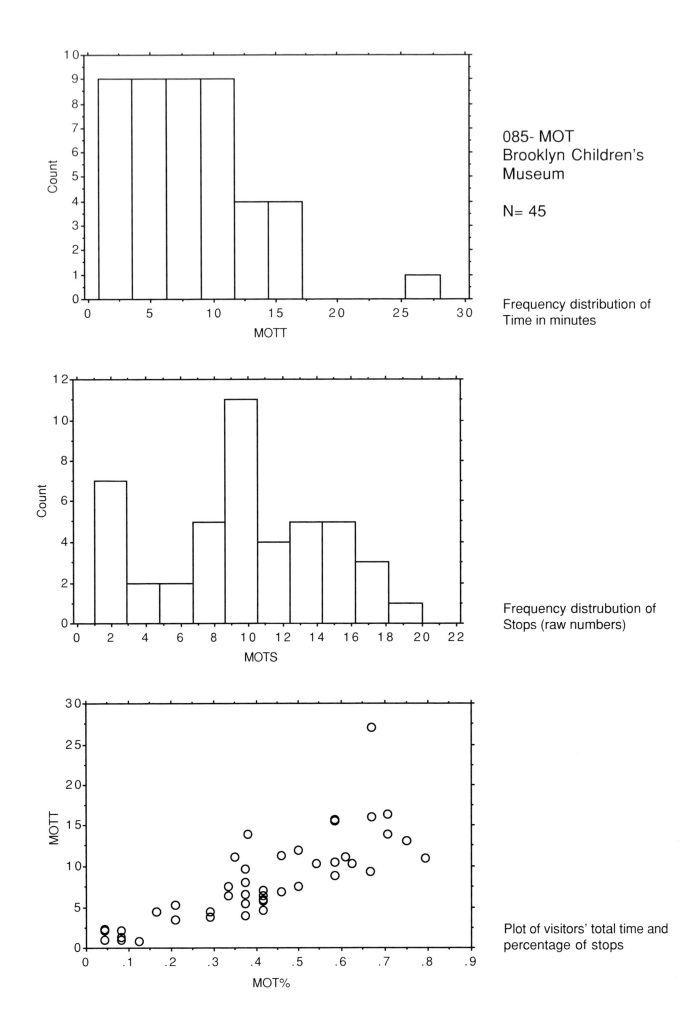

085- MOT
Brooklyn Children's
Museum

N= 45

Frequency distribution of
Time in minutes

Frequency distrubution of
Stops (raw numbers)

Plot of visitors' total time and
percentage of stops

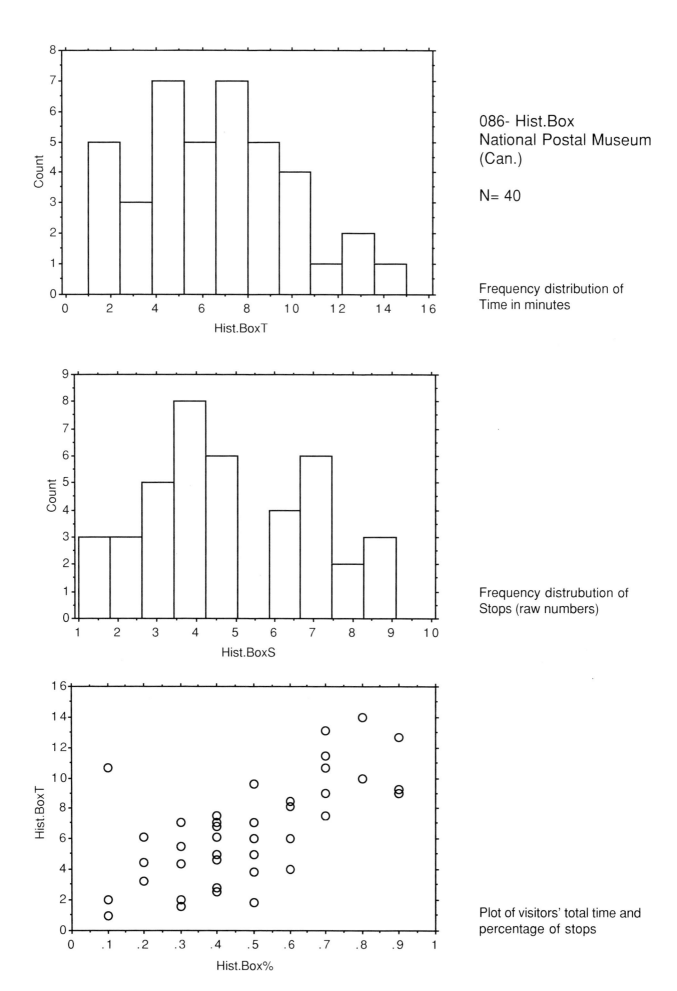

086- Hist.Box
National Postal Museum
(Can.)

N= 40

Frequency distribution of
Time in minutes

Frequency distrubution of
Stops (raw numbers)

Plot of visitors' total time and
percentage of stops

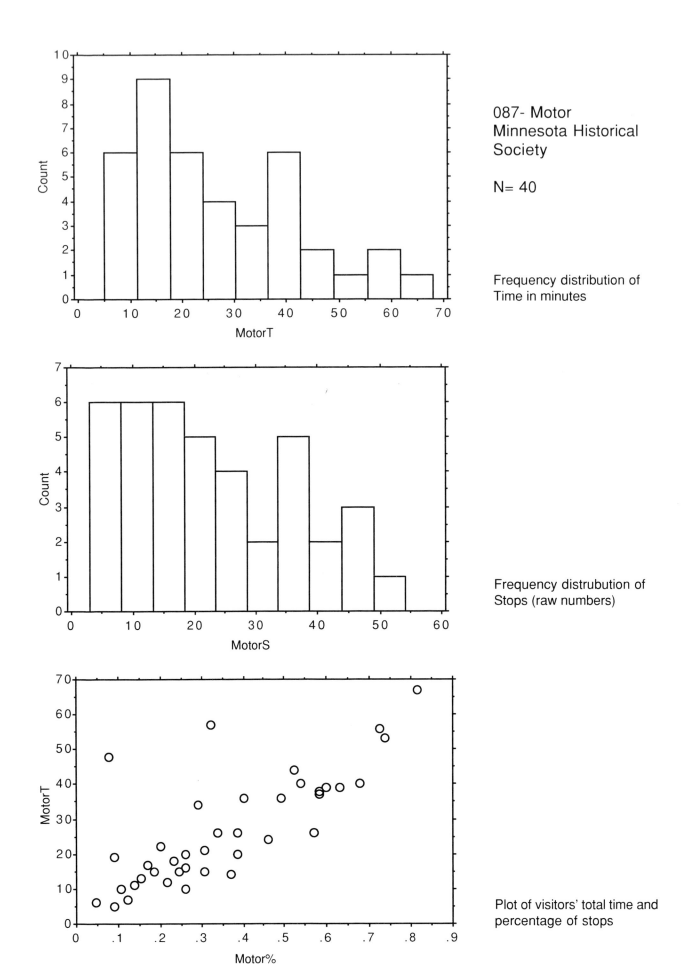

087- Motor
Minnesota Historical
Society

N= 40

Frequency distribution of
Time in minutes

Frequency distrubution of
Stops (raw numbers)

Plot of visitors' total time and
percentage of stops

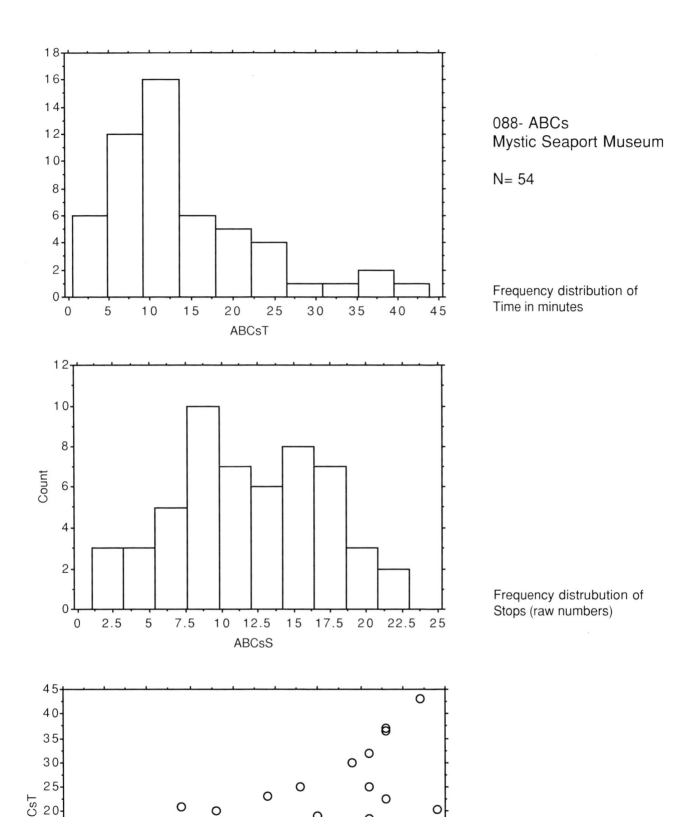

088- ABCs
Mystic Seaport Museum

N= 54

Frequency distribution of
Time in minutes

Frequency distrubution of
Stops (raw numbers)

Plot of visitors' total time and
percentage of stops

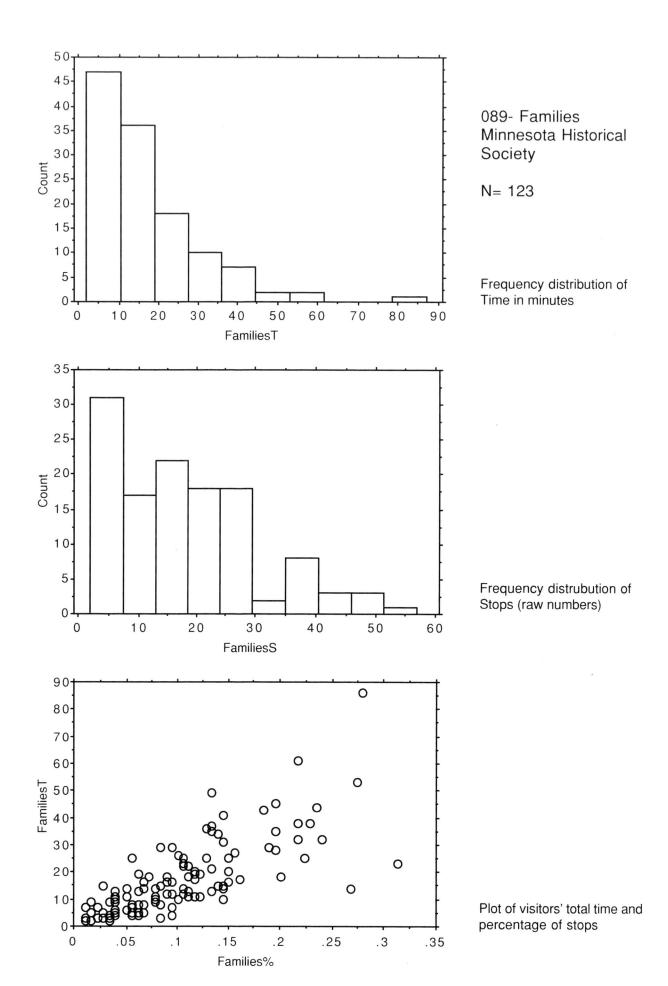

089- Families
Minnesota Historical
Society

N= 123

Frequency distribution of
Time in minutes

Frequency distrubution of
Stops (raw numbers)

Plot of visitors' total time and
percentage of stops

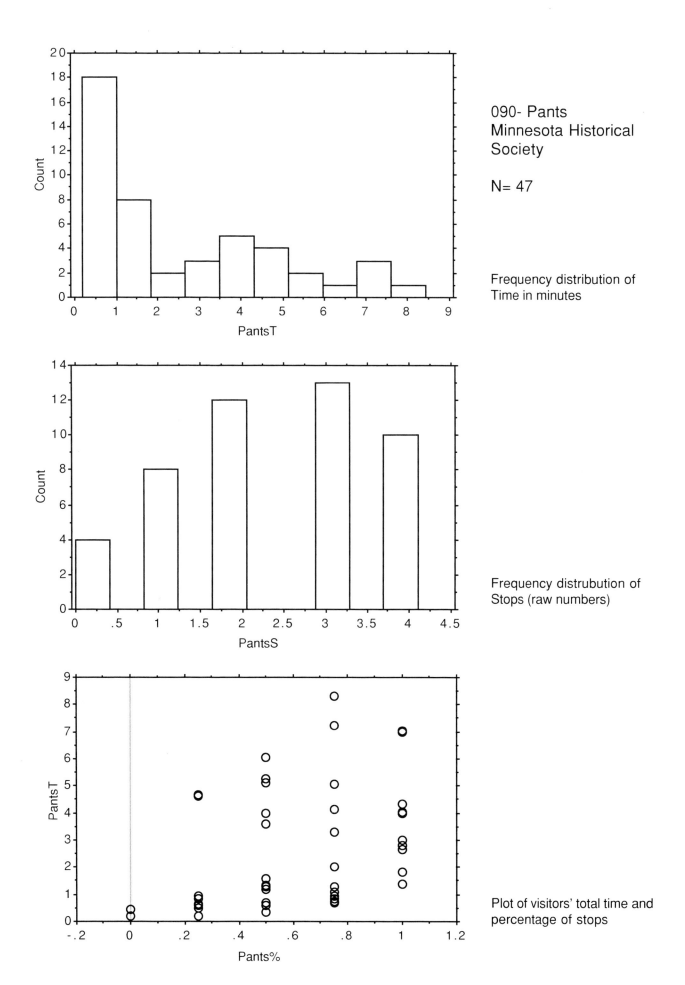

090- Pants
Minnesota Historical
Society

N= 47

Frequency distribution of
Time in minutes

Frequency distrubution of
Stops (raw numbers)

Plot of visitors' total time and
percentage of stops

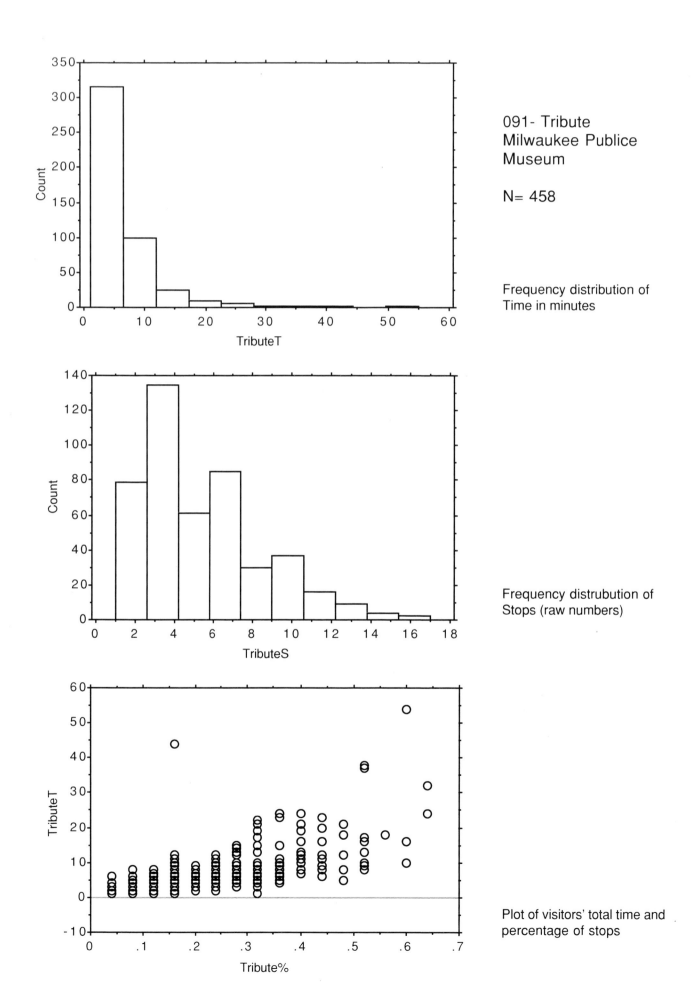

091- Tribute
Milwaukee Publice
Museum

N= 458

Frequency distribution of
Time in minutes

Frequency distrubution of
Stops (raw numbers)

Plot of visitors' total time and
percentage of stops

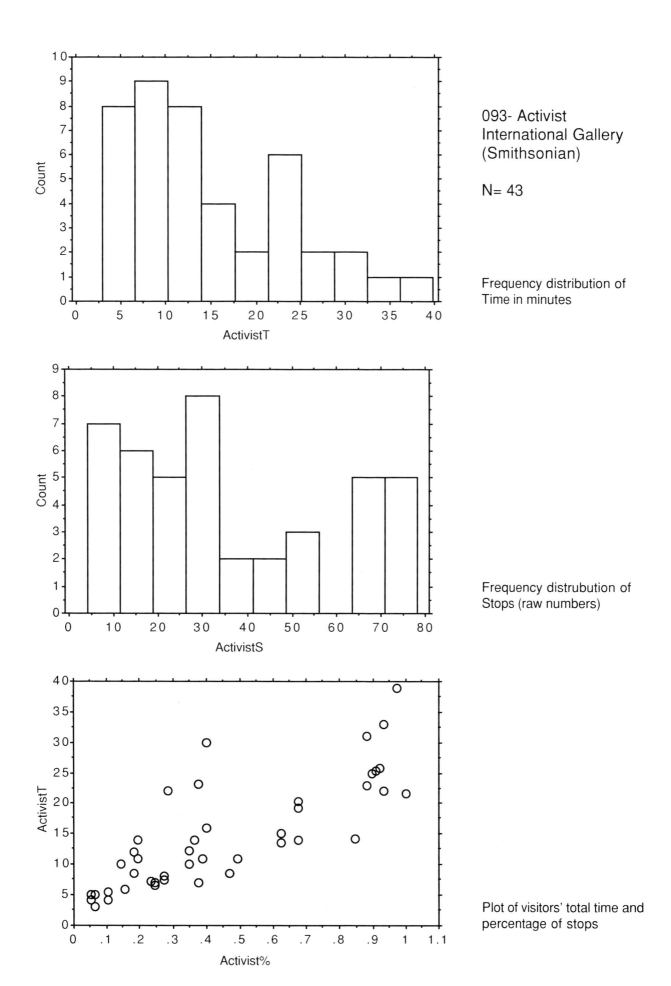

093- Activist
International Gallery
(Smithsonian)

N= 43

Frequency distribution of
Time in minutes

Frequency distrubution of
Stops (raw numbers)

Plot of visitors' total time and
percentage of stops

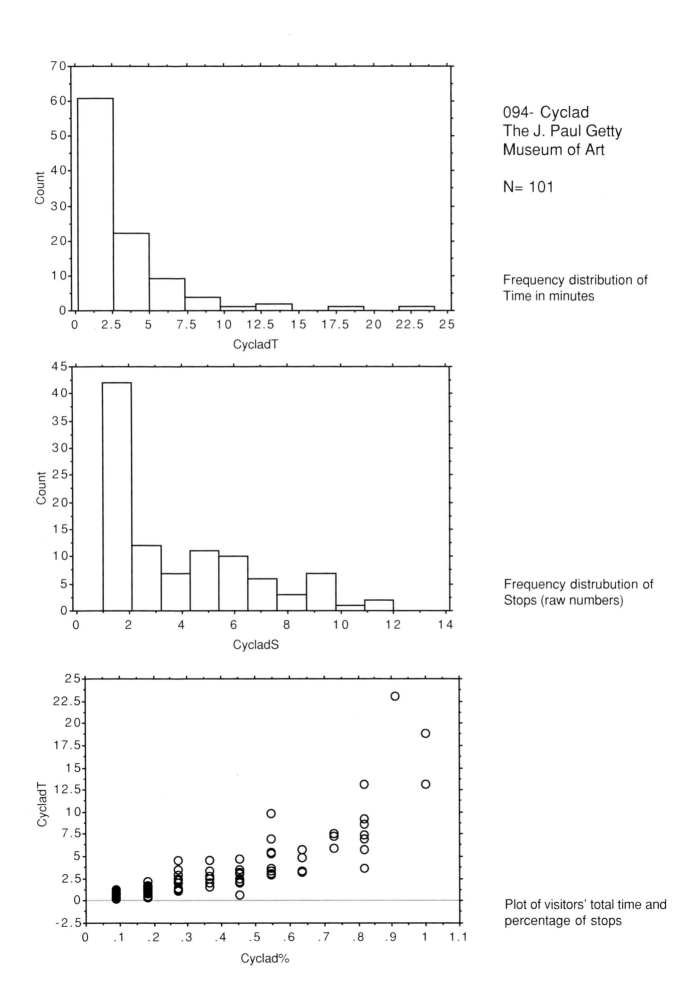

094- Cyclad
The J. Paul Getty
Museum of Art

N= 101

Frequency distribution of
Time in minutes

Frequency distrubution of
Stops (raw numbers)

Plot of visitors' total time and
percentage of stops

In "Discovery and Deceit: Archaeology and the Forger's Craft," a tracking study showed that visitors to the art museum paid above average attention to the labels and interactive experiences but did not make exceptionally thorough use of the whole exhibition. Exhibit developers concluded that fewer elements probably would have worked just as well.

Photo courtesy of the Nelson-Atkins Museum of Art

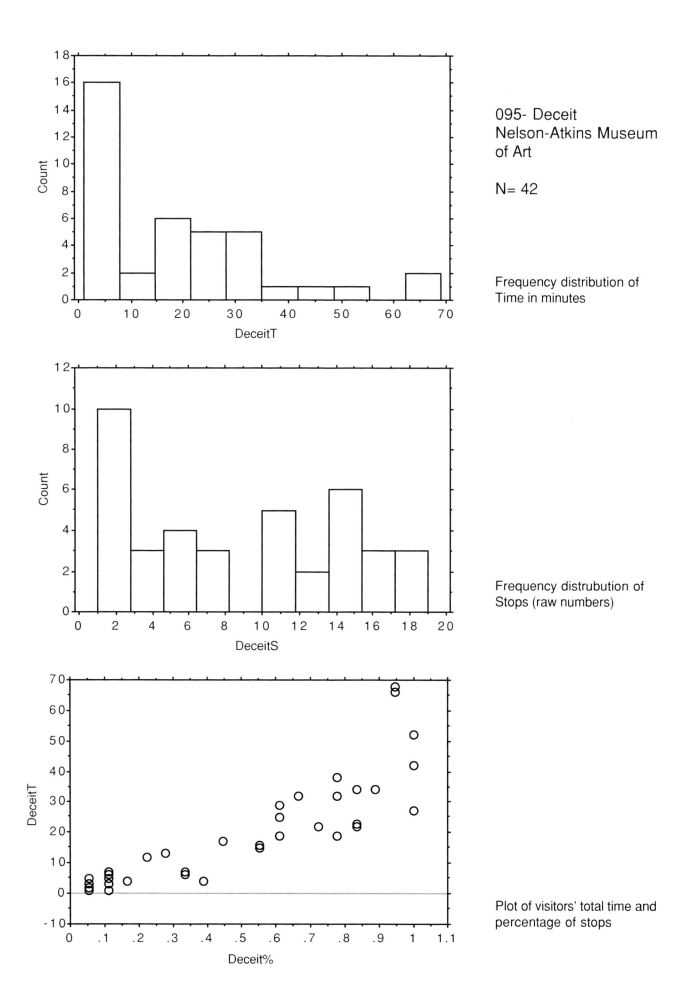

095- Deceit
Nelson-Atkins Museum
of Art

N= 42

Frequency distribution of
Time in minutes

Frequency distrubution of
Stops (raw numbers)

Plot of visitors' total time and
percentage of stops

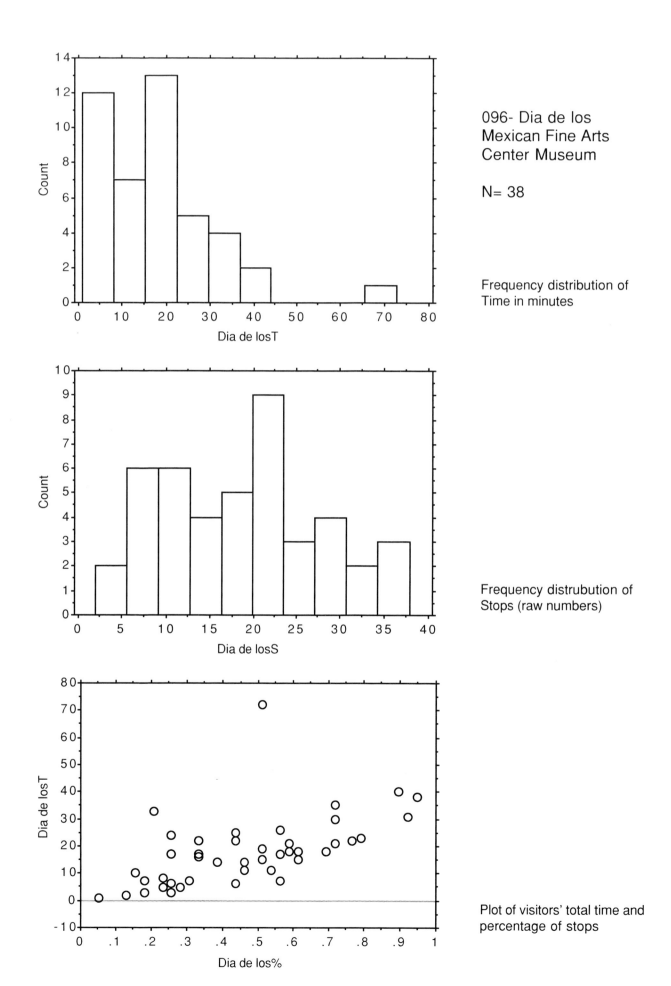

096- Dia de los
Mexican Fine Arts
Center Museum

N= 38

Frequency distribution of
Time in minutes

Frequency distrubution of
Stops (raw numbers)

Plot of visitors' total time and
percentage of stops

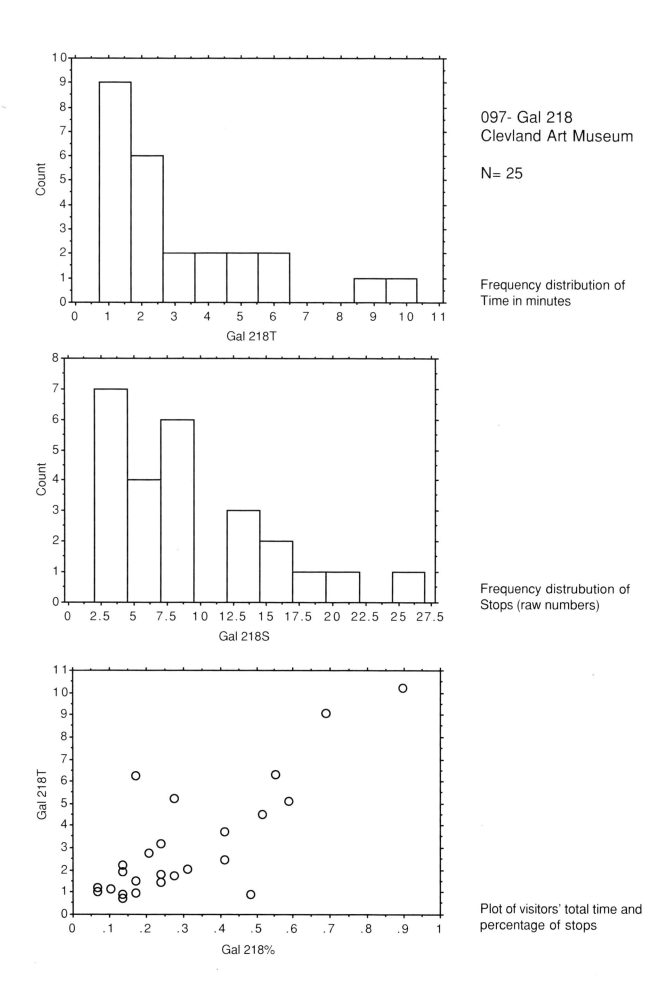

097- Gal 218
Clevland Art Museum

N= 25

Frequency distribution of
Time in minutes

Frequency distrubution of
Stops (raw numbers)

Plot of visitors' total time and
percentage of stops

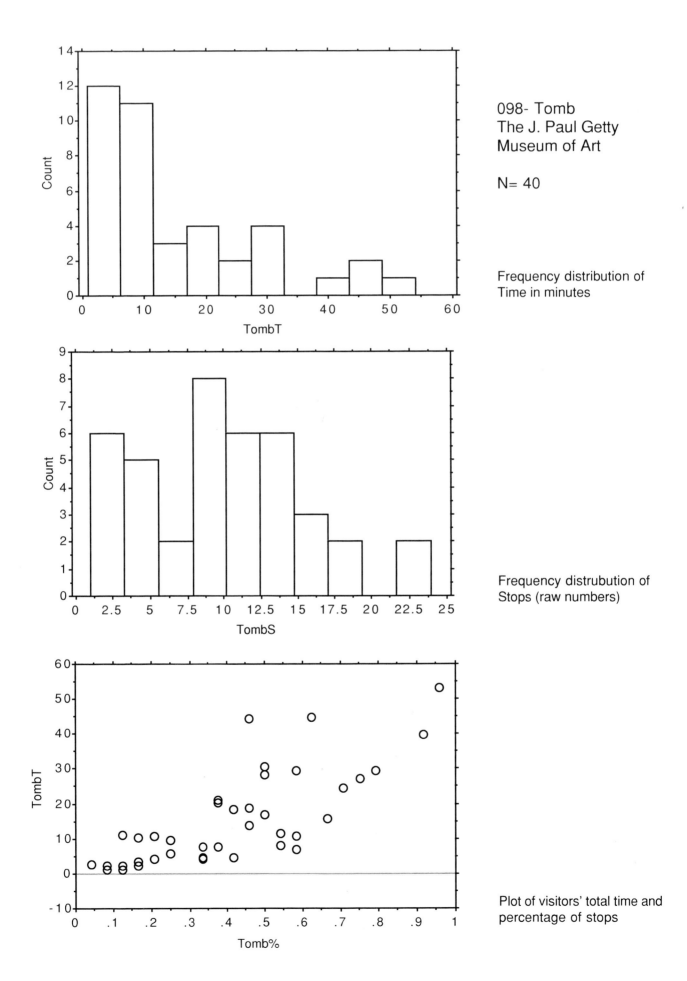

098- Tomb
The J. Paul Getty
Museum of Art

N= 40

Frequency distribution of
Time in minutes

Frequency distrubution of
Stops (raw numbers)

Plot of visitors' total time and
percentage of stops

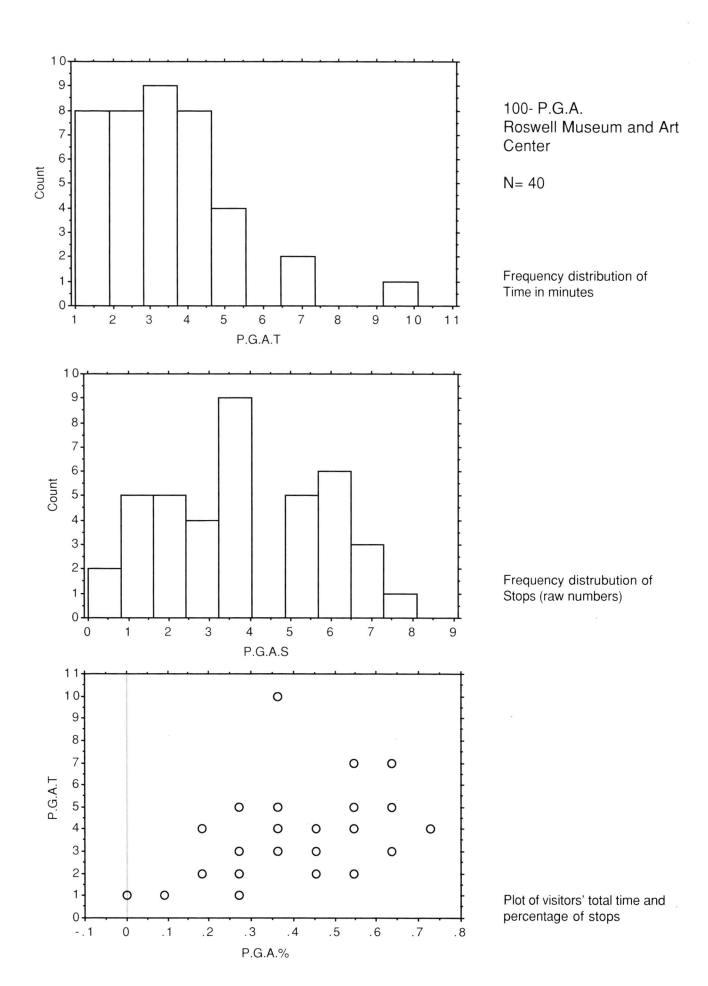

100- P.G.A.
Roswell Museum and Art Center

N= 40

Frequency distribution of
Time in minutes

Frequency distrubution of
Stops (raw numbers)

Plot of visitors' total time and
percentage of stops

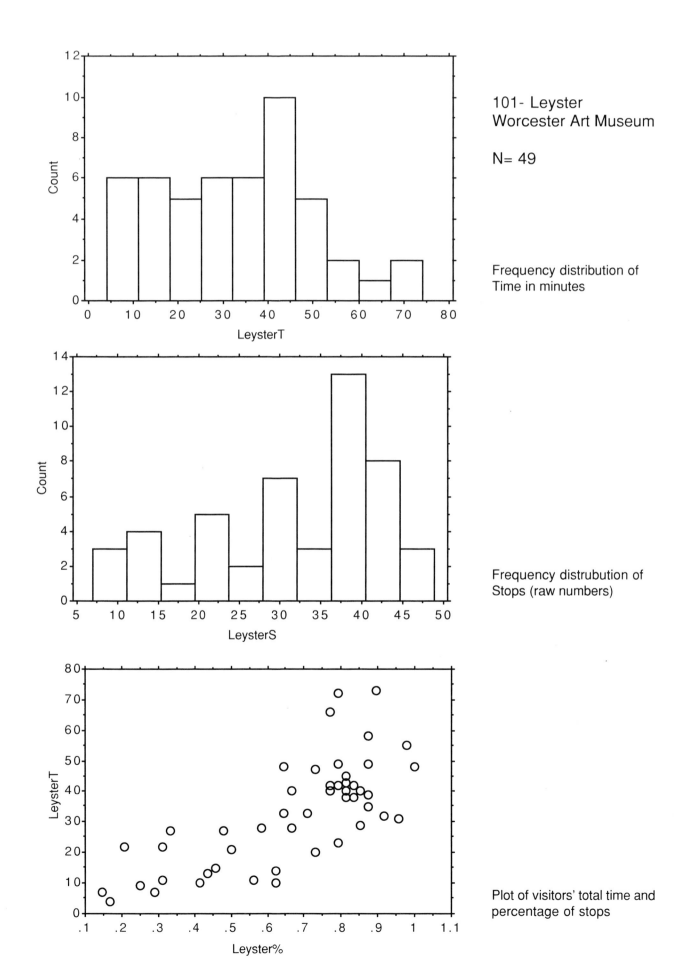

101- Leyster
Worcester Art Museum

N= 49

Frequency distribution of
Time in minutes

Frequency distrubution of
Stops (raw numbers)

Plot of visitors' total time and
percentage of stops

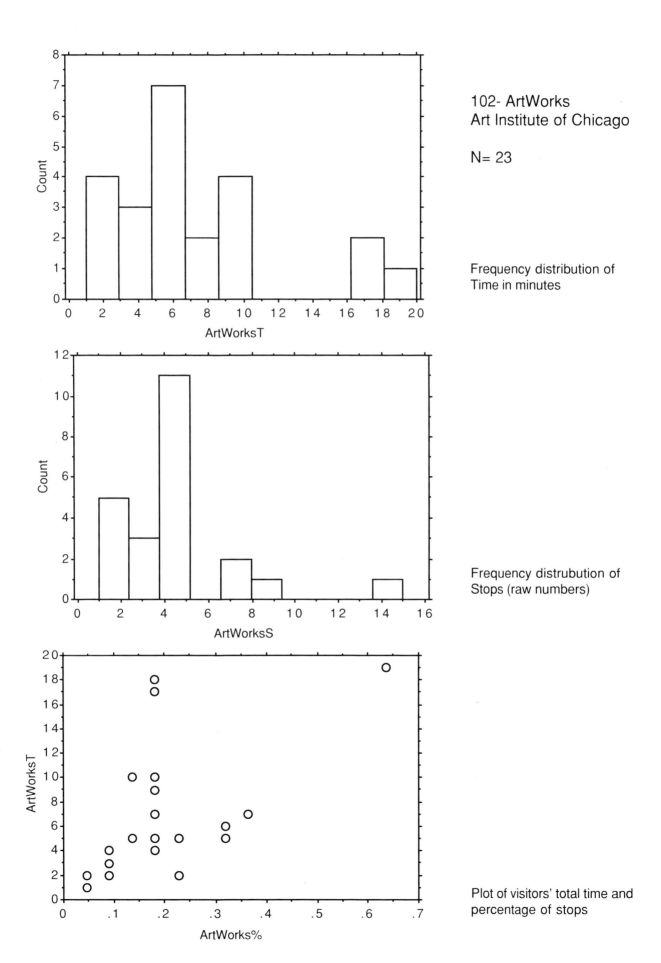

102- ArtWorks
Art Institute of Chicago

N= 23

Frequency distribution of
Time in minutes

Frequency distrubution of
Stops (raw numbers)

Plot of visitors' total time and
percentage of stops

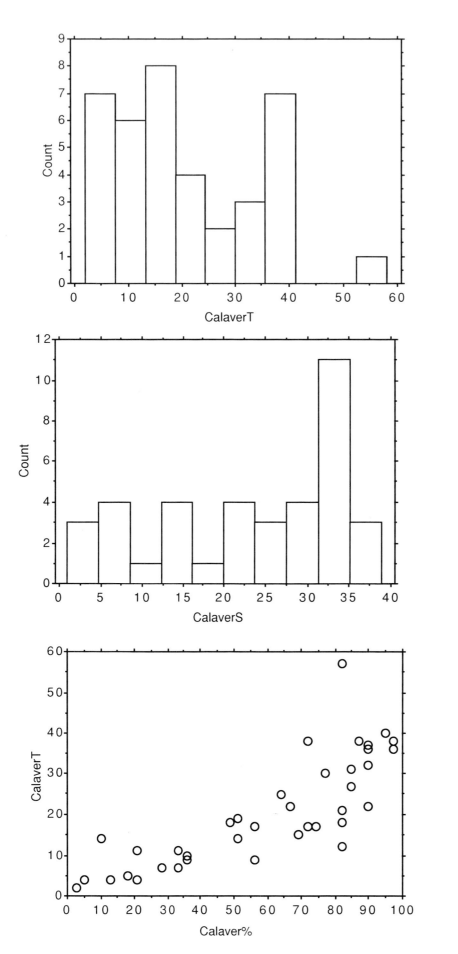

103- Calaver
Mexican Fine Arts
Center Museum

N= 44

Frequency Distribution
of Time in Minutes

Frequency Distribution
of Stops (raw numbers)

Plot of visitors' total time
and percentage of stops

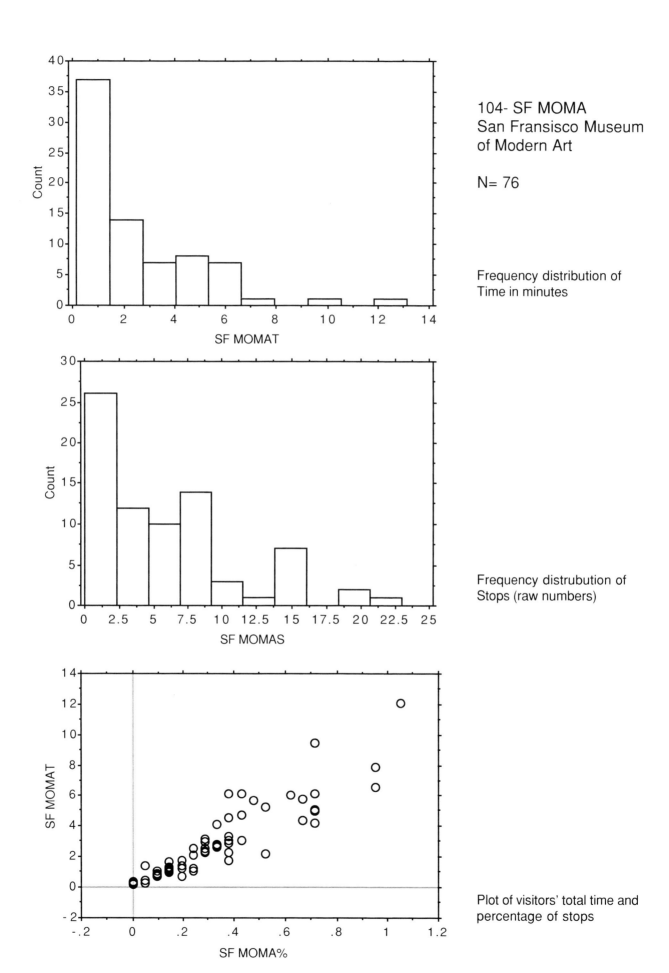

104- SF MOMA
San Fransisco Museum
of Modern Art

N= 76

Frequency distribution of
Time in minutes

Frequency distrubution of
Stops (raw numbers)

Plot of visitors' total time and
percentage of stops

In the old Hall of Birds at Field Museum, "stuffed birds on sticks" was the prevailing exhibit technique. Most visitors browsed through quickly, but they still got an overall idea of bird diversity. One of the developers' goals for the renovated hall was that visitors would spend more time.

Photo by author

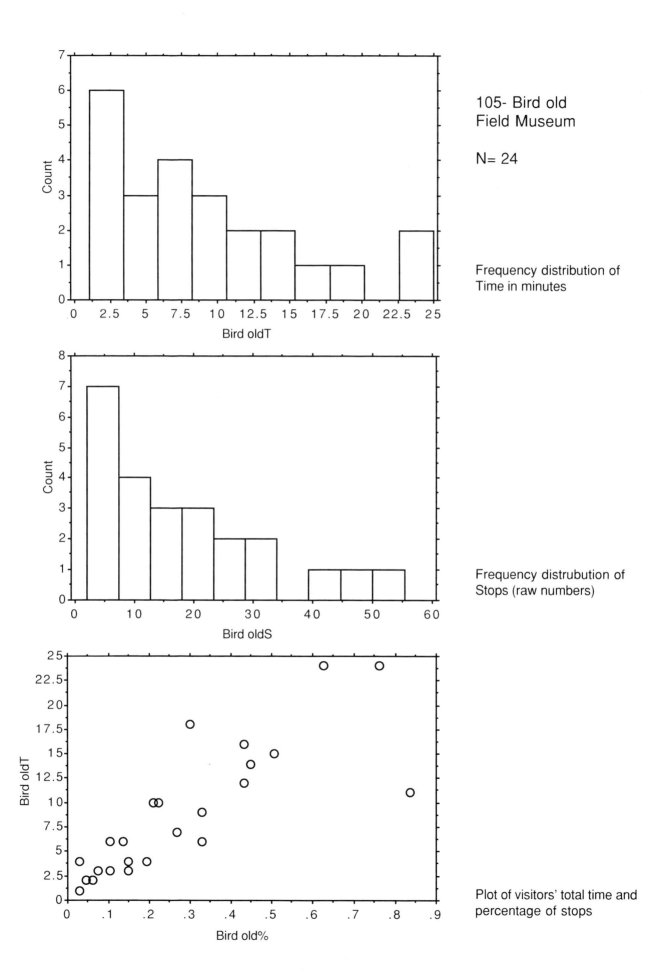

105- Bird old
Field Museum

N= 24

Frequency distribution of
Time in minutes

Frequency distrubution of
Stops (raw numbers)

Plot of visitors' total time and
percentage of stops

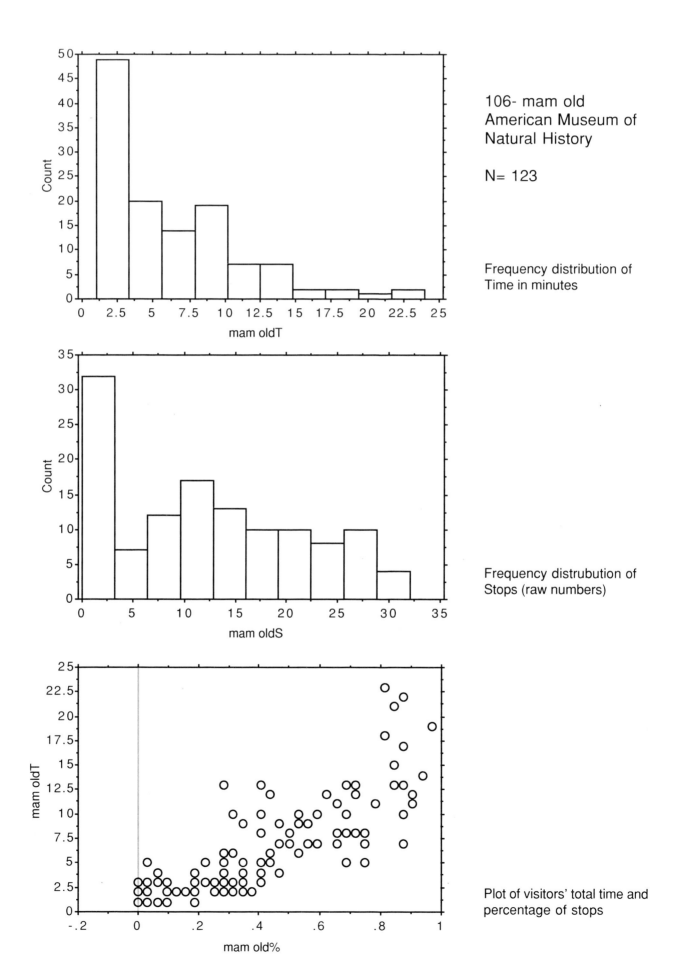

106- mam old
American Museum of
Natural History

N= 123

Frequency distribution of
Time in minutes

Frequency distrubution of
Stops (raw numbers)

Plot of visitors' total time and
percentage of stops

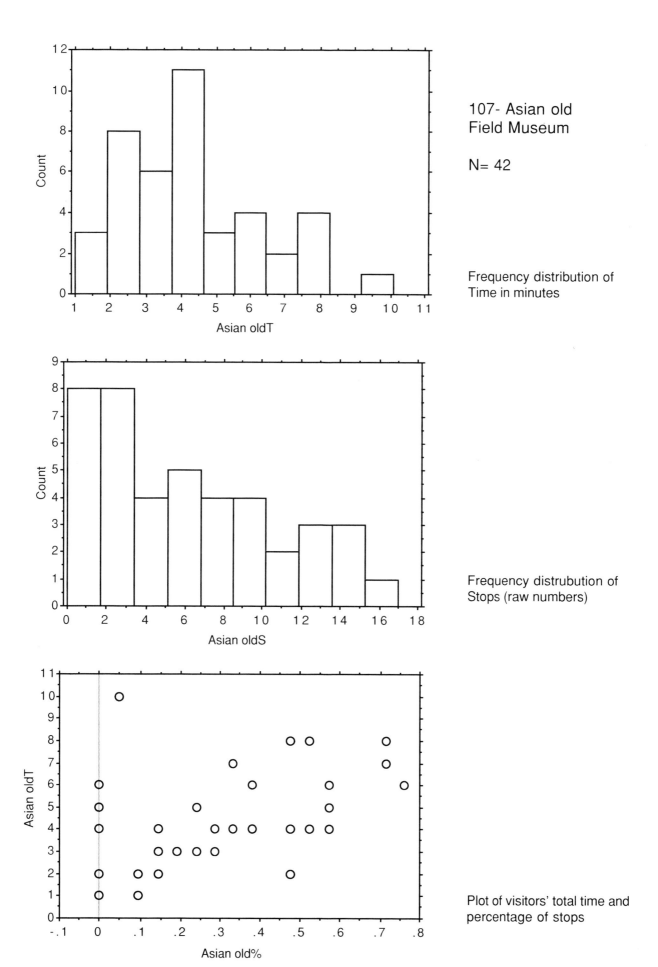

107- Asian old
Field Museum

N= 42

Frequency distribution of
Time in minutes

Frequency distrubution of
Stops (raw numbers)

Plot of visitors' total time and
percentage of stops

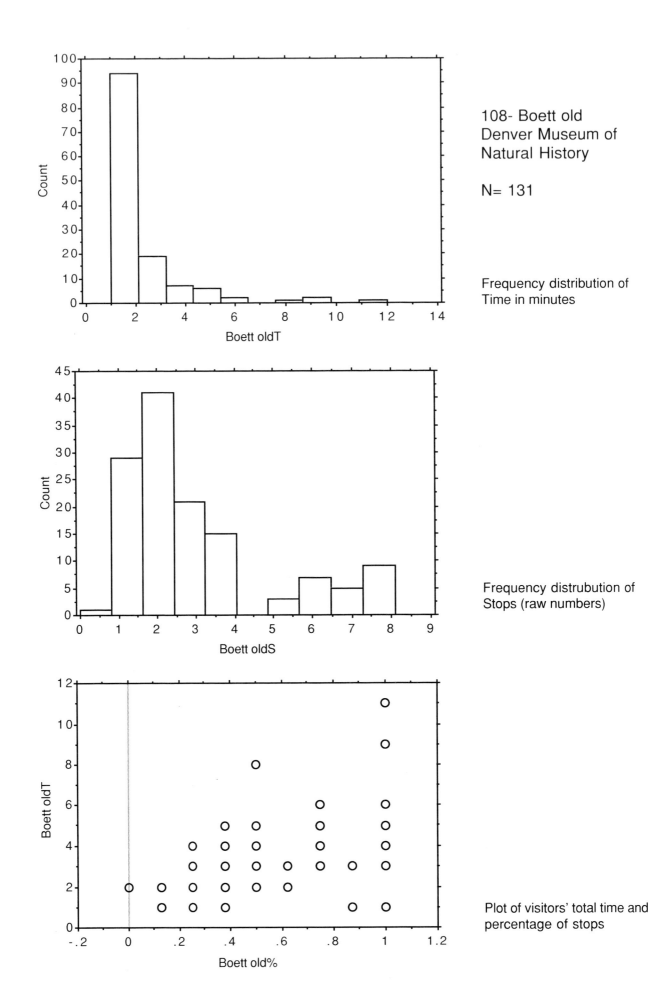

108- Boett old
Denver Museum of
Natural History

N= 131

Frequency distribution of
Time in minutes

Frequency distrubution of
Stops (raw numbers)

Plot of visitors' total time and
percentage of stops

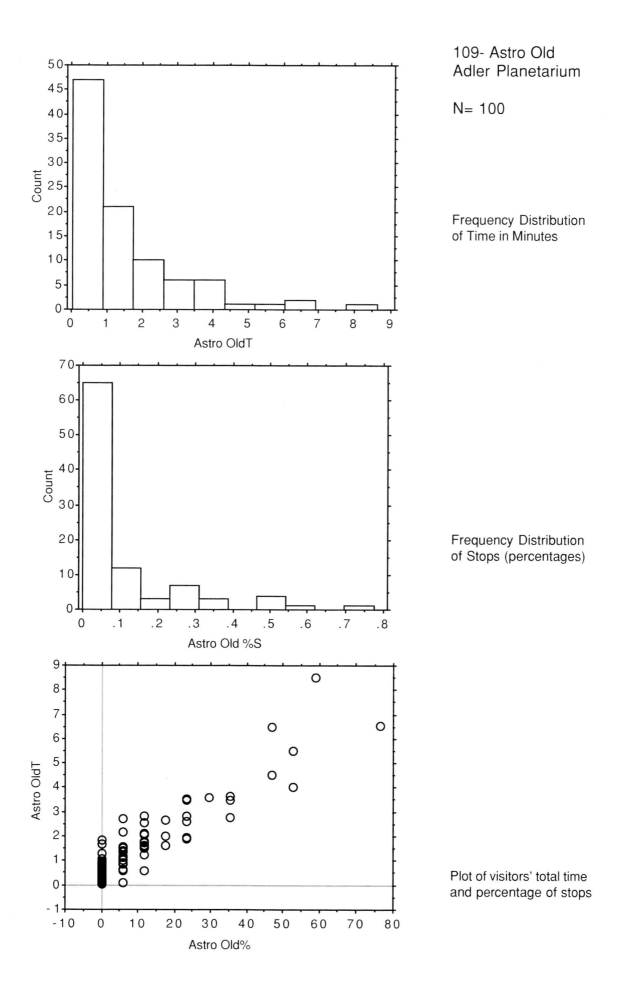

109- Astro Old
Adler Planetarium

N= 100

Frequency Distribution
of Time in Minutes

Frequency Distribution
of Stops (percentages)

Plot of visitors' total time
and percentage of stops

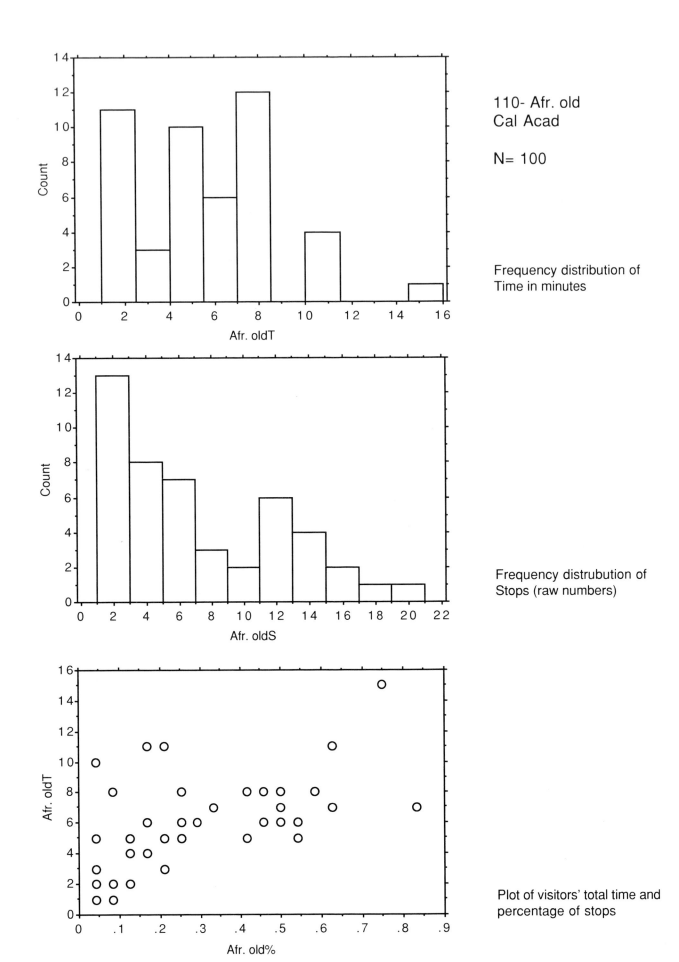

110- Afr. old
Cal Acad

N= 100

Frequency distribution of
Time in minutes

Frequency distrubution of
Stops (raw numbers)

Plot of visitors' total time and
percentage of stops